# Cultural Narratives

# Cultural Narratives

## Hybridity and Other Spaces

*Edited by*

**Jasbir Jain**

**Rawat Publications**

Jaipur • New Delhi • Bangalore • Hyderabad • Guwahati

ISBN 978-81-316-0496-0





*Published by*
Prem Rawat for **Rawat Publications**
Satyam Apts, Sector 3, Jawahar Nagar, Jaipur 302 004 (India)
Phone: 0141 265 1748 / 7006 Fax: 0141 265 1748
E-mail: info@rawatbooks.com
Website: www.rawatbooks.com

*New Delhi Office*
4858/24, Ansari Road, Daryaganj, New Delhi 110 002
Phone: 011 2326 3290

Also at *Bangalore, Hyderabad* and *Guwahati*

Typeset by Rawat Computers, Jaipur
Printed at Chaman Enterprises, New Delhi

# Contents

## II
## Personal is Political



## III
## Community Narratives

# Acknowledgements

Our special thanks to the creative writers who have contributed to this volume Geetanjali Shree, Rajee Seth, Joya Mitra and Vijay Lakshmi; to the translators Raji Narasimhan and Sarabani Sinha for carrying the stories (of Rajee Seth and Joya Mitra), across languages; to Santosh Gupta for delivering the Keynote Address at the Hybridity Seminar and allowing us to include it in this. We gratefully acknowledge the contributions of all our writers who have explored texts across languages, cultures, time and media. Many of the writers whose essays are here were present and participated in the debates which constituted the basis of this collection. We express our deepest thanks for their contribution to this venture.

# Introduction: Hybridity and Other Spaces

This work is about 'space' and 'location': the two work in consonance. Literary and critical theory have been for more than two decades preoccupied with the 'politics of location' and there is an increased consciousness of identities and cultures being constructed through spatial categories. Prison walls, ghettos, town planning, village outskirts – all are markers of segregation and separation as well as of social and economic status. Foucault's *Discipline and Punish* (1975), a work that explored the relationship between the moulding of the individual when subjected to the gaze and Homi Bhabha's *Location of Culture* (1994) which foregrounded the interstitial spaces and worked with the concept of the 'third space', where 'the *place of utterance* – is crossed by the *difference* of writing' (36) have prominently influenced contemporary theory. Bhabha links this 'third space' directly with acts of enunciation and interpretation. The 'third space' is a meeting point, not of similarities but of differences, and it moves beyond communication to create an ambivalence of interpretation. Apparently it is the coming together of two entities initially located in different origins.

Moving further back into the multiple histories of humankind, one realises that space has always played a dominant part in setting up demarcations, supporting power, confining freedom in various social and gender stratifications. Royalty, class structures, territorial boundaries, outcasts and fugitives, military cantonments – all are created by space dynamics. One doesn't have to go very far in order to realise the all-pervasive nature of space. Antahpuras, zenana/mardana divisions, purdah and veils, segregation of sexes even in social and community get-togethers and the different gender roles are all marked by spatial categories. Thus identity, freedom, nationhood, religious constructs – each one of them is dependent upon it and shaped by it. The intensification and foregrounding of diaspora studies, in the various contexts of colonisation, decolonisation and now globalisation, have not only further emphasised space as an important aspect of socio-political life, but they have also created a divided space. The diasporic imagination is very often ambivalently located, the physical location does not necessarily correspond to the cultural location and besides this the diaspora claims affiliation to dual territories.

bell hooks, a gender theorist, has identified the margin as the 'space of radical openness' (206). It also works as a starting point for resistance and opposition. The phrase 'pushed to the wall' explains it very well; when one finds no viable option, one is compelled to rebel. Gandhi, if he had not been thrown out of the railway carriage by a white man in Pretoria, may never have become a 'mahatma'.

Yet, while on the one hand one desires inclusive space, on the other the need for privacy is equally urgent. Both requirements are dominantly governed by political and class factors. As for instance the long-drawn battle for women's voting rights was primarily a fight for political space, for a role in decision-making and as a move towards equality. Segregation had, in this case, worked as an exclusive division and a perpetuation of inequality. The interaction between gender and space has been intricate and problematic in almost all societies at some point of time or the other. Rape, assault, molestation all of them imply the violation of the individual's right to bodily space.

Strangely enough, even as exclusion is discrimination, visibility does not necessarily promise equality. Caryl Phillips in his autobiographical work *The European Tribe* writes about how he became conscious of his blackness. In this awareness both his physical visibility and his social invisibility interacted. The white men standing in a queue at a bus station talked across his body, thus rendering him invisible and violating his space at the same time. In New York he felt the whole city 'seemed a testament to migratory patterns' with its little Italy, Spanish Harlem, Chinatown, Harlem and other exclusionary spaces. Everywhere he was viewed with suspicion and the police questioned him both in Detroit and Chicago; their questions, Phillips observes, 'centred on the simple fact that I was black and in the wrong street at the wrong time' (6). When similar experiences of neglect and suspicion followed him in Salt Lake City he walked straight to the bus station. There too, he found men talking across him about his blackness (*The European Tribe* 6–7).

This self-hurt, the experience of being humiliated and ignored, forced him to escape the city and move to Los Angeles. Phillips reiterates the feelings which Frantz Fanon had pointed towards in his work *Black Skins, White Masks*, 'Look a Negro ... Mama see the Negro! I'm frightened' (112). The fact of blackness makes a person an object to be viewed, as if on exhibition, leading to the creation of stereotypical images, questioning or subverting which becomes a lifelong struggle for the subject.

Dalits in India have had similar experiences of social rejection and erasure. The psychological impact of this double consciousness as it works simultaneously can be devastating, especially when visibility is ignored or when the individual has to announce his difference publicly. Both aggression and imperialism have founded themselves on the invisibility of the 'other'. George Orwell, in his essay, 'Marrakech' written during his stay in French Morocco in 1938–39, writes:

> ... when you see how people live, and still more how easily they die, it is always difficult to believe that you are walking among human beings. All colonial empires are in reality founded upon that fact. The people have brown faces – besides there are so many of them! Are they really the same flesh as yourself? ... They rise out of the earth, they sweat and starve for a few years and then they sink back into the nameless mounds of the graveyard and nobody notices that they are gone. (388)

Similar is the fate of the punkah-puller in Forster's *A Passage to India*. Imperialism, like racism, thrives on ignoring the other. This erasure is a spatial erasure, a refusal to see the body.

In the nineteenth century novel, women had few outlets for freedom of movement and often they were described as going out for a walk. One notices this in Jane Austen's novels. This is a shift from Fanny Burney's writings, where women commuted in sedan chairs. In Austen's *Pride and Prejudice* the significant turns in the narrative take place when Elizabeth goes for a walk. We find this being repeated in novel after novel right up to Elizabeth Gaskell's *Wives and Daughters*. Yet when we read them we do not problematise the significance of this space which moves into two kinds of spaces simultaneously – personal and public.

The search for freedom is double-edged. Virginia Woolf's *A Room of One's Own* problematises it as a woman's need for privacy, away from the claims of family and matrimony. She considers it a necessary condition for personal growth. We have similar situations depicted in Ashapurna Devi's *Suvarnlata* and Kundalika Kapadia's *Seven Steps in the Sky*. The degree to which space lacks stability is extremely problematic. These very rooms which promise privacy, freedom and individual growth can also become places of confinement and exclusion: the Red Room in *Jane Eyre* and the 'dark room' in R.K. Narayan's novel, *The Dark Room*. The spatial divisions resulting from economic levels may provide an open space, in the sense of absence of walls, but they also fail to provide freedom or equality or even privacy. Slums or ghettos where more than half of one's life is spent in the open, open one to the gaze of others; low-income housing, crowded tenements or chawls deny privacy and constantly expose a person to the public eye.

All concepts of 'otherness' and feelings of alienation are marked by this difference. Thus, whether it is open access or a wide expanse or a closed space, the kind and quality of space invariably plays a dominant role in moulding societies and people, even ideologies.

The essays in the present volume have all been presented at various seminars organised by the Institute for Research in Interdisciplinary Studies (IRIS) over a period of two years. They are a representative selection of some of the main issues. The first section examines the concept and meaning of hybridity; and the second looks at the intimate tie between the personal and the political, concepts and positions of significance to cultural and gender formation, as they explore relationships between 'self' and 'other', diasporic positions, border politics and cultural theories. The last two sections are more directly focused on space and narrativity with special attention to oral and community narratives in the third, and in the fourth moving on to urban narratives. They explore the interaction of space, the narrative and its telling. Together they seek to express the problematics and the multiplicity of spatial discourses where identity formation, nation construction and politics converge; where traditional modes of storytelling make place for technological innovations and the rapidly changing environment of urban spaces, and where inner consciousnesses collide with history. Writing itself is an inscription on empty space as is the performative act.

Thus, it follows that narrativity or the manner in which a story is told is governed by the space it inhabits or the space which inhabits it. A village narrative conceptualises relationships in an entirely different manner from an urban narrative. The morphology works altogether on a different plane. The outsider is seen as an exotic element, at times even as a threat and gains power in the local hierarchical structure, while the urban narrative is more impersonal and distant, and moves at a much faster pace than its rural counterpart. Relationships have a faster turnover.

Oral literatures and folklore are travelling narratives. They very often take journeys to distant spaces within their fold without necessarily concretising them. They are concerned with movement, not with fixity. But a community adopts a slightly different route; it decentralises the narration as well as the narrator. Multiple, often unformed, perspectives join multiple narrators to carry the tale forward. Community narratives can function in myriad ways; they are half way between the oral and the single-narrator narrative, yet they often acquire a postmodern disjunctiveness.

We also have three very sensitive narrations. Geetanjali Shree takes the reader with her as she walks along the blurring and shifting boundaries between the personal and the political; Rajee Seth uses the narrative of a border crosser, to transcend territorial boundaries through recollection, memory, affiliation and a literary relationship while Joya Mitra uses ideology, gender and class to identify the markers of space.

The essays, short stories and other critical examinations of different kinds of narratives, brought together under one cover, represent our attempt to understand the relationships between space and the individual, space and time and space and narratology in the context of power dynamics, new migratory patterns and culture wars. Above all, they reaffirm the role of the human imagination.

## References

Devi, Ashapurna. *Suvarnlata.* (Bengali, 1977). Translated into Hindi by Hanslal Tiwari. New Delhi: Bhartiya Jnanpith Prakashan, 1979.

Fanon, Frantz. 'The Fact of Blackness' *Black Skins, White Masks.* (1952). Translated Charles Lan Markmann, 1967, London: Pluto Press, 1986, 109–140.

hooks, bell. *Feminist Theory: From Margin to Center.* New York: South End Press, 1984.

Kapadia, Kundanika. *Seven Steps in the Sky.* (Gujarati, 1982). Translated into English by Indira Nityanandan and William Anthony. Bombay: Navbharat Sahitya Mandir 1994, 2004.

Orwell, George. 'Marrakech' in *Collected Essays, Journalism and Letters of George Orwell.* Eds. Sonia Orwell and Ian Angus. London: Secker and Warburg. 4 vols. Vol. 1, 387–393.

Phillips, Caryl. *The European Tribe.* New York: Vintage Books (1987), 2000.

Woolf, Virginia. *A Room of One's Own.* London: Granada Publishing House, 1979.

# I

# Hybridity

## Exploring Hybridity

*The term 'hybridity' has, over the last couple of decades, acquired a certain notoriety, as locations have become increasingly important. Ironically, a term initially used to describe cultural interaction and one which, through its agency, created the 'Third Space', has been relegated to the category of 'jargon', a word very often used like a handy aspirin available to the tired scholar.*

*No longer is hybridity a neutral term. Perhaps it never was in the colonial context; it rests on inequality, malleability and mimicry; in the diasporic context it often assumes the status of day to day survival and involves a separation between inner and outer space and between physical and emotional locations; and in the postcolonial context, it demands recognition on terms of equality.*

*How does one cope with power, racism and past histories through hybrid formations? Do we search for other words, other terms to express the evolving shifts in the cultural matrix? Increasingly the inadequacies of the term have begun to haunt us pointing towards the need to explore its myriad dimensions.*

*In this section the term and its development are set in the historical context by Santosh Gupta, who cites the several examples pointing to the different nuances of interpretation and application. We also have an autobiographical account of the experiences of a sensitive creative writer who now lives in America in Vijay Lakshmi's essay. Gerda Unnithan Kauffman, who migrated to India after her marriage and has lived here for half-a-century, moves into a close examination of Madeleine Slade, a Gandhian follower who transformed herself in great measure. The question which she asks is: does this writing over erase the original?*

*Madhuri Chatterjee, in her essay on Pico Iyer, shifts her stand from both Vijay Lakshmi and Gerda Unnithan Kauffman, to explore it in the context of globalisation, where technology and development have brought about a free floating identity, an identity which is more like a kite or a balloon which has broken away from its anchor, with nation, stability and identity calling aloud for redefinitions. Jasbir Jain brings the discussion home to India and explores the power of words as they mould cultures and attitudes. Language has the power to both articulate and camouflage and terms if overused acquire a fixity which deters human thought, Together, these essays lay open the layers of hybridity.*

# Locating Hybridity in History

*Santosh Gupta*

Hybridisation has been experienced variously by different people all over the world. A crucial factor in cultural mutation, its transformation and evolution, it has become an important issue in the recent discourse of hybridisation and the postcolonial search for the formation of a decolonised identity. Postcolonial studies and cultural studies have examined the impact of diaspora and exiles on the making of an intermediate culture that is either placed in between or on the margins of the cultures of both the homeland and the adopted land. This modern discourse explores the repercussion of western imperial expansion all over the world in the post Enlightenment era and the way these violent intermixings have impacted the deeply diverse cultures, religions and social practices of the colonised people.

Intermixing of philosophical and cultural traditions has long and fruitful histories. Jawahar Lal Nehru writing about ancient

---

Expanded version of the keynote address delivered at the IRIS seminar on "Exploring Cultural Locations".

India's absorption of foreign invaders, settlers and the accompanying cultures considers the outcome of hybrid art forms as one of the constant sources of the strengthening of Indian civilisation (Nehru 1946). Similarly, Edward Said, in a completely different context, views the travelling of ideas and cultural values between the East and the West as having mutually benefitted each other. Edward Said would place colonial history of modern Europe out of the 'binary oppositions' dear to the nationalist and imperialist enterprise because he finds that 'partly because of the empire, all cultures are involved in one another; none is single and pure; all are hybrid, heterogeneous, extraordinarily differentiated and unmonolithic' (Said 1994: xxviii). This heterogeneity, he remarks, is as true of the 'contemporary United States as it is of the modern Arab world' (xxix). In such a situation the pro-nationalist claims of a pure and unitary national culture go against the historical reality of western empires all over the world. Cultural intermixing has occurred, as these scholars suggest, voluntarily or forced by the collisions caused by colonial impositions. Said refers to some very well-known examples of philosophical and political ideas travelling between the east and the west: the eastern ideas about transcendence were imported into Europe during the early nineteenth century, and the European ideas about society used by the traditional eastern societies during the later nineteenth century (Said 1983: 226).

The hybridisation of cultures seen as the aftermath of modern European colonial experiences has not always had a uniform pattern or received respectful reception. The multidirectional development of the hybridity discourse in postcolonialism has drawn attention to the pain, humiliation and loss of a stable sense of belonging as forced contact with totally strange ways of life, language and cultures was created. Nehru's appreciative view of the hybridity in Indian cultural tradition and Said's perception of the fruitful exchange/borrowing between the east and the west are different from the views of other postcolonial scholars such as Homi K. Bhabha, Gayatri Spivak and Michael Dash. Homi Bhabha and Gayatri Spivak, amongst others, examine the sites of the 'hybrid' taking shape under British colonial domination in India. Bhabha, in his analysis of the nineteenth century, encounters between British rulers and the native Indian masses who tried to form their own resistance practices, finds that 'hybridisation' is an outcome of the colonial effort of creating discriminatory and repressive system, in which the colonial authority, race, nation and culture are 'fixed' by an essentialism (Bhabha 112). When the oppressed, colonised subject returns the gaze of the ruler, the reversal causes all the deformation and displacement to become public and build up a new kind of tension, which according to Bhabha, not only 'unsettles the mimetic or narcissistic demands of colonial power but reimplicates the identification of the strategies of subversion that turn the gaze of the discriminated back upon the eye of power' (112).

The making of the 'hybrid', in Bhabha's view, is not a single 'dialectical power struggle' between the authority of the colonial self and the ruled race (or individuals). It is also not the discrimination between the 'mother culture' and the 'alien culture'. 'What becomes visible is not the self as a reflection, but a "split" within the self'. The 'hybrid' is not a coming together of two distinct cultures; it is not simply a repetition but a double, that represents the trace not of what is disavowed or depressed, but 'something different, a mutation, a hybrid' (111).

The representation and institutionalisation of the hybrid art, cultural forms and behavioural practices go through a struggle within the cultural site where they emerge. These struggles for recognition often become politicised and tend to be governed by the metropolitan concepts of 'norm', 'authenticity' and 'aesthetic' values. Having dislodged the binary opposites the hybrid can be constructive, creative and forward facing. The differing locations in history and geographical spaces lend hybrid developments a different politics of identity and self-validity.

As the discourse has emerged in different locations, its interpretive engagements in histories of colonial experience also include the re-reading of literatures and other art forms. New interpretations can emerge through the recognition of hybridity, a viewpoint that Stuart Hall, Paul Gilroy, Kobena Mercer and Michael Dash, for example, maintain.[1] For the artists and critics who locate their hybridity in an aesthetic frame, transfer from the place of one's origin may have valuable impact. In Kobina Mercer's views, 'Across a whole range of cultural forms there is a "syncretic" dynamic which critically appropriates elements from the master-codes of the dominant culture and "creolises" them, disarticulating given signs and re-articulating their symbolic meaning'. These acts of appropriation and transformation can have a subversive role when employed at the level of language, where creolisation of English, the language of the master, can 'decenter, destabilize and carnivalize the domination' of the English language (Mercer 57).

An important direction taken in the hybridity discourse is a reconsideration of the shared histories of the colonial period, histories shared between the different races. Although shared, these histories are seen very differently by the ruled and the rulers, for each experienced that period in a radically different manner. For the slaves, indentured labour, and subjugated societies, the forced transportations and transformations led to the making of translated beings. Hybridisation of languages, cultural practices and other aspects of life were, for the most part, extremely painful and humiliating.

Homi Bhabha explores this relationship between the coloniser and the colonial subjects as inhering in ambivalence. The ambivalence is located in the colonised's presence, through the sense of anxiety and desire that the coloniser experiences (Bhabha 112). Bhabha uses the idea of the ambivalence of mimicry, which is 'almost the same, but not quite' (86). This ambivalence creates a split-consciousness in the coloniser, and the subaltern's counter-gaze serves to intensify colonial control mechanism and also to threaten the disciplinary power of the coloniser's position. Fludernik argues that in Bhabha's analysis hybridisation is 'said to be produced by the ambivalence and undecidability of traditional discourses of authority, a formulation that paves the way for the recurrent phrase "the ambivalence of hybridity" (Bhabha 113, qtd. by Fludernik 41).

The painful awareness of the demeaning treatment meted by the coloniser and erasure of one's cultural heritage are depicted poignantly in several novels, poems and other writings by writers of Caribbean descent. V.S. Naipaul's *A House for Mr Biswas* (1961) makes a subtle and comprehensive analysis of the transformative processes of a society that shifts imperceptibly from being a colony of indentured labourers and slaves to a hybrid social entity. Mr Biswas's struggle for success in the larger world, outside the small world of his wife's prosperous family, reflects the colonial urge to gain acceptance in the white man's world, represented in the novel through the figure of Mr Burnett and the journalism that he tries to teach Biswas.

Another remarkable novel that has dealt with the trauma and misery on one of the Caribbean islands is Austin Clarke's *The Polished Hoe* (2000). A West Indian who now lives in Canada, Clarke presents the oppression of the mulatto men and women on the small island, Bimshire, focusing on one woman's narration of her lifelong subjection, sexual oppression, and finally, her revenge; the novel moves beyond the individual story to that of an entire social group. Mary Gertrude Mathilda, the central character of the novel, has been, since she was eight years of age, under the power and control of Mr Bellfeels, the plantation manager, who rules the population of the small village on the island. When she makes her 'statement' to the police Sergeant, Mr Percival, after she has killed the master, she recalls her entire life's story. Her individual story interweaves the experiences of three generations of women – her mother and grandmother who were born on the island and her 'great Granma' who remembered how she had been transported, along with several other Africans, from their native land. Gender, race and class histories pour forth through the combined narratives of Mary, Percy and the constable who comes to the 'Big House' for a short while. Most painful to these people is the continued and unrelieved harassment from the white men, even though they may have fathered many of these mulattos.

Mary has been fortunate to some extent in that her one surviving child, Wilberforce, is the only son that Mr Bellfeels has. He educates him in the best of British educational institutions and provides well for the upkeep of both Mary and their son. But having a separate, big, well-furnished house to maintain, however, does not bring to Mary the dignity of a legal status. Instead, hinted through Percy's memories, is the fact that Mary has been sexually exploited by Mr Bellfeels, whose guests were often 'entertained' by her (135).

All these indignities and humiliations have created a rage in Mary, which she keeps well under control. She carries out Mr Bellfeel's orders and wishes with a polite humility, never giving a hint of the murderous intention with which she polishes her hoe at night. She and her son are brought under the impact of the European classical art forms, such as painting, music and architectural forms, through the magazines and other objet d'art that are displayed in the 'Big House'. Mary's own personality has undergone a refinement of manners, language and taste which are taken further in the case of her son. She and Wilberforce are the resultant 'hybrids', come into being through mixed parentage and other direct and indirect influences.

The hybrid native however brings together the inherited traits of both lineages. Their internalisation of the language, songs, religion and ritual of the white master makes an uneven mixing up with their African lineage, customs and forms of knowledge. Practicing the white master's religion, rituals, language, nursery rhymes and games, the natives come within the cultural domain of the master. Christened with European/English names, their children have played the games of their children and shared their popular music and dance steps. The cultural erasure, however, is at a deeper level, a problematic intermixing, for the responses of Mary and Percy to the English society's sexual practices and marital relations reflect a distance between the master and these adapted/adopted natives.

Fluency in the language and manners of the 'other' remains a problem for these hybrid people. Mr Bellfeels, himself of a mixed origin, reflects this in his use of the dialect of the natives. It is his white colour that gives him a superior position of authority which he constantly flaunts. Talking to the sergeant (a Black Police Officer) one evening, Mr Bellfeels says 'I is the law round here, boy'. Putting his arm round the sergeant's shoulder, he continued, 'and I intend to take the law round here, Sarge-boy' (Clarke 71). Showing off his authority, he emphasises the position of unquestioned power he occupies.

The mulattos, metisse and others of mixed origin, like the Eurasians, Anglo-Indians in China and India did not enjoy any special favours or privileges from the rulers. These children were further subjected to the ignominy of being disowned by their white parents. They often ended up as policemen, housekeepers, or 'kip' women, and were placed at the lowest rung in the social order.

Antoinette, the creole Jamaican heiress of the plantation, in *Wide Sargasso Sea* may have money and a higher social status among the village population, but as she gradually learns that for her English husband, Rochester, her social place is at a low level. 'Looking at her smiling at herself in the mirror, he reflects, "Looking up smiling, she might have been any pretty English girl"' (Rhys 499). Despite her fair coloured skin, Antoinette's creole descent prevents her from ever claiming a social status at par with a European or English lady (Rhys 496). Her childhood proximity to her mixed and native associates marks her out as 'savage' rather than one capable of rational or affectionate behaviour. This attitude reflects 'the metropolitan view' (Hogan 97) of people of non-European/white descent. They were stereotyped as barbaric, uncivilised and irrational.

Charlotte Bronte's 1847 novel *Jane Eyre* depicts the commonly held view of creoles through Mr Rochester. Describing Bertha Antoinette Mason, the rich Jamaican woman he has married, to Jane, he speaks of her as wild, with 'a pigmy intellect', 'violent', 'unreasonable' and 'unchaste' (Bronte 302). Jean Rhys reconstructs the narrative of the silenced, estranged and 'mad' woman whose agony of marrying into a totally different cultural ethos needs to be recognised. The creole's sudden loss of her cultural background worsens as she travels across the seas to a radically different and overwhelmingly hostile social world. Her financial status may have attracted colonial masters (not necessarily Mr Rochester) but her social ostracisation finds an extreme isolation in the attic of Mr Rochester's grand mansion, Thornfield.

Social ostracism and devaluation was also the lot of Eurasians in nineteenth century Bengal. An agitation, in fact, took shape as the aggrieved group found a reverse discrimination against them by the British rulers who banned their entry into England, British universities and the civil services.[2]

Linguistic hybridity becomes an apparent marker, reflected in the speech of the British speakers as well as the natives. The colonial Indian society formed its own mixed pidgin as the diverse nationalities came together on land and sea. The British officers of the East India Company in Calcutta and their business associates who were reaping the benefits of expanding opium market between India and China and the staff on the ships travelling all around these limits, did not speak standard English as reflected in Amitav Ghosh's *Sea of Poppies* (2008). In a conversation at dinner where the British officer Mr Burnham, Zamindar Raja Neel, Mr Doughty and another Britisher, almost unconsciously use local words within their English. 'Here, Mr Doughty suddenly joined in, "The trouble, you know, is that Johnny China man thinks he can return to the good old days, before he got his taste for opium. But there's no going back – just won't *hoga*" ' (Ghosh 112 emphasis mine). The Hindi word '*hoga*' is the verb that completes the meaning 'just won't happen'. Speaking further he used the word '*gudda*' to indicate 'fellow' (person): 'Damned hard headed *gudda* is Johnny long-tail' (Ghosh 112). 'But they've never made a tumasher about it in the past' – *tumasher* for making a show, a fuss about something (113). Mr Burnham also uses some of the other local words, words from Indian languages like '*desturees*' (bribe) *lattee* (stick), *bobachees* (cooks) (113–114.) Mr Doughty and Mr Burnham are not the only English characters whose language is mixed with local words, Mrs Doughty also speaks in pidgin as she converses with Pauletta and other persons in the household: *jadoo* (261) *puggly* (271) *gupping about, shaytan* (272) *butcha* (274).

The colonial domain became a fertile site for the intermixing of languages. While ships are at sea Naval officers, sailors and labourers work together, a heterotopic space develops, where men and women from several different countries converge and form one unique community. In the *Sea of Poppies* the young enterprising lad, Jodua, runs away from his dull life in the village than, from Calcutta. He becomes an ordinary sea-man where he comes across Zachary Reid, an American of mixed white and Black parentage, a Chinese, Serang Ali from Malaya, other langa boys and lascars who have come from different ports from Malay, Burma and other islands scattered over the Indian ocean. Their language is a curious mix of several dialects from different countries. Mr Doughty's command 'Heave, you dogs, heave!' is translated immediately into a different accent, and language 'Habés, habés, Kutte, habés! habés! (171). Ghosh takes time to depict how the songs of the Bihari indentured men and women are trancreated as they are transported with them, along with their marriage customs; rituals are modified according to the availability of space and resources and slow mutations begin to take place (397). *Sea of Poppies* reconstructs the transportation of indentured labour from the central states of India to a totally unfamiliar land, landscape and work. The dislocation immediately loosens the stronghold of a fixed stable cultural self rooted in a particular space and history; the self-contained, heterotopic space of the ship itself begins to mould these Indians. They experience a new form of violent authority that brings out their ingrained innovativeness as well as resilience. Their stories at the new locations need to be seen within these diverse histories of colonial and self-willed displacements.

In re-reading the histories of colonial rule of the Caribbean islands, Edward Brathwaite looks for new interpretive possibilities. The exploration of these pasts brings forth memories of the anguish of that deterritorialisation. The pangs of separation and an awareness of a sense of destruction of all routes back home create in these people 'an impossible mourning' as Vijay Mishra puts it. Deterritorialised societies and the communities which have lived through the sense of un-belongingness and exilic alienation, gradually developed in these conditions new survival strategies. While the compulsion to retain the native inherited identities and resist its forced modification by an 'other' were strong, forced living in close proximity with those who showed open contempt, disregard, and hostility also moulded them. In analysing this situation, especially on the Caribbean islands, Michael Dash refers to 'the emergence of new cultural forms and practices that were neither extensions of the culture back home, nor the one imposed from above by the ruling class'. The creole, metisse and mulattos were created by the settlers, and migrant rulers, 'through a pattern of apparent consent, opposition and overt resistance' (Dash 1988: 57).

'Creole' and 'hybrid' writers have articulated the deep pain and uncertainties experienced in these transformations. Jamaica Kincaid looks at the loss of self and national identity suffered 'by the millions of people' of whom she says she is also one: 'people' made orphan: no motherland, no fatherland, no god … and worst and most painful of all, no tongue'. The bitterness of using the language of the oppressor, of having to speak of this 'crime' in the 'language of the criminal who committed the crime', silences and humiliates even as one uses that language (Kincaid 43). The hybridised writers' work expresses the complex emotions that anger, hatred and the sense of inner void create in there people. David Punter relates these sentiments of Kincaid's words to the awareness of 'hidden histories' of the criminal consequences of colonial desire 'where the white men fathered children on 'native' women and acted out the further wish to obliterate the trace of this crossing of the boundary by removing those same children from situations in which they might learn something of the truth of their parentage' (Punter 48). The recognition of these 'ruins' that lie at the source of 'origin' generates a kind of trauma that is expressed in different tropes, metaphors and symbols in their writing.

Jamaica Kincaid's fictional works and autobiographical texts reflect her alienation and loneliness in a society deeply fractured by colonial domination. She also reflects upon the difficulties that are faced in the formation of an identity in social structures where gender discriminations continue to prevail, along with the legacy of colonial hierarchies. In an interview she expresses her realisation that at one point in her life she came to see that the central theme of all her writings 'was about the relationship between the powerful and the powerless' (Ferguson 164). The underlying current of anger against these discriminations in Kincaid's work has been noted by various critics (Gupta 236), as is the sense of anguish and betrayal by the past history of Jamaica, although Kincaid has migrated to USA and writes from there.

The emergence of Caribbean writers and others of mixed origins in the twentieth century has created a literature which seeks to articulate their experiences from their perspective. Ramabai Espinet discusses this aesthetic and cultural self-expression of the Caribbean writers; she herself was inspired by the efforts that the writers were making to 'carve out' their 'literary space' (Savory 261). Writers like V.S. Naipaul, Wilson Harris, Arnold Itwaru, Derek Walcott, who are hyphenated (sometimes doubly hyphenated) identities, explore their unique cultural locations as they further migrate from one area to another, from colonial contexts to metropolitan centres.

The hybridity discourse attempts to articulate the desires, pains, beliefs and the political projects from below. An anxiety of 'authenticity' of identity haunts many of the hybrid social communities and the languages, experiments in literary and other art forms that they have developed. The hybridised faces an uncertainty not only about heritage, but also of the yardstick by which it can be measured. The poetics of hybridity must be created from within the existing systems, yet, as several artists, writers and critics of postcolonial belongings realise, such 'poetics' must struggle for recognition. The hybridity discourse draws attention to the constant movement between the 'origin' (al) and the hybrid, and the destabilising impact of the latter; when a nomadic transfer takes place the deterritorialising impact unsettles the frontiers associated with the national (or the other source) identities.

The historical role played by the hybrid societies and of the hybridisation of slave societies has begun to be viewed positively by critics like Edward Brathwaite and Paul Gilroy, giving the discourse a new direction. Brathwaite's book *The Development of Creole Society in Jamaica 1770–1820* (1971) reviews the role of the British ruling class and the West Africans brought to Jamaica, in the formation of a society which developed its own distinctive character as a creole society. This society, he says, gave rise to customs, festivals, social practices which were basically the result of the interconnections between the two main presences, for there were other ethnic groups too. The African, Indian and European social groups shaped together this society. Their shared experiences brought together the different races, along with their music, dances, festivals, and languages. Brathwaite's analysis links together the history of Jamaica with that of Europe, America and the other parts of the world. He argues that these different geographical units were linked in their trade and commerce, mercantile projects and also influenced one another in the development of ideas. He brings out the flow of ideas between France, America and Jamaica when different revolutions occurred in this region during the eighteenth and nineteenth centuries. Brathwaite places the so far neglected and ignored creole society on a very different political status, a presence to be recognised in the international scene.

A somewhat similar agenda is noticed in the writings of Wilson Harris who celebrates the hybridity of Caribbean culture in *The Palace of the Peacock* (1988) using both European and Caribbean cultural myths in such a way 'as to stress the mutual benefits brought about by alternative perceptions of a colonial past otherwise assumed to take its place within the self-authorising annals of European history' (Huggan 29). Graham Huggan in his analysis of Harris's *The Palace of the Peacock* foregrounds Harris's 'belief in the possibilities afforded by a new cross-cultural poetics which participates actively in the transformation not just of postcolonial, but of all cultures' (29). Harris and Brathwaite both build up the idea of 'interculturative' process of creolisation'. It is useful to distinguish this productive idea of creolisation from the 'monolithic perception' which come from the usual negative forms of creolisation which 'either subscribe to the values of and therefore, reinforce the social hierarchy presided over by the dominant (white) culture or, alternatively, which claim to have effected the total recuperation of the marginalised (indigenous) culture in terms which now exclude external influence of any kind' (Huggan 29).

The relevance and value of Huggan and Brathwaite's model of interactions and cross fertilisations between the European and creole cultures lies in providing a space in between the two positions and working out of 'binary structures', an idea also supported by Said. This process provides a perception of integration through 'a dialectical process involving the interrogation, displacement and ironic refiguration of the hegemonic practices of European cultures' (Huggan 31).

Paul Gilroy's re-reading of European/Western history seeks to move out of binary oppositions that postcolonial studies are caught in, and the essentialism that forms the basis of many writings on race, ethnicity and nation. In *The Black Atlantic* (1993) he considers Black writers, travellers and political activists and even slaves: Gilroy finds that several figures like Crispus Attucks, Frederick Douglass, Marcus Garvey, George Padmore, Claude McKay, and others who were sailors, played an important role in bringing about a new political awareness leading to a 'Pan-African communication' in the entire region around the Atlantic (Gilroy 61). He further refers to 'Notable black American travellers, from the poet Phyllis Wheatley onwards who went to Europe and had their perception of America and racial domination shifted as a result of their experiences there' (Gilroy 64). Ida B. Wells, a radical journalist, Lucy Parsonus and Nella Larsons are some of the other black writers and intellectuals whose perceptions of the race, nation, class underwent very significant shifts, due to such travels to Europe and other kind of dislocations. Naming such writers and persons, Gilroy wants to emphasise how the black travellers/diaspora brought together diverse units of Black people spread out around the Atlantic, and also to highlight the opening out of the Black mind to wider, diverse influences – creating a new intermingling of cultures. That there were mutual influences and awareness of these diverse cultures Gilroy argues with reference to European thinkers (53). Gilroy in *The Black Atlantic* argues about the adoption of the west's cultural and ideological traditions by generations of Blacks who had been brought there. The concepts of nationality and race were opened up when the processes of adapting to new cultural conditions took place, by which the Blacks become linked with their 'adoptive cultures'. Gilroy says, 'I have become fascinated with how successive generations of black intellectuals have understood this connection and how they have projected it in their writing and speaking in pursuit of freedom, citizenship and social and political autonomy' (Gilroy, 51). This positive view of the vital role played by the intermixing of diverse cultures in the modern age allows for recognition of hybridisation as worthy of respect and celebration. In his book *Between Camps: Nations, Culture and the Allure of Politics* (2000) Gilroy goes ahead with the idea of loosening the nationalist frames, to develop out of entrenched 'camps', i.e., the nations, and create a 'unifying planetary humanism' as a strategy of moving beyond ethnic identities, including hybrid and diasporic identities. Nations divide humanity, and thinking beyond nation allows for greater unification among people.

The concept of a large universal brother/sisterhood of the entire world as one family (*Vasudha Kutumbkam*) is an ancient Indian ideal. In more recent past the cultural homogeneity of Indian civilisation, even when different foreign groups regularly entered the land, was highlighted during the nationalist discourse beginning in the middle of nineteenth century. Indian nationalist discourse used this assimilative, syncretic and evolving aspect of Indian civilisation as one of its important qualities. The baffling diversity of ethnic, racial, religious presences in India was treated as a constituting phenomenon of the old and, so, of new India. In the imagining and narrating of the new India various scholars foregrounded India's diversity, pluralism and most important, the assimilation between the different streams of people/communities into a heterogeneous culture which tolerated difference readily. Indian scholars, historians and political activists emphasised the rich diversity that had arisen in Indian social and cultural scene as diverse religious and cultures entered India and gradually settled down, contributing to formation of a complex culture that incorporated new elements/influences, allowing the differences to prevail without causing clash of civilisations.

Such intermingling led to the emergence of hybrid people, communities, art forms and festivals. Languages came together, giving rise to new dialects and creole languages which found general acceptance. Urdu (Hindustani) is an important development of this kind. Rabindra Nath Tagore's poetic expression is given below to express this constant process of assimilation that is found in India civilisation. In his poem *Sanchayita*, he wrote:

> No one knows at whose call
> Arrived waves of humanity in tumultous currents
> And became absorbed in the ocean (of India)
> Here are the Aryans, the un-Aryans, the Dravidians,
> The Chinese, the Sakas, Huns, Pathans and Mughuls
> All merging into one entity .... (quoted in Sharma 140–41)

This spirit of absorption is noted by Jawahar Lal Nehru in the *Discovery of India* which, he says, created 'a multi-dimensional tapestry of stunning richness and depth, as bewildering as it is compelling, as subtle as it is exuberant'. He refers to this integrative process; with the presence of the different new immigrants there was 'a gradual and hardly conscious approach towards these foreign ways both in thought and life. A synthesis worked itself out: new styles of architecture arose; food and clothing changed, and life was affected and varied in many other ways' (Nehru 260). He further elaborates upon these new developing forms: 'This synthesis was especially marked in music which, following its old Indian classical patterns, developed in many directions' (261).

The persistence of integration of diverse external influences raises several questions about the 'authenticity' and 'purity' of the 'true' Indian civilisation. New influences were absorbed within the mainstream creating new hybrid forms in architecture, literature, different art forms, and in the socio-cultural practices. The nationalist discourse highlighted the assimilative process, as perhaps a strategy to contain and homogenise the variety and diversity within the new nation that was being imagined and narrated by them. A careful analysis of the 'unity' that has prevailed within the nation in the pre- and post-independence period belies to some extent this optimistic view. Yet the importance of this discourse in creating a multi-racial and multi-cultural nation is undeniable.

India continues to bring diverse elements from different cultures in its characteristic way attaining new hybridisation in art forms, fashions, literary genres and ideas. One of the recent examples of this hybridity is the new musical instrument called 'Mohan Veena' designed by Pt. Vishwamohan Bhatt, in which he has combined features of the guitar (a western instrument) with 'veena' (a traditional Indian instrument). The new innovation has been well appreciated in the art world. Bhatt is a recipient of the Grammy Award. Hybridisation here is substituted by the word 'fusion' and it plays a creative role, by bringing together diverse elements and contributing to the formation of a global culture, which incorporates local traditions.

## Notes

1. See Stuart Hall, 'Negotiating Caribbean Identities' (1995) rept. *Postcolonial Discourses: An Anthology.* (Ed. Gregory Castle. Oxford: Blackwell Publication 2001), 280–292.
2. The Indian Eurasian community began to organise itself in Associations and took care of their educational, financial and social problems. In 1830, some of these persons together presented a petition to the British authorities to consider how the lot of the Eurasians could be improved, mainly through financial support for a 'high class liberal education'. The petition expressed pain at the social discrimination that these persons of mixed (English, French, Portuguese, and others and Indian) origin experienced. Though these associations of Eurasians and their members expressed loyalty to the British Government, they also acknowledged that 'India is the home, the native land of Eurasians in a true sense as it is of men of pure Indian blood' (Edwards 227). The distinct sense of hierarchical placing of 'pure' and 'mixed' origins is sensed in the wordings of the petition. 'Appendix A', The Petition of 1830' in Thomas Edwards, *Henry Derozio,* (1884, New Delhi: Rupa & Co. 2002), 177–217.

## References

Bhabha, Homi K. 'Of Mimicry and Man: The Ambivalence of Colonial Discourse' in *The Location of Culture*, London: Routledge, 1994, 85–92.

——. 'Signs taken for Wonders: Questions of Ambivalence and Authority under a Tree Outside Delhi, May 1817', in *The Location of Culture*, London: Routledge, 1994, 102–122.

Brathwaite, Edward K. *The Development of Creole Society in Jamaica* 1770–1820. Oxford: Oxford University Press. 1971

Braziel, Jana Evans and Anita Mannur., eds. *Theorizing Diaspora: A Reader*. UK: Blackwell, 2003.

Bronte, Charlotte. *Jane Eyre* (1847) World Classics, UBS Publishers Distributor, New Delhi n.d.

Clarke, Austin. *The Polished Hoe*: New York: Harper Collins, 2003.

Dash, Michael. *Haiti and United States: National Stereotypes and the Literary Imagination*. London: Macmillan, 1988.

——. 'In Search of the Lost Body: Redefining the Subject in Caribbean Literature'. *Kunapipi* XI, No. I, 1989, 17–26.

Edwards, Thomas. *Henry Derozio*. 1884. New Delhi. Rupa & Co. 2002.

Ferguson, Moira. 'A Lot of Memory: An Interview with Jamaica Kincaid'. *Kenyon Review* XVI. 1, Winter 1994: 163–188.

Fludernik, Monika. 'The Constitution of Hybridty: Postcolonial Interventions', *Hybridity and Postcolonialism. Twentieth Century Indian Literature*. Ed. Monika Fludernik (1998). Jaipur: Rawat Publications, 2006. 19–54.

Ghosh, Amitav. *Sea of Poppies*. Penguin: Viking India, 2008.

Gilroy, Paul. 'The Black Atlantic as a Counter Culture of Modernity', *Theorizing Diaspora*. Eds. Jana Evans Braziel and Anita Mannur, UK: Blackwell 2003, 49–80.

——. *The Black Atlantic: Modernity and Double Consciousness*. Cambridge. MA: Harvard University Press, 1993.

Gupta, Punam. '"I Cannot Always Be a Little You". Daughter–Mother (country) Relationship in Jamaica Kincaid's *Annie John*'. *Writers of the Caribbean Diaspora: Shifting Homelands, Travelling Identities*. Eds. Jasbir Jain and Supriya Agrawal. New Delhi: Sterling Publication, 2008, 235–246.

Hall, Stuart. 'Negotiating Caribbean Identities' (1995) rept. in *Postcolonial Discourses: An Anthology*. Ed. Gregory Castle. Oxford: Blackwell Publication 2001, 280–292.

Harris, Wilson. *The Palace of the Peacock*. London: Faber and Faber, 1986

Hogan, Patrick Colm. 'Colonialism, Patriarchy and Creole Identity', *Colonialism and Cultural Identity: Crisis of Tradition in the Anglophone Literature of India, Africa and the Caribbean.* Albany: State University of New York, 2000, 83–102.

Huggan, Graham. 'Opting out of the (Critical) Common Market: Creolization and the Post-colonial Text'. *Kunapipi.* XI No.I. 1989, 27–41.

Kincaid, Jamaica. *A Small Place.* London: Virago, 1988.

Mercer, Kobina. 'Diaspora Culture and the Dialogic Imagination' *Blackframes: Critical Perspectives on Black Independent Cinema.* Eds. M. Cham and C. Watkins. Cambridge, MA: Cambridge Univ. Press, 1988. 52–61.

——. *The Story of the Voice.* London: New Beacon Publication, 1983.

——. *Welcome to the Jungle.* London: Routledge, 1994.

Mishra, Vijay. 'The Art of Impossible Mourning'. *In Diaspora: Theories, Histories, Texts.* Ed. Makarand Paranjape. New Delhi: Indialog Publications, 2001.

Nehru, Jawahar Lal. *Discovery of India* (1946). New Delhi: Penguin, 2004.

Punter, David. *Postcolonial Imaginings: Fictions of a New World Order.* New Delhi: Atlantic: Edinburgh UP, 2000.

Rhys, Jean. *Wide Sargasso Sea.* In the complete novels. Ed. Diana Athill (1966). New York: W.W. Norton, 1985.

Said, Edward. 'Introduction', *Culture and Imperialism.* London: Vintage 1994, xi-xxxiii.

——. 'Travelling Theory' *The World, the Text and the Writer,* Cambridge Massachusetts. Harvard UP, 1983. 226–238.

Savory, Elaine. 'An Interview with Ramabai Espinet'. *Writers of the Caribbean Diaspora: Shifting homelands, travelling identities.* Eds. Jasbir Jain and Supriya Agarwal, New Delhi: Sterling Publishers Pvt. Ltd., 2008, 257–274.

Tagore, Rabindranath, 'Sanchayita'. translated and quoted by Proshanta Nandi, in 'Visions of Nationhood and Religiosity among Early Freedom Fighters in India' in *Nation and National Identity in South Asia.* Eds. S.L. Sharma and T.K. Oommen. New Delhi: Orient Longman Ltd. 2000, 135–150.

# Diasporic Imagination: Memory, Space and Hybridity

*Vijay Lakshmi*

It all began after I immigrated to the United States. The memory of the homeland left behind dictated every thought, mood, and action in the adopted home. The language I spoke, the food I ate, the clothes I wore, the thoughts I thought were no longer 'purely' Indian or American. I spoke a hybridised Hindi or English at home, cooked in a hybridised way, wore hybridised clothes, and thought hybridised thoughts. On the street, I heard people speaking Hindi. Among a bank of daffodils, I breathed in the fragrance of *champa*. The psychological as well as the physical distance was frightening; the danger of losing my identity, terrifying. The notion of who I thought I was clung to me like the vestiges of a beautiful dream that lingers on in the mind even after one is awake. It took me some time to understand that identity is not a finished product, that it is 'a matter of "becoming" as well as of "being". It belongs to the future as much as to the past' (Hall 225). Once this awareness had sunk in, I could give free reign to my imagination to cross the oceans, though in the beginning, it was not a comfortable sensation. Going back in imagination is never without risk. Having stepped through the looking glass, as Chamcha in *The Satanic Verses* says, 'You step back at your own peril. The mirror may cut you to shreds' (Rushdie 58).

The anxiety about loss and longing, about belonging and not belonging, about having and not having, however, gave me a very strong vantage point, a kind of oblique angle, both on the world that I had come into and the world that I had left behind. Straddling two worlds, a whole process of integration and exclusion had begun to take place in my mind. Divided by two sets of possibilities, I began to understand the nature of a schizophrenic dialogue which lies at the centre of diasporic writing.

If a dialectical transaction is at the basis of all art, nowhere is it more visible than in the works of diasporic writers who have crossed national boundaries, who have exchanged the currency of their cultural codes for a new set, and yet who still inhabit their 'imaginary homelands'. Their work is fraught with the polarities they learn to wrestle with, and subdue, everyday. They write with the memories of the imported, but conscious of the visions that the 'circumambient' American phenomenon creates.

The diasporic author constantly draws upon two temporalities and two spaces. Exchanging one tradition for another, one culture for another, and one home for another, the writer creates and inscribes 'alternative worlds,' which, vibrant and demanding, resist the prospect of annihilation. A diasporic writer has no other worlds to live in but the ones she creates. She writes with the memories of the imported, a blend of the old and the new, of the real and the ideal.

What shapes this fiction, then, is the silent dialogue that goes on between the inner voices that keep on whispering at the writer's elbow and the imaginary audience – one familiar, yet not quite known. In Bakhtian terms, such a writer's fiction is shaped mainly by a special kind of dialogic imagination where the writer's voice is the imported one and the reader's is the one with whose accents and tones the writer is not altogether at home. Fiction then becomes not only a dialogue between the writer and the reader of the same community, but the conversation between representatives of two groups, two places, two beliefs, two histories, and two cultures. It is this kind of relationship that can explain the presence of other languages, and non-English idioms, maxims, and fresh metaphors. That, I believe, accounts for the polyphonic, the alien, the refreshing nature of diasporic fiction.

Initially, a writer survives by memories of what was, of the life left behind. Here I must emphasise that nostalgia, the first step into the domain of art sustains memory, even creates memories. And memory is the psychological scaffolding that keeps the self from collapsing, that prevents the present from wiping off the past. Memory is the only weapon for fighting what Milan Kundera calls the 'organised forgetting' forced upon us by the new world. Akin to the Proustian memory, it solders the past with the present.

Of course, this can't happen overnight. It takes a writer a while to come to terms with the dialectical transaction which is so visible in the works of writers who have crossed national boundaries, who have exchanged the currency of their cultural codes for a new set, yet who still inhabit their homelands. The writer learns to wrestle with, and subdue polarities. This is where memory steps in as an accomplice rather than an adversary. The house, the garden, the country she has lost will remain forever as she remembers them. In fact, memory makes them more vivid. Sometimes even recreates them, imbuing them with a different colour, which the writer takes to be the one there was.

Memory, however, may not always be accurate. It doesn't have to be, unless one were writing historical fiction. Even there, I believe, we can have different versions of the same event. The point is that the writer's memory is the golden stuff from which she spins out her variegated yarn. And to thrive, the imaginative memory of the writer needs excess. For it is through plenitude alone that it can stall the forgetting forced by the crowding new impressions. Narrative of displacement then recreates, 'the endless desire to return to "lost origins," to be one again with the mother' (Hall 236). This tension is conducive to creativity. In a struggle for survival, the diasporic writer's memory, real or invented, helps her escape the deadening conformity, allowing her the space necessary for the formulation of a new literature – a hybrid literature – which does not conform to any one tradition or culture, but mints a fresh world with new alloys of the two. The writer becomes a creature 'of selected discontinuities, of willing re-invention' (Rushdie 47). The only way one can go home is through one's imagination, through one's fictive constructs. Home is not the place where our possessions and accomplishments are deposited and without which as Loren Eiseley says 'man is lost, not only man, but life' (79). Wherever we perch, or burrow, or nest, becomes our home. Implicit in this is the notion of disassembling and reassembling our psyche so that, 'It is the willingness to pioneer the one trek we all can make ... no matter what our station or location in life ... the existential reality that wherever there is life ... we are at home' (Giovanni 167).

As to the nature of imagination in this writing, it may well be argued that the pre-articulation process would be the same for all writers, diasporic or not. One could, certainly, argue that all imaginary countries of literature are set up by literal or metaphorical exiles, anyways. And nor is the existential state of nothingness, or the consciousness of apartness peculiar to the diasporic writer, either. All true – but the alienation of the diasporic writer is more than psychological. It is physical, linguistic, and cultural. But the insidious dialogue, a continual activity of the immigrant's mind, cannot be the common experience of all writers. It can hardly be the same in a self that was shaped elsewhere and then shipped to survive in a different clime, treated to different customs and expectations, greeted by different gestures and accents.

The diasporic writer, like Macbeth, stands in a double trust, to the distant homeland as well as to the immediate country. The double citizenship, a form of new cosmopolitanism, is the source of creativity. The instinct is to tell a story whose artistic function is even richer. Working in conjunction with the writer's present environment, the memory works, like Coleridge's 'esemplastic imagination,' to dissolve, dissipate, and recreate the world of past fixities. It modifies the present, even as the writer's present modifies the memory's past. It is this parallel activity that re-mints both the worlds – of here and now as well, as that of there and then.

Naturally, the future of this hybrid creation lies in tomorrow's lap. Just as sure as the world moves to globalisation, the stock of this literature will rise, for it shall offer something new and something old, blending the familiar with the unfamiliar, casting a strange glory on both.

To conclude, one may say that, for the diasporic writer, memory is more than a luxury; it is her lifeline. It is through the mediation of memory alone that she can get re-connected to what has formed her. Lacking the familiar sites, sounds, smells, and seasons, she comes to rely on the memory-tissue. She finds her space in the confines of her environs.

## References

Eiseley, Loren. *The Brown Wasps: A Collection of Three Essays in Autobiography.* Mount Horeb: The Perishable Press Limited, 1969.

Giovanni, Nikki. 'Pioneers: A View of Home.' *Sacred Cows ... and Other Edibles.* New York: William Morrow, 1989.

Hall, Stuart. 'Cultural Identity and the Diaspora'. *Colonial Discourse/Post-Colonial Theory.* Eds. Patrick Williams and Laura Chrisman. New York: Columbia UP, 1994.

Rushdie, Salman. *The Satanic Verses.* New York: Viking, 1989.

# From Madeleine Slade to Mirabehn: Not Really so Different After Crossing Over

*Gerda J. Unnithan-Kauffman*

> 'The call of the Eternal, heard most clearly in India, can make them (some Europeans) throw all caution to the wind. There is then a reckless rush towards a merger with the herald, be it a Hindu god or guru. I am afraid Mira may be heading for heart-break, if not worse. But I shall not warn her. It is perhaps better to foolishly heed this particular call than be wise and close the ears'.
>
> *(Romain Rolland's diary)*[1]

Madeleine Slade or Mirabehn, Gandhiji's companion from 1925 to 1948, was well-known because of her close association with Gandhi during the tumultuous times of the freedom struggle, but also because of her own writings and a more recent book by Sudhir Kakar named *Mira and the Mahatma* (2004). I was fascinated by Madeleine's life and her experiences of crossing over from England to India with a total surrender to a life so different from the one she was born to. Her crossing over was not just a simple spatial relocation, but a cultural relocation consisting of *multiple* crossings over: of class, gender, politics and religion. Madeleine was to the manor born, she belonged to an upper class English family, her father being an admiral in the colonial navy. But as Gandhiji's devoted companion and disciple she lived an extremely simple life in voluntary poverty. She negated her womanhood foregoing marriage and children and lived like a sannyasin. She crossed over from Christianity to a Hindu way of life and was directly politically involved in the freedom struggle of India diagonally opposite to her own colonial background. Her cultural relocation appeared to be almost total. Does she display a hybrid identity?

The reason for my fascination with Madeleine's crossing over is of course a personal one. As a twenty-year old, or rather young, woman born in The Netherlands before the Second World War started and with my formative years during this devastating war and immediately after that, I became intrigued by Gandhiji's writings and messages promulgating non-violence as the ultimate Truth. My future husband's doctoral dissertation on 'Gandhi and Free India' introduced me to a world of thought and actions I was unaware of. Gandhiji's work for and with the downtrodden stimulated a social consciousness in me which must have been latent till then. For me this became eventually 'the reckless rush' to cross over to India fifty-two years ago. My cultural relocation was considerable, but certainly not as total as Madeleine's. And I think I have kept my own, albeit flexible, identity.

Through observation I have found that more women than men have crossed over from elsewhere to live in India; their motives and experiences have been as varied as they are individuals from different cultural backgrounds. For women marriage to Indian men has often been the main reason, and seeking spiritual enlightenment is another. A few of these 'firengis' in India are well-known through their writings, work and actions, most have not put their experiences on paper or have preferred to remain invisible.

Let us search for the causes or motivation why people are abandoning what is familiar to them for a future that promises greater fulfillment. Emigration westwards from India has mostly been for economic reasons, for higher education, better employment, an improved standard of living, or greater freedom from oppressive social customs. Cultural relocation and cultural integration have naturally brought with them great demands of adaptation, and if not, then of conflict, polarisation, unhappiness and loss of identity. The great Indian diaspora has come into existence with ever widening organisations in all countries and a literature full of richly textured narratives. Except for Sri Lanka, Indian origin people abroad have as yet not demanded their own territories, although parts of England could qualify for this. In some countries, Mauritius, the Fiji Islands, the Caribbean, South Africa, etc., Indians have blended in well over the generations. In most of the so-called western countries they often remain a distinct group and their integration has remained sometimes problematic on both sides.

We are looking at the crossing over of Madeleine Slade, becoming Mirabehn. After personally cropping her hair soon after Madeleine reached Sabarmati Ashram, Gandhiji said he had a present for her – a new name, Mira. He adopted her as his daughter, although their relationship grew into an unusually platonic one, as between guru and female devotee. There took place a sublimation of Mirabehn's yearning for a deep emotional, passionate bond, remarkably like the saint Mira with the God Krishna. Madeleine belonged to a high class landed family in England. She was a very sensitive, somewhat lonely child. As a young woman she had experienced passionate emotions for the Scottish pianist Lamond. 'Her magical fascination was no longer confined to Lamond's music but had begun to inhabit his person. To put it plainly, she had fallen in love with the fifty-six-year old pianist who had a wife and a daughter, and who enjoyed her admiration but was oblivious of her infatuation'.[2] Her unfulfilled, almost neurotic yearnings for Lamond's love and her great obsession with the composer Beethoven and his music sent her on a journey to Europe. In Vienna she purchased the French philosopher Romain Rolland's *Jean Christophe* and his *Vie de Beethoven*. She was so infatuated with Beethoven's music that she studied French in Paris for six months to be able to read the ten volumes of *Jean Christophe* and then requested a meeting with Romain Rolland. By their third meeting Romain Rolland had adopted Madeleine as his 'spiritual daughter'. During their fourth meeting Romain Rolland casually mentioned Mahatma Gandhi whose biography he had just published. 'Who is he?' Madeleine asked. 'He is another Christ', Rolland told simply.[3]

Madeleine bought a copy of Gandhi's biography and while reading it she found, to quote 'the dawn in my heart glowed brighter and brighter, and by the time I had finished, the Sun of Truth was pouring his rays into my soul. From that moment I knew that my life was dedicated to Bapu. That for which I had been waiting had come'.[4] She then wrote to Gandhiji and literally begged that she may come over to India and join his ashram. He persuaded her to think it over for a year and to prepare herself for this major change in her life. On 31st December 1924 Gandhiji wrote to Madeleine: 'I am glad indeed that instead of obeying your first impulse you decided to fit yourself for the life here and to take time. If a year's test still impels you to come, you will probably be right in coming to India'.[5] A year of extreme preparations began: Madeleine changed her diet to pure vegetarian, started sitting cross-legged and sleeping on the floor, learnt Urdu and started carding, spinning and weaving, devoured literature by Tagore, the Bhagawat Gita, Gandhiji's writings, and to toughen herself physically worked with Swiss peasants in their hayfields during the summer months. Fortunately her parents somehow understood the spiritual character of the urge that impelled her and never said a word in disapproval. In October 1925 Madeleine sailed to India, 'The voyage was one long dream of spiritual ecstasy – leading on and on towards the blessed goal'.[6]

Undoubtedly, Mirabehn and her life-long committed work for the downtrodden in India and the various rather unusual health and nutrition experiments of Gandhiji have been greatly admired and appreciated in India and elsewhere. She lived extremely simple in the most remote and difficult circumstances. She was also incarcerated several times during the freedom struggle. Her attachment to and care of Bapu was extraordinary. To give one example: she would sit at the entrance of his door to keep visitors away while he was eating, sleeping or observing silence. Apparently, she did keep herself aloof from other people and was more attracted to looking after the animals, a similar character trait of her early years at her ancestral home in England. Kasturba tolerated all this devoted almost wifely attention to her husband, since Bapu did not seem to object to it.

Interestingly, while re-visiting Romain Rolland along with Gandhiji in December 1931, Mira's joy was tempered by a strange disquiet as she revisited the scenes of her former free and independent life, but now under conditions of the strictest discipline. 'In order to maintain that discipline,' she writes, 'I had, without realising it, shut myself up in a self-imposed inner prison …… *something was wrong; wrong in the sense that I was not my full self* …. I could not emerge from that inner prison. It seemed to be a part of the tapasya which Fate had ordained for me, in answer to these prayers of long ago. So the days passed in a haze of inner sadness, which I could not, at that time, explain to myself'. (emphasis mine) After spending a year in jail and later travelling to England and the United States as Gandhiji's unofficial ambassador she lived in a small village near Wardha to work on rural development programmes he had planned out. 'She was restless, but maintained an iron control on her emotions in relation to him, living out his script for her without complaint or rebellion. There were several breakdowns in her health, though.' Mira had hoped to live alone with Gandhiji in Seagaon (later Sewagram), but initially he insisted that she lived separately and she departed for 'the hut on the hill where I lived alone with my little horse as my companion'.[7]

Mirabehn's intense longing for a deep emotional relationship with Gandhiji was only partially fulfilled. Sudhir Kakar's book also mentions her infatuation with another follower of Gandhiji which came to nought and left her again extremely distraught. Towards the end of her life she returned to Europe and lived in Baden (Austria), the place where Beethoven had also lived. His music, which she so passionately loved, now filled her days and 'she walked the same paths which her beloved Beethoven had also walked'.

Crossing over often results in crossing back to one's roots later in life, because the basic identity and longing remain there. Mirabehn remained the Madeleine of her youth in spite of the vastly different experiences and exposures she had had during the main part of her life. As the well known psychologist Erik Erikson (1968) has mentioned: 'personal identity is an individual's subjective sense of a continuous existence and a coherent memory'. We notice this in the case of Madeleine/Mirabehn.

Hybridity more often takes place in persons of the second generation who have crossed over. Their roots are in the new country, although their doubts linger and the construction of their identities between the ancestral and mainstream cultures can cause confusion and conflict. This was not to be the case of Madeleine who constructed a social identity of her own choice, although her personal identity remained in tact. Still, an intriguing life which deserves great admiration, especially in the Indian context.

## Notes

1. Quoted by Sudhir Kakar in *Mira and the Mahatma* (Penguin Books, 2004), 133.
2. Ibid., 73–74.
3. Ibid., 79.
4. *Bapu's Letters to Mira*. Ed. Jivanji Dahyabhai Desai, (Navjivan Press, Ahmedabad) 1949, 4.
5. Ibid., 9.
6. Ibid., 6.
7. *Mira and the Mahatma, 212–213.*

## References

Desai, Jivanji Dahyabhai., Ed. *Bapu's Letters to Mira*. Ahmedabad: Navjivan Press. 1949.

Kakar, Sudhir. *Mira and the Mahatma*. New Delhi: Penguin, 2004.

Rolland, Romain. *Romain Rolland and Gandhi Correspondence and Diary Extracts*,. New Delhi: Publications Division, Ministry of Information and Broadcasting, 1976.

# Working Through Cultural Histories: The Meaning and Politics of Words

*Jasbir Jain*

In the beginning was the Word and the Word was with God[1] – and words are loaded with power. Not only are they a means of communication but they govern and shape our responses. Thus, their origins, directions of movement and the manner of use become increasingly significant in determining human relationships. Over the centuries different terms have been employed to indicate the interaction between cultures, the shifts and the accommodations they have made for each other – words like syncretism, accommodation, pluralism and blending. Racial crossovers have ordinarily been dismissed with pejorative terms like mulatto, Eurasian and later Anglo-Indian; 'Miscegenation' was a term very much in use till the 1960s. Some States in the US had legal provision for action against miscegenation till 1967. Other words that have been used for mixed races have been words like half-breed and freak. We have also traversed the whole course through hyphenated, translated and now transnational identities. The hyphen is done away with, the doubleness, the *douglaness* however is recognised, specially in the Caribbean context.[2] Almost all these terms work with the idea of purity as the defining norm notwithstanding the fact that racial purity has perhaps never been a reality. In recent times we have shifted to words like pluralism and multiculturalism. Each one of these terms conveys a different meaning, a different concern and mindset. While pluralism means co-existence specifying harmony, multiculturalism indicates a separateness, the need for tolerance and at times, withdrawal into ethnicity.

Placed against this context I wish to take up the different meanings of 'hybridity' as they have permeated the cultural discourse of our times, as well as the power behind this word and its inadequacies for our times. A free-floating adjective and a fixed noun, 'hybrid' can be used for anything – culture, language, space, mind, thought, philosophy, cuisine and what not. A botanical term in its origins, in its application to the human, it has lost its flexibility. And now it is more than ever before locked in the postcolonial discourse and carries with it a sense of inequality. Incidentally, postcolonial is another word which I feel, it is time to discard. Primarily because it no longer serves any purpose and secondly that as it has generated a whole lot of discourse which is circular in its movements, unable to get out of the maze of coloniality. An additional reason is that whatever the justification in terms of description, both 'hybrid' and 'postcolonial' are an ongoing deterrent to the very process of decolonisation which we talk about but hardly ever work towards translating it into reality. The last few decades have thrown up polarised concepts such as hybridity, indigeneity, multiculturalism, fundamentalism, centre-margin and other similar groups. These terms have now been caught up in what we call 'jargon', a safe label which nobody opens out or reads the small print – not even the practitioners.

More than a decade ago I wrote an essay 'Problematizing Hybridity' for a conference in the mid-nineties. I am not going to repeat the argument here, except for explaining that even at that time, I found the term both inadequate and grossly misused. So many years later, I have not changed my stand. Hybridity is a word is loaded with the substance of Macaulay's *Minute* (1835) and carries within it the Machiavellian theories of erasure of conquered cultures by erasing their language (and religions).

Several years later (2004) when this essay was published, the same volume contained an essay by Nayantara Sahgal 'Some Thoughts on the Puzzle of Identity'. She makes an even stronger statement against the passive acceptance of unequal terms of existence. Sahgal critiques the framing of our epistemological discourse by the west through its selective interpretations, rejections, erasures and suppressions. Resistance movements were dismissed as 'unrest' and the pageantry the Empire constructed around it painted it larger than life. Bernard Cohn has written in detail about the artificial rigging of the Empire (1997). Sahgal recalls her own disapproval of the TV version of *The Jewel in the Crown* and the memories it recalled of her childhood, of the 'crude white arrogance', the 'hurts and humiliations' – a period when 'West was the World and the rest a fringe on its edges' (25). The West, however, 'still continues to be the World' (29) and the fringes are dismissed as hybrids, some of whom have taken well to the grafting while others have succumbed to other pressures.

We find this debate going in Sahgal's novels. As for instance in *Plans for Departure*, we have the character of Anna Hansen, a Danish woman caught between several cultures and trying to make sense of them. She succeeds in this by trying to relate her external experience to her internal growth. It is the interrogation of the socio-political realities surrounding her that render the shifts in her being meaningful even in later life. Anna's search for freedom is related to her attempts at understanding the nature of both colonial power and missionary interventions, these she places frontally with her experiences as Sir Nitin's secretary and the Indian freedom struggle marked by her leaders like Tilak. Thus it is through these multiplicities that she works out her resolutions or partial resolutions, which are search for values rather than 'hybridity' through passive surrender. In *Mistaken Identity*, Bhushan's interrogation and response in the court scenes is a powerful commentary on the gradual evolution of cultures as they absorb outside influences and resist stereotypes. When asked about religion, his answer is Hindu Muslim When he is asked about the language he speaks, the answer is not in the singular:

> 'Your mother tongue?
>
> 'Poetry. But if you're going to be finicky about it, my mother tongue is Hindi, and my father tongue is Urdu, she – illiterate

> though she is – hailing from the Sanskrit script and paraphernalia and he from everywhere that hit us when Islam rode in. Let me assure you Father wouldn't know Hindi letters from a crab's crawl. His tongue doesn't rise to the higher pillars of Hindi pronunciation. The glories of Sanskrit are Greek to him. The capital of his culture is Persia.' (144)

In *Lesser Breeds*, the young Shān's walks with her tutor Nurullah are, in themselves, a lesson in keeping resistant frames and alternative epistemologies alive. The novel works with multiple cultural traditions: Leda, the Czech collector of fairy tales and Shan's opera-loving admirer Otto all bring in different cultures and experiences.

Indian culture has always been subject to other interactions, imperial conquests and foreign powers. Were all these phases 'hybrid'? Bhabha published *The Location of Culture* in 1994, but some of the essays were written as early as 1985. Three of his essays specifically deal with the 19th century India, and one of them 'Signs taken for Wonders', examines the role of the missionaries in some detail. It is this essay which unravels the complexity and the negativity of the term and needs to be read closely. Power seeks to impose, yet resists from 'sameness' and hence one of its important strategies is discrimination (112). The colonial subject is left with the 'disturbing questioning of the images and presences of authority' (113). When a symbol, a category which represents continuity and evokes thought turns into a sign, then perhaps hybridity sets in with all its negative implications. Susan K. Langer in her essay, 'Logic of Signs and Symbols' defines a sign as denotative, it is something to act upon, while symbol is connotative, it does not depend directly on memory, it is a space for thinking (Langer 143). It is this difference which Bhabha's title indicates. Bhabha in another essay 'Articulating the Archaic' draws attention to the ambivalence present in the colonial discourse (129–131) and goes on to observe that what is articulated is 'a splitting of discourse'. Both the essays question the meaning and implications of hybridity. How far are the belief systems transferred and who is it that changes in these cases and what kind of a resistance emerged are some of the issues he addresses. Conversions took place as early as the 16th century. A large number of convertees on the western coast were from the upper castes. The first half of the 19th century was no different in Bengal. This was an acceptance of ideas not of a way of life – no reproduction of the 'brown sahib'. Today, the Church in India has adopted regional cultural practices almost all over the country. Is it hybridity working the other way?

Going back further into our history, the early Turk invaders were not identified as Muslim on the grounds of their religion but on the basis of their language as 'Turks' or 'Turkish' (Eaton 10). As conversion to Islam began to take place there was a great deal of going across from one language to another from one literary tradition to another, and from one genre to another. And people who converted often took their customs and habits along. Architecture also accommodated cultural shifts. A mosque need not always look like one. In pre-colonial Malabar, a mosque maybe quite different from a mosque of the same period in Kashmir or Bengal (6) being more in tune with local culture. In fact, the Indo-Islamic period witnessed an ongoing double movement between the local cultures where art, culture and languages were concerned. The rise of the Sufi and Bhakti movements, the poetry of Kabir and Guru Nanak, the dargahs which attracted all alike, were all products of an opening out of cultures, some of which had been peripheral so far. Hegemonic structures like culture were porous. They did not clamp on us any grafting. If there was any, it was a chopping off on both sides followed by a gentle convergence signifying an acculturation. Khushwant Singh's *History of the Sikhs* deals in fair amount of detail with the intermixing of cultures especially in the convergence of the Bhakti movement and the Sufi impact.

Histories do not always remain the same. Human imaginaries, arrangement of facts and their recasting go a long way in defining our perspectives. I need not remind you of Said's *Orientalism* and the burden of his thesis that any continued projection of an idea, creates a climate of opinion. Hence, the need to read the past over and over again in order to identify the political directions of the interpretations; hence also the need to deconstruct terms and terminologies. Hybridity as a term leads us into complacent evaluations, without taking the trouble of dissecting situations or identities. Today, the word has even moved away from Bhabha's use of the term. For him it was a process not a position; it enabled the possibility of dismantling polarities (see Bhabha, 38, 113, 181). Bhabha felt that it had the capacity to work as resistance and render any position of power untenable. But today it has increasingly become a comfort zone with 'third space' following close on its heels. As I have already said, western hegemony underlines the concept: it hinders the process of decolonisation.

Early in the 90s, a conference was organised in Amsterdam with the purpose of enabling scholars to deconstruct and decode the images created by the West. Jan Nederveen Pieterse and Bhikhu Parekh in their 'Introduction' to the subsequent volume titled *Decolonization of Imagination* (1997), observe that western imperialism, by the mere fact of being accompanied by capitalism and industrialisation, has lingered on even after territorial occupation has ceased. It is a much more complex phenomenon than any earlier conquest or domination, mainly because it has infiltrated ideas of progress, evolution, modernity and development (1). In effect it thwarted the evolutionary process at work in these societies (see Irfan Habib) and also pushed India into various religious reform movements such as the Brahma Samaj, Arya Samaj, Prarthna Samaj and others, creating fresh fixities and divisions that had not existed earlier. In some ways they were subversive of the spirit of the more than six-century-long Bhakti movement which had travelled from one end of the country to the other, forcing us to think of larger issues than fixities like rituals, boundaries and places of God.

The process of colonisation had a centre, a policy and a strategy: processes of decolonisation are represented by minority voices and often adopt the terminology of centre and margin freely yielding authority to the erstwhile masters. Pieterse and Parekh point out that the decolonisation of imagination involves both the colonisers and the colonised (5), but in actuality has this happened and can we make it happen? Instead we often separate 'culture' and 'development', accept a monolithic representation of 'modernity' and succumb to economic pressures. The circulation of power has not taken place except marginally through resistance movements. Ethnicity has deteriorated into another kind of exhibition (as contrasted to museumification), nativism has failed to thrive in India, though negritude still survives in pockets especially in Afro-American and African writing. Is it that we have suffered mutation beyond redemption? Or is it that we do not question enough? Or our littlenesses take possession of us?

I return to Sahgal for comfort and hope, she who acknowledges a mixed heritage and who refuses to 'squash' herself into European categories. She writes: 'There is a whole other universe of value waiting to come to light which does not lend itself to European terms [...]'. A world, she feels, that will come into its own the day the 'white man lays down his burden and holds out his hand in equal partnership' (36). To this I add, this world will come to light the day we learn to examine critical terms more closely rather than allow our minds to be ridden by those who have outlived their utility. Decolonisation begins with the mind: and any placid acceptance of hybridity with its implied subordination of one to the other has no place in it.

## Notes

1. Genesis 1:1. The opening lines of the first book of the Bible.
2. I heard this term from Brinda Mehta, a scholar on Indo-Caribbean writing, when she visited Jaipur in 2009. Later I found this was properly explained in her work, *Diasporic (Dis)locations. (2002).* The word, in India, would imply a double-facedness, an untrustworthy character but in the Caribbean its pejorative usage has been wiped off, it is equated with creolisation, mixed race, half-breed, doubleness and similar other meanings carrying within them the notion of hybridity. Quoting Shalini Puri, Mehta points out that Puri argues that' the figure of the dougla could provide a vocabulary for figuring disallowed Indian identities; furthermore they could offer ways of reframing the problematics of black-Indian party politics and race and gender relations (14).

## References

Bhabha, Homi. 'Articulating the Archaic' (1990), *The Location of Culture*. London: Routledge, 1994, 123–138.

——. *The Location of Culture*. London: Routledge, 1994.

——. 'Signs Taken for Wonders' (1985), The Location of Culture. London: Routledge, 1994. 102–122.

Cohn, Bernard S. *Colonialism and Its Forms of Knowledge: The British in India*. Delhi: OUP, 1997.

Eaton, Richard M., ed. *India's Islamic Traditions 711–1750*, New Delhi: OUP, 2003.

Habib, Irfan. *Essays in Indian History: Towards a Marxist Perception*. New Delhi: Tulika (1995), 1998.

Jain, Jasbir. "Problematizing Hybridity: The Diasporic versus the Stay-at-home Writer", *Critical Spectrum: Essays in Literary Culture*. Ed. Satish C. Aikant, Delhi: Pencraft International 2004. 37–47.

Langer, Susan K. 'The Logic of Signs and Symbols' in *A Reader in the Anthropology of Religions*. Ed. Michael Lambek. Oxford: Blackwell Publishing House, 2002. 136–144.

Mehta, Brinda. *Diasporic (Dis) locations: Indo-Caribbean Women Writers Negotiate the Kala Pani*. Jamaica: West Indies University Press, 2002.

Pieterse, Jan Nederveen and Bhikhu Parekh, eds. "Introduction *The Decolonization of Imagination* New Delhi: Oxford University Press, 1997, 1–20.

Sahgal, Nayantara. *Lesser Breeds*. New Delhi: Harper Collins, 2003.

——. *Mistaken Identity*. London: Heinnemann, 1988.

-——. *Plans for Departure*. London: Heinemann, 1986.

——. 'Some Thoughts on the Puzzle of Identity' *Critical Spectrum: Essays in Literary Culture*. Ed. Satish C. Aikant, Delhi: Pencraft International 2004. 23–36.

Said, Edward. *Orientalism*. New York: Random House, 1978.

Singh, Khushwant. *A History of the Sikhs 2 Vols., Vol. 1 1469–1839*. (1963). London: OUP, 1965, 20–28.

# Hyphenated Identities and Global Cities in Pico Iyer's *Global Soul*

*Madhuri Chatterjee*

Pico Iyer's travel memoir *The Global Soul* (2002) is an inventive take on the increasingly elusive nature of cultural identity in the modern world. With the help of Tielhard de Chardin and Emerson, Iyer first defines the idea of global soul as a collective unconscious. He then gradually shifts to designate the individual and his heritage: Iyer himself claims an Indian parentage with a childhood spent in England and US lives in California: 'The country where people look like me is the one where I can't speak the language, the country where people sound like me is a place where I'll look highly alien, and the country where people live like me is the most foreign space of all' (*Global Soul* 24). He is constantly on the move as he travels through multiple modalities of space – lived, conceived and perceived. Iyer recognises the blessings of being unaffiliated and one who can get anywhere in no time and for whom no destination is ever final. A sense of rootlessness runs through the book and, in a way, *The Global Soul* is a search for self and community in an accelerating hi-tech, fast paced world where cultures, borders and cities are increasingly blurred.

In this context, the terms – globalisation, collective identity, hyphenated existence, definition of place, and the various other contesting terms like city, nation and urbanscapes – all become significant as the notion of identity is explored. Wittgenstein has pointed out, 'Identity is not a thing (sometimes tangible and measurable in a determinate way) but is not nothing either (formless, indeterminate, a single expression of social construction) (143). That is, identity is a problem of living, a contentious and ambiguous force in everyday life. Now, if we intend to explore the interface between globalisation, cultural identity and social space, we need to conceptualise space as a territory which can be 'mental as well as physical, and … capacity to demarcate social, political and cultural boundaries make it the core of public and private projects' (Berezin and Schain vii).

Interestingly, globalisation and urbanisation have in their own way influenced the formation of identities. Iyer first establishes his position as a representative 'global soul' and then draws a complex portrait of his friend Richard who, with his briefcase full of phone call cards and plane tickets, needs no office. Though Richard lives in Hong Kong, his sense of home is similar to Iyer's – nowhere and everywhere, necessarily foreign and finally only a state of mind, 'He talks like a robot, I don't really need to exist in real time and real place at all' (121). Home is reduced to a fondness for where one lives when one is not touring, an idea of where you are at the moment and one or two objects that ground you. There are other socio-cultural identities and characters somehow liberated from their traditional ethno-cultural moorings and becoming a part of 'creolisation'. Himani Banerjee is the sharpest exponent of this trend and Henri Lefebvre critiques the right to city and notion of space. Chaffe describes the 1970s as a watershed marking the end of domination by one constellation of forces and the beginning of domination by another. In this context, 'Globalisation can be understood as a shorthand label referring to a multiple or interlinked process all related to the increasing interdependence of once disparate parts of the world' (qtd. in Hardt and Negri 443). It is also facilitated by mass-migration, new transportation and communication technologies. In the cultural sense, globalisation has been associated with a shift from modernity to postmodernity and is in a sense a 'time-space compression' (Harvey 270). Hence, under globalised condition of fragmented identities – the conception of community makes no sense and calls for alternate social space. Thus, Los Angeles International Airport becomes the new social space – a symbol of the cultural movement of and border crossing. LAX is a place of fluctuating identities, global local flows of all kinds and the Disney-inspired discovery that it is a Mall world, after all. Iyer persuasively argues that such places are increasingly the places where the pivotal moments in people's lives are played out, where travel and technology have burst the horizons and where modern-day nomads move around and who like the idea of transplanting and trying to integrate. The borderland emphasises ethnic diversity, rejecting all notions of community and recognises the complex nature of today's ethnoscape – a term which Arjun Appadurai uses to get away from the idea that group identities – necessarily imply that 'cultures need to be seen as spatially bounded', or as 'ethnically homogenous forms' (183). Thus, home becomes divorced from homeland and is placed in borderlands. For Pico Iyer, the world is increasingly both interconnected and disjunctive. Also, this borderland concept of space sees borders as zones of interaction which open up new possibilities, not walls which enclose; such spaces also allow add to knowledge and further communication. It is in them that the benefits of hybridity and cross-pollination shape new ways of 'being'. Arata Isozaki, another character in *The Global Soul,* describes his hybrid identity and echoes this sentiment – 'I am double binded, but ... I am also in a position that generates a great deal of creativity' (116). In the words of Deleuze and Guattari however this can lead to re-territorialised and de-territorialised identities – one who are in the state of being made (new cultural identity) and 'those who are immersed in a state of becoming (seeking to finalise their identity) or in an articulate state of existence' (*A Thousand Plateaus* 402). This mixed world, Iyer suggests, can mean greater friction and misunderstanding. He quotes a character in Paul Anster and Walfre Wang's film about New York – *Blue in the Face* – 'Best thing about Brooklyn? All the countries of the world are here. Worst thing about Brooklyn? None of us get along' (189). In Atlanta, for the Olympics, Iyer happens upon a choice example. Three Iraqi tourists are being shown around the headquarters of CNN, where they unintentionally terrify the other visitors by revealing their nationality. Also, the fact that we sing of Planet M and Planet Reebok, yet none of us necessarily feel united.

As a writer and traveller, Pico is always traversing borders, cultures, cities and genres. The book's focus also shifts to urbanscapes and cities and how they provide the condition of emancipation from class, gender and other identities. One-third of *The Global Soul* consists of fascinating, though anecdotal, contrasts between Atlanta and Toronto. His Toronto surveys hint at social polarisation and spatial segregation – where the city's growing underclass had etched a U-shaped curve around downtown. Still for him Toronto is a more authentic and workable experiment in ethnic and socio-economic diversity. And, because there is no shared mainstream culture (Canadian) Toronto becomes the Creole or the diasporic city. To quote Pico Iyer a 'global city of mongrel identities and miscegenated mindsets, nothing sits still, everything, including all manner of collective identity is in a postmodern flux' (Stamintz interview). For him it is a city willy-nilly speeding into a postnational future, full of fusion restaurants (Little China Restaurant advertising Pakistani-style Chinese food is Iyer's favourite), and home to quintessential diasporic events, such as the Caribana festival. Pico comes alive here as these global cities represent an indispensable condition for liberation and growth. He enjoys the rich diversity of life they offer with their ethnic diversity, rich variety of languages, clothing, culinary styles and cultural experiences but deep down there is also the importance of place that typically pervades everyday life in the cities. For him, Atlanta represents the hypocrisy of the new money culture – the globalised homogeneity and placelessness of endless malls and chain stores – anxiety of discriminatory racialisation still rampant. It is also a city given entirely to self-promotion, civic amenities and business, straining to establish the international status. He sums up his visit as 'walking through a curriculum-vitae'. The multicoloured present actually redeems an unaccommodating past. Pico describes this redemption as one brought, 'Not by bureaucratically erasing it (as in Singapore) or by turning it into a court, but by offering unorchestrated cacophony (*Imagining Canada*). The way the question of collective identity is addressed and shaped in the city hints at the coherence and fragility of the problem and because the construction of social spaces is not fixed – it puts the cities in a constant state of redefinition.

Iyer however chooses cities which are able to bear the pressures of the globalisations and modifications of collective life and which in the process, come to represent an indispensable condition for liberation and growth. In the words of social scientist Alan Blum, 'Globalisation appears to be producing a more urbanised world making cities more important than ever as centers of power, each stressing to make their mark as players in the world market. But urbanity itself may be disappearing as a powerful notion in social life' (Culture of Cities Project 11). This is reflected in *The Global Soul* in the commodification of social values, the primacy of efficiency, the loss of civility and the lack of connection between different groups in the social mosaic (Toronto), all settling for a polymorphous identity. There is a subtle tension at the ideas of world citizenship and loyalty to place in Pico but then as Blum says, 'A world citizen without a sense of place would be spaced out' (Culture of Cities Project 14) Only in disalienated city that is wholly produced by global citizens can creative human beings find true identity amidst difference. Also, interestingly, the book opens with a 'Burning House' in California and concludes with a alien home in Japan with Iyer searching for a Walden – like simplicity. But both home and identity for Pico Iyer are not a form but a process and I conclude with Iyer's interview where he sums himself thus – 'I am a mongrel citizen inspecting a mongrel world and definitions all dissolve. So, the old dialogue of self and other (space) becomes more porous floating exchange between two bodies, which overlap and merge in some ways and separate in others' (Montogomery). Thus, the search for identity remains an ongoing process in this global urban space.

## References

Appadurai, Arjun. *Modernity at Large: Cultural Dimensions of Globalization*, Minneapolis: University of Minnesota Press, 1996.

Banerjee, Himani. *The Dark Side of the Nation: Essays on Multiculturalism Nationalism and Gender.* Toronto: Canadian Scholars Press, 2000.

Berezin, Mabel and Schain, Martin. Eds. 'Preface' *Europe without Borders: Remapping Territory, Citizenship and Identity in a Transitional Age*, Baltimore: John Hopkins University Press, 1999.

*Culture of Cities* Project York University, Toronto: http://www.yorku.ca/culture of_cities/about.html,(7.06.2010)

Deleuze, Gilles and Guattari, Felix, *A Thousand Plateaus: Capitalism and Schizoprenia*. Minneapolis: University of Minnesota Press, 1987.

Hardt, M. and A. Negri. Eds. *Empire.*, Cambridge Harvard University Press, 2000.

Harvey, David, *The Condition of Postmodernity*, Malden: Blackwell, 1990.

Iyer, Pico 'Imagining Canada: an outsider's hope for global future', Hart House Lecture, University of Toronto, 5 April, Toronto: http://www.utoronto.ca/harthouse/lectures/images/HHL2001 .(7.08.2010)

Iyer, Pico. *The Global Soul: Jet lag, shopping malls, and the search for home*. New York: Vintage, 2002

Lefebvre, Henri. *Writings on Cities*. Trans. and eds. Eleonore Kofman and Elizabeth Lebas. Oxford: Blackwell, 1996.

——. *The Production of Space*. Trans. Donald Nicholson-Smith. Oxford: Blackwell, 1974.

Montogomery, Tom. Interview with Pico Iyer. *Christian Century Foundation*, 30 August, 2000.

Stamminz, Kati. 'Turning The Telescope in the Other Direction: Postcolonial Writers Pico Iyer. '13 November1997. Letter Interview (mhtml:file:/D:PICOIYER/Post-%20%Travel%20 Writers.mht (6.09.2010)

Wittgenstein, Ludwig. *Philosophical Investigations*. Translators and Eds. G.E.N. Anscombe and R. Rhees. London: Basil Blackwell, 1953.

# II

# Personal is Political

## Crossing Lines: Marking Difference?

*The assertion that personal is political has gained importance primarily in the feminist discourse because gendered roles and spaces have been marked in politics, architecture, morality and till quite recently in law. The struggle has been long and arduous as the oppressed of all categories – women, disadvantaged people, classes and castes – have worked at questioning and transgressing this division.*

*But was this separation natural? And if so, why was it oppressive? Personal lives enter the political space in everyday existence; and the journey is never one-way. There is a constant movement between the two. Our attitudes, prejudices, political choices, migrations, memories all inhabit and are governed by both the spaces.*

*Geetanjali Shree discusses the overlapping in feminist terms; Joya Mitra works at it through class relationships; and Rajee Seth problematises both memory and politics. The narrative form works through its own imaginative expanse as the writers use the fictional form involving human life and situations in both their capturable and the uncapturable nuances. The creative form acquires an additional dimension through its ability to express silences as well as psychological situations.*

*The two essays on the two near contemporaries Gandhi and Ambedkar by Jain and Mathur respectively, work out the parameters of leadership as the political concerns invade individual lives. Our choices of how we dress, what we read, where we go all acquire some degree of political texture whether it is the sartorial choices that Gandhi and Ambedkar made or the veil which women in Iran were compelled to wear through a diktat of the rulers.*

*Nidhi Singh in her essay on Uma Parameswaran's novel opens out another dimension altogether when she shifts the discussion to grafting of culture on each in the diasporic context, linking up the question of hybridity with the cultural question and the difficulty of retaining either its singularity or its purity in a multi-cultural society, especially where the outsider/immigrant is concerned.*

*These essays debate the issue of how far and how meaningfully is the personal political, and where do we draw a line to assert free will and individual choice. Would transgression not be another political action?*

# Uneasy Synonyms: The Personal and the Political

*Geetanjali Shree*

I am a writer. Is that personal or political? Let me say it straightaway. My entire existence hangs in this balance. The personal and the political intertwined as if one. Maybe they are one, maybe they are not. All my tension, all my excitement springs from this unresolved paradox – they are one and I must try and separate them but also they are separate and I must overlap them.

How else should a writer speak except in stories? So let me recount at the start a sort of story. A rather mundane one, daily and uneventful in occurrence. The Walk, let me call it. The writer's. From her home to her studio.

## The Walk

It takes less than ten minutes from her home to her studio. But, still, even as she reaches out a hand to creak open the gate, she feels again that great wave of tiredness. A whole life-long

Keynote address delivered at the IRIS seminar on 'Personal is Political'.

tiredness! Or just the dust and smoke that will trail her way at the start of the day.

In this part of the world the early morning air shows up the blackness of the rest of the day even more clearly. School buses, chartered buses, milk vans, tempos loaded with bread, eggs, bananas, race along spewing smoke that is no gas but a solid block which only a knife can chip away.

The first thing she does is to adjust her dupatta so that it covers not just her chest but also her head and across her nose too! So that instead of that blackness, she only inhales the staleness she exhales!

The street is already up and alive, and, lost in the stench of the shit of humans and animals in all variety of hues and blobs strewn across the side walk, lies a long-forgotten dawn.

Boys wait for their bus and chat raucously and, even in between the much pampered lingua franca of English, mouth rude abuses in Hindi. She always feels uncomfortable walking past these groups. All abuses in their etymology obscene a woman's body. She has even wished on occasions to stop and give them a piece of her mind, but the boys are innocent, just growing up as if in the naturalness of such abuses, unmindful of their etymology.

And unmindful of the abuses, more mindful possibly of the English dividing them, sit the women from villages herded here from far and near to build global apartments and offices. Their saris hitched up to their thighs, unmindful even of the much-trumpeted lure of the female body oozing down the Bollywood posters, high on the road just behind them.

It is a street where the world mingles. Village and town and East and West and animals, from the two-legged to the many-legged kinds. The gutter stinks, the refuse from it piled high and squiggling with worms and waiting for the municipality trucks to come, whisk it away. Before which the dust-laden, pollution-laden breeze will do it, whisk it not away but right back into the gutter. And everywhere! On to the road now full of air-conditioned cars, playing high quality Indian or Western classical music if the driver is of a respectable age, and pop quality Indian or Western if the age is carefree and wanton. On to the tent-like shelters of the migrant construction workers made of left-over bricks, plastic sheets, tyres and tatters and rods and rubbish, the inmates sitting crouched around a television set, a top priority procurement got going by pulling, twisting, and definitely stealing wires and electricity and cable connections, from nearby electric poles and houses.

While their children play badminton with a discarded shuttlecock and discarded, unmatched, sandals for rackets. It is not by magic, but politics, that these sandals and such things can turn into knives or pistols or at least a tool, not just to hit a shuttlecock!

She trudges past them, bag in hand, well covered from top to toe, like it is a cold winter's day on this hot summer street, or else like it is not mere body parts but gold and silver that she has tucked away in the folds of her clothes. The vegetable vendor, who is hollering out advertisements in local Hindi to attract buyers to his cart, suddenly breaks out into an interspersed-with-English invite, to show he too is educated, has dignity, so what if he is, and she is not, a vegetable guy.

It is ten minutes past. She stands before the door of her studio, ready to push it open. Will it be like crossing over into another world? Shutting the door behind her and with it this world of teeming, troubled, relationships of class and caste and community and gender and race and age, full of the geo-politics of the region? Enter a moment personal and hers and free?

She shuts the door behind her and the first thing she does is to throw off her dupatta and breathe as if freed.

Let me stop here and not move to the story part of the story. Instead I shall move right back into this whole tirade of the personal and the political. Taking off from the uncompleted story which is so trite and ordinary – just stereotypical images cascading endlessly one upon the other. Not in dramatic collisions of plot and event. As much in the story as out of it. As much in the room as out of it. As much in the personal as in the political.

Take it step by step if you will. And every sentence, which in itself is just the description of personal experience, is in fact also political and often with volatile political implications. The wave of tiredness. The drudgery of the walk. The pollution of urban modernisation. Classical and pop generations. West and East and elitism. The covering of the body. The machoness of innocence. The game of badminton. The readiness of violence.

The baring of the body. Women and their bodies. Television Culture. Stealing electricity which is-it-stealing? English and other languages. The studio. A studio? A room of one's own? Virginia Woolfe's or a new connotation? Throw off the dupatta. Free and freed. The illusion of it.

Every act, as has become commonplace, is a political act. Framed in a social and ideological reality. The most personal and private too. Defecating where and how? Says it all! Constipation is an elitist malady! Diarrhoea may reflect a whole politics and history of class! Food, quality, quantity, manners...!

History. A key word. We are now, like never before, 'handcuffed to history'. Like Saleem Sinai in *The Satanic Verses*. Therein lies the intertwining of the personal and the political. History itself got invented recently. For a thing *is* only when it is felt to *be*. The awareness of history is what I refer to. A new relationship with the past, rather. The story of man – a given, seen in some kind of wholeness – changes. The Past becomes, now, something to be probed and interpreted to explain the present, prodded to prop up something in the present. To create another world. Much like the novel which Milan Kundera says was born the day Don Quixote looked out on the world and finding he no longer recognised it, began to conceive of that world as a question! The Past to connect with the Present not in answers in the garb of myth but in questions and challenges. Inciting a new language – of the personal and the political. Inciting also, if I may labour the point somewhat, not the story of man but more and more the story of *woman* and man!

Yes, that is the point, a different awareness of history and the past, or the story of persons, has created this new experience of personal and political. Academics can expound on this far better than me. But I realise and feel it too.

It was my kind, we women, who first gave the slogan 'Personal is Political'. The Women's Movement in the '60s, was it not? I do not know what conglomerate of factors led to this way of discovering the world and history. But what I can imagine is how liberating an awareness it must have been. Such a source of inspiration. Such an opening up of uncharted territories. Such possibilities of clipping away the undergrowth and walking along new paths. So enlightening even in its full square recognition of oppression.

No, I do not posit a linear move forward from blindness to seeing. Rather another way of seeing. Another way of contouring the world. Another way of living. And to the extent that new modes of perception come from the imperatives of living, not from an arbitrary whim, it would have been so relevant to our existence, so edifying, so, I repeat, liberating.

The personal is political, and in one stroke a whole language of new meanings became available. Couched in overarching dictates, and exhilarating in their revolutionary potential. Everything needed to be and could be questioned. The current and the commonplace would change. A proverb like 'An Englishman's home is his castle', suddenly, importantly, valuably, necessarily, could be deconstructed as a metaphor for much of history, society and the makeup thereof. An example of a world vigorously being learnt and lived anew.

To continue a bit more on this, the imperious assertion of the personal, epitomised in the proverb 'an Englishman's home is his castle' – that assertion sat atop an earthquake! The English, the man, the home, the castle, all would be toppled now and arranged in a new set of relations and power alterations. Because the new awareness exposed the cunning that valorised and preserved as personal that which was *not* personal. The use of Englishman, home, castle, in the old equation, laid bare not just domestic politics, but politics in the largest as also the narrowest sense of the term. The new gaze showed up the devious side of an all-pervasive patriarchy.

And showed up much else. Nothing remained the same any longer. Nothing remained just *it* any longer. Every personal and private had political implications. Every act denoted political – and therefore power – relations of sexism, racism, communalism, class, gender, on and on. All individual experience had larger connotations. Nothing, as in nothing, remained untouched – colours denoted something; words, smells, tastes, gestures, entire body language, all languages, became repositories of political signification.

It might be disturbing, as any overturning of social orders is, but it must also have been truly exciting. To hold the world and shape it anew. To challenge oppressions and inequalities. The rethinking of differences. A time of great fluidity and ferment. Creativity. Discovery. Self-discovery.

Was this modernism? A derivative discourse? Acquired from the West in a relationship of inequality?

Many here can speak of this problematique with greater knowledge. But I would like to wonder whether language, even so acquired, cannot, is not, imbibed, applied with a criticality and dialogic honing, in a new way, *my* way? Does history make such idiots of us? That we can only parrot and not make our own and reinvent? I will venture to say that a 'modern' awareness of the Past/History, showing up the political masquerading as personal, has stood us in rich stead.

> And we are now in the habit of peeling away to get to the 'truth' behind layers!
>
> Exciting, painstaking, agonising as all search for truth is.
>
> Exciting, painstaking, agonising as the political in all personal is.

So there! The world opened up. The drive was the same age-old. To grab our life with both hands and make it better. Not to be fooled or misled by the apparent inevitability of everything as it is. We *knew* now why it is what it is and we moved from the personal to the political, finding and forging links between them and finding so many that the gap just narrowed and kept narrowing and it looked like there was no gap, there should be no gap, for the personal is political and how can we not realise it?

Go back to the last bit of the story I did not complete:

She opens the door to her studio, shuts it behind her, is alone with herself. Seemingly in a personal space. Wishing it to be a personal space. Away from the politics imbuing the 'outside' she has shut off.

And here lies the paradox. Exhilarating as the movement from the personal to the political has been, how very oppressive too it is! Assuming a frighteningly kaleidoscopic totality over the individual's fate. The realisation that there is no autonomous space can be such a burden. To reclaim that personal space then joins up with the drive to not let the underbelly of politics go unnoticed anywhere.

So henceforth I expound on the story of this paradox – the sashaying back and forth from the personal to the political.

*And* (underscore the *and* please) from the political to the personal. One move was towards acquiring a room of one's own. The other is to acquire a room of one's own! The first in the primacy of politics, the second in the primacy of personal! In dignity and equality and trust and freedom.

Illusory, is it, to maintain a separation? Desirable, nonetheless, it is.

Let us go back to the story. Remember she is a writer. But that is to highlight the point. It is not just writers who require personal space. A writer, though, might manifest the need in its extreme. In her desire to be unique, even – within quotes – mad!

The writer enters her studio and throws off her dupatta as if throwing out the world. Shuts the door behind her as if shutting out the world. In quiet and solitude and privacy. But that world outside has become so loud and visible, overbearing and garish, so full of political ramifications, that wanting to turn away from it looks like luxury, self-indulgence, irresponsibility, moral decay.

She throws off her dupatta, remember? That simple act is imbued with history. And its awareness. The female body is seated in the midst of acute politics. The act is not innocuous. It is personal and private but not without politics. Is personal life at all possible?

History has killed it – personal life – Boris Pasternak said.

I agree!

What are the fulminations about, you may get indignant, impatient? We must have antennae that pick up signals sensitively. The environment has acted upon her of the story, as it must, and does, on all of us. Refining our senses, providing interconnections, informing, even entertaining us.

But the problem is that we find it impossible, increasingly, to carry our learning with lightness. Nor are we allowed to. Nor we should. Outer and inner censors both monitor us. If gender sensitivity is constantly being challenged/violated, how can we ignore it? We *cannot*, not even in our most personal, private moments, not even when we are so alone with and in our own body.

And that is why once inside, so what if she throws off her dupatta, she is not free or carefree. She is heavy and too mindful of purpose and politics. This one act bespeaks a whole particular gaze she has physically left outside. It is that awareness that imbues her act inside and continues to imbue her thought. If perchance she has reclaimed her body for herself and no longer looks and feels it as man has been doing, even then she is still carrying the awareness of that oppressive gaze in her act. And if she continues to look at herself in male desire then too the point remains.

That politics intrudes into her most personal moments too!

Let me meander along my sojourn a bit longer. Does this awareness augur well for the writer? I am not sure. Though many might disagree.

Too many answers, too many needs, are already there, out there, in politics. In its shadow looming so large and imminent, many things gasp for breath. Adventure and creative wantonness go for a sixer. Flexibility and open-endedness turn tail. Sense of humour jumps out of the window. And – and now I enter the area of dangerous thought! – freedom is lost. Freedom, almost irresponsibility. To leave the world behind. And aside. And get into another innermost being. And fly! And drown! And leap! Creating/reaching another world. Which may or may not sync with the world outside. Unmindful in any obvious sense and uncaring of the laws of the land, of the Constitution, of ideologies, politics, history. Free to invent. Daring and baring. Even outrageously. Under some other impulse which is let-me-call-artistic, secret, personal.

Allow me to quote Proust who said of the writer: '... in fact it is the secretions of one's innermost self, written in solitude and for oneself alone, that one gives to the public ... the innermost self which one can only recover by putting aside the world and the self that frequents the world.'

That is what the writer wishes to do. Embark on a search freely, prying, probing, experimenting, even irresponsibly, even irreverentially. Fiction deals with stories. And stories, as Coetzee says, 'are defined by their irresponsibility'. 'The feel of fiction', to continue with Coetzee, 'is one of freedom, of irresponsibility, or better of responsibility towards writing something which has not yet emerged.' Creating another world, not a replica of this one.

What an anxiety then our writer carries of how to be free in the face of political imperatives, how to protect herself from lapsing into an impoverished aesthetic of merely political writing.

To play – for art is also a game – create, shape, rearrange, destabilise, demolish, go to risky edges, desiring, needing no plaudits from the world outside or legitimacy from history. To write a novel which, again as Coetzee says, 'operates in terms of its own procedures and issues in its own conclusions, not one that operates in terms of the procedures of history and eventuates in conclusions that are checkable by history (as a child's school work is checked by a school mistress).'

Premchand spoke of *adarshonmukhi yatharthwad*, social realism pointing towards an ideal, as the guiding principle for literature made in troubled times. Literature as the hand-maiden of social reform. Maybe there are times when such an imperative dominates all other concerns. Maybe the worry is misplaced – the times are so powerful that they themselves creep into literature without you and I needing to make the effort. But, I do believe, that must not be the 'sword' hanging on the writers' neck even if it does! The writer wants to transgress, almost as if born to do so! Born free!

Do I here glorify the freedom of the writer, hence the personal? Forgive me, for that is not my intention. I know as well as anyone that we are and always have been products of history and all and any of our expressions will never be neutral but instead resonate with all manner of subliminal and political echoes. But must it become such a pressure, a domineering, all-time anxiety?

Such seems to be the curse of our times.

This is the final point I make about the uneasy synonymisation of the personal and the political. In a less urgent atmosphere than today's they may have made a congenial pair. They would be related, but in healthily sanctified different spaces. Politics would have won the writer a room of her own, and the personal would grant her the space therein to flower. There would be time and solitude to shut the door and the world outside, proverbially speaking, and have 'fun' inside, also proverbially speaking. There would be that important line between the personal and the political, full of time, space, trust, dignity, humour.

But something has happened. In the world of today the line between the two has faded or else springs like a noose any minute to strangle our voice, and thought too. The outside barges in and demands instant explanations for our expressions. Almost imposing on art and thought a shortness of life which shouts 'now, right now'.

I started my presentation with an ordinary walk full of ordinary things. But violence lurks just round the corner. Individuals, whole peoples, are at risk. How can she, the writer, turn away and not feel guilty? The urgency of politics does not permit the time and space for self-indulgence or spontaneity. No place to wait, mull, let it be ... see where it will go ... forget about it! Nadine Gordimer condemns such 'creative self-absorption', which she says must be checked by 'conscionable awareness'.

Our writer feels weighed down by the extraneous pressure. By the dictate of politics saying you must write on this and thus. The writer craves that 'feel' for a non-ideological, even amoral, locus. Unrestrained, in her own self. It is embarrassing. It feels like a luxury. And worse. It is as if she wants to masturbate! As if that is what art is. Self-appeasement! In distress she realises even masturbation can be a political act – echoing the whole narrative of sexual politics and of guilt and/or liberation therein!

At the end of the day I feel confused, compressed, constrained, incapable, and perhaps ashamed of the abandon I so desire. The urgency of our political and politicised world forms an outer censor that threatens to dominate the inner censor as well. The fusion of the personal and the political is increasing even as the desire for their separation persists.

So what does our writer do? She moves uneasily around her studio, putting pen to paper, in some agony negotiating the obliterated line between the personal and the political.

The outcome too easily can be one of the following. Either like a Hussain she may be dragged to explain her lines to whosoever has power in the over-intrusion of the political, the lumping together of all spaces into the art space. Or else she could end up reducing artistic expression to uncomplex, innocuous transparencies, in seeming immediate value and influence. Not like the geniuses who said complex things simply, but merely saying simplistic things simplistically. Politics will be the big bully and the personal will be pushed over into exile.

# Wait, Intezaar Hussain

*Rajee Seth*

This happened around the time Intezaar Hussain's *Bastee* was published. Straightaway he went to the bookshop and bought a copy, slipped the brand new book into the rack at the head of his bed.

Slipping it in, he counted the books in the rack again. *Bastee* was the tenth book to come out on Partition. In these ten books lay enclosed an important part of his life. He was sure he would need these books some day compellingly. Reading them he would be reading his own past, his own life.

But life, his or others', moved on. And his compelling need didn't arise. One day his wife said, 'Take these books away. The children need the rack'.

He stared hard at his wife. She told him to stop staring like that. She was not scared of him as she was in earlier days. Calamities had hardened her. Nothing scared her now, nothing whatsoever.

He made an effort to put force into his retort. He did succeed in this, sometimes. How did the saying go – 'one stroke of the ironsmith's equals one hundred of the goldsmith's ....'

'I have said not once but many times that this rack will stay where it is, at the head of my bed. And these books too. Whoever moves it will see me dead'.

It was the kind of argument he'd always called female: threatening with death and dying when intelligence failed. Emotional blackmail.

He was the one speaking this language now, because he could not, in all honesty, think of a more clinching argument to shore up his refusal to empty the rack.

Her sagged cheeks quivered in a kind of helpless rage. She didn't set much store by her husband's threat, but she couldn't bring herself to laugh away a threat of this kind, either.

She flung down the cardboard box she'd brought along for storing the books in, and called out in a resounding voice in the direction of the children's room. 'No rack, no nothing for you, you hear? Your grandfather has to have everything he sets his heart on'.

The children were nowhere around. It was for him, he knew well enough. For him, to show him up as a mean old man: by setting off the children's needs against his stubbornness. But he knew well enough too that the rack was to stay where it was, was simply not to be moved from there. These books had to be near him, within reach. In the contents of the books, the pulse of his life throbbed quietly. Some day he was sure to get time. Some day, for sure, he would be sitting amidst them reading his past. What if the day hadn't come so far: given his strong longing for it, it was bound to come. And God forbid, that, out of sight they got buried in cellars.

His stung wife didn't speak to him all evening. The next day too she kept up the face-off. On a pile of things in a corner of the room after the white washing, she flung the children's books higgledy-piggledy. It was one more fling at him. She could have looked for another corner if she'd wanted to.

He decided not to take notice of it. And getting smaller day by day, one fine morning the heap vanished. He didn't think it necessary to find out which other corner the children had found. As on all days he left for work at his furniture factory.

If...If...If...If he had known that his wife's life span was so short, that she would die so soon, he would most certainly, have given way. He would have spread out the books on a plank under his bed.

He did not know. Nobody knows anything. Things meant to happen, happen, without as much as a by-your-leave. A sharp pain in the chest does not always augur death ... why then did she die? Slumped into his arms within the blinking of an eye, as if taunting him, 'O.K! Here you are, all yours now, children, rack, books, the whole caboodle, never would she be butting in now!'

He felt cheated, almost enraged. Rage not so much over the squabble about the rack, as over a lot of other things. Her rank disloyalty at leaving him half way. Flare ups and bickers were their agreed terms of exchange between them, not this rude exit.

The cold winds now cut deeper into his rib cage. His heart also hurts more. But why crib now about aches and pains? Now there is no need to spread out the books on a plank under the bed. He himself has given up the room, made it over to the children, and set up camp on the takht in the front room. For the children he has bought a new rack. His, he has put at the head of his bed. Exactly as before, in anticipation of his dire need.

When she was alive it never, ever, crossed his mind that between wife and books no relationship gets built. Books lie around because they have no link with the life that goes through living. No give and take, no incursion into each other's territory. If they did, would he have assembled just this handful of books on the carnage after the country's partition? Just ten book bearing witness to the massacre of lakhs! The Jews have proved cleverer, wiser, smelting their tragedy and sending it afloat into the arteries of the world. Was there no lion-heart in this country to describe this indescribable tragedy it had suffered?

No, he is thinking wrong, the correction comes on its own. Those who write are one class, and those uprooted, another. The uprooted have no time for words, nor the nerve to feel in their palms the embers smouldering under their soles and study them. Look at his own self. For years the books have been calling him from the head of his bed, and he...he...

If he'd read these books, perhaps he'd have been free of their spell, his heaviness of heart lessened. He could have read them like fiction. They would have gone, gone clear of his mind. Right now he doesn't even know what's in them. All he knows is that in them lies buried the balance sheet of his past and its mute pains.

Today…

On the morning of Independence Day, sitting before the TV, he is feeling different, stirred beyond reckoning. This day comes every year – twice a year, in fact – when he sees the screen as he would, happenings in other people's lives but today…. Perhaps to certain events we are ever sensitive, with or without knowing. Perhaps it is like dampness under the roots that never dries up and ever courses. Otherwise why would he stand head bowed, hands folded, springing from his chair on hearing the notes of the national anthem on the screen? Alone in the room, he finds himself standing till the, last, fading echoes of the refrain 'Jaye hè, Jaya hè, Jaya Jaya Jaya Jaya hè, …'. It happens to him involuntarily, like an instant awakening the whole of destiny. You never come to know what and which branch of the tree of memory is being shaken, where. Our leisure hours perhaps bring to our door the saga of the past.

His granddaughter Sweetee comes into the room. The sky in the TV screen is a-wash with balloons painted the colours of independence, and he sinks within.

It is the fifteenth of August today, the fortieth year of the country's freedom. What a length of time! He re-winds time to his own speed and site. He was nineteen years old when he left Lahore, Nikkee's image housed in his eyes like an intransigent, riveted there.

Now he is forty plus nineteen. That is, forty years past the freedom war. From then to now, forty plus nineteen, full fifty nine. Fifty nine – a half-baked age, neither centre field, nor to the boundary.

To see grandfather lost thus, to see him 'not there', makes Sweetee impatient. This is just the kind of thing that makes her flee her father. 'Papa is useless, grandpa', she complains. 'Never listens to me. Work, work, work – all the time, work'. Even today when it is a holiday for her, and he has to take her out to see the lights.

'The lights will be at night, child', he reins in Sweetee's mounting rage.

'Not night. Evening', she bridles.

'All right, evening. But evening's still a whole afternoon away, and anyway what's the point going with me? If I go, it'll be on foot ...'

'I too will go on foot ...'

But by evening it is peace between Sweetee and her papa. He'd known all along it would be so, that Sweetie would not go with her grandpa. That she'd go in the car with her father. And she wouldn't look grandpa in the eye, would look away, and say, 'It's like this, see, grandpa, why don't you also come with us ....'

He laughs, so long and so much that tears sprout from his eyes. How would Sweetee know that he is not to go anywhere today? That he is to sit around the house alone! A something has been knocking at his attention for God knows how long now. He has to bring it close and see it, see it face to face. Surrender himself.

Everybody has gone. A hush lies all round, but the mind is not at peace. Why is it not? If there's silence without, and din within, how fearsome it seems! In a daze he sits down by the books. *Jhoota Sach* first? No. *Aag Ka Dariya*? No, not that either .... Then *Udas Naslein*? No, this too, no. Finally he pulls out Intezaar Hussain's *Bastee*. A slim volume, easily folded: its slimness decides him.

He knows well enough that a book is a book only till it remains in the rack, holding between its two covers long, horizontal lines. Once out of the rack it becomes something else, something other.

Intezaar Hussain had begun the book in the name of the city, swearing by it. But which city can this be? By what the book says, it is where the hero, Zakir, is in search of his first day in a new city of a new country. This variety of displacement puzzles him from the word go.

In God's name how could a new country come up on old soil...and, in the new country, a new city? And in the new city a stranger, an unknown citizen, is looking for his first day in it: the first sacred day bathed by the first flush of freedom.

He cannot for the life of him decide whether to laugh or cry at this irony of a new country on old earth. To feel the 'sacred' in the fire of freedom is the sole gain to bear in mind, forget all this groping around. Mostly it is the same dark, the same gloom, the same sadness he has never forgotten: the very same sadness, foreboding and darkness about which Intezaar Hussain writes farther on. On each succeeding page a shadowy nervous agitation quivers. A lot is being said, but nothing is clear. In place after place are accounts of trickery, firing, of curfews in the offing, heated debates in coffee houses about 'agents of imperialism' and 'mongrels of compromise'. Nothing but straws in the wind and motes of dust heralding a major catastrophe brush his understanding as he turns the pages.

He loses heart, feels outside it all even while stationed dead centre in a circle of flames.

His unhappiness grows. No! None of this is what he had been wanting to, waiting to, read. But...but...wanting to, waiting to, read what? He cannot tell. Which part of the past is he so avid to touch?

In great agitation he turns the pages indiscriminately. So far he hasn't even got the name of the city where the hero is drifting about. Roads, turnings and by-lanes appear but without names. Nothing to identify them. Not that he does not know the names of the cities! Flashing forth in his mind as if by the wave of a wand the names of the cities would not have changed so soon.

So far, the hero's loafing around is all that he has gleaned, when abruptly breaks in a name he knew so well. Anarkali Bazaar. He reads: 'Anarkali Bazaar – partly open, partly closed. A heavy crowd but no big buyers ...'

The bare name 'Anarkali Bazaar' stops him in his tracks. Uphphph. Now at last Intezaar is identifying the city. He sits up, feeling the need to sit up. This, yes this, is his own city! Lahore, Lahore, wait a while, Intezaar Hussain ....

The narrative ahead, he feels, is about to take a turn to Mall Road. You must halt, Intezaar. Let me get my breath back

But perhaps in Intezaar Hussain's hand the text of the novel is tugging at its reins. It is raring to wing forward. He stops on his own. Pausing long and repeatedly to read the passages twice over, thrice, over. Sitting on this side of the border now, he is reading the face of his city there, on that side. Rapt. Swallowing the lumps in this throat.

Now, a new eye opens in him. He walks in step with the hero. The hero, Intezaar Hussain writes, 'is relishing his walk in the new country. From the first road to the second, from the second to the third ...' God knows how long he keeps pace with the hero. 'After ages, after countless numbers of years he is walking there free, free of the nagging fear that somebody scraping past him would stick a knife into him'.

He is reading about the caravans of refugees entering the city, and his mind is in a turmoil. He, among the myriads forced out of Lahore. If it is Walton Camp this side, it is the D.A.V. College camp that side.

Moving with Intezaar's text he advances farther. 'In Sham Nagar so many houses stood empty. Doors and windows wide open, whole sets of furnishings were visible through the open windows. It looked as if the people going away just rose to their feet, wrapped themselves and stepped out'

Uphphphph. How did you know all this, Intezaar Hussain? But you should have known, still, that it was not Sham Nagar, a vicinity of Sant Nagar. Sant Nagar...his home, his locality.

The evening hadn't waned yet. Father came in fast and halted dead centre in the yard. Heavy lines of tension were on his forehead and his hands sank into the dip of his waist. Eyes fixed on the tongues of flames on the *choolah*. A cooking vessel was on it.

A knob of ginger in her hand, Mother came in, and he said, 'Take down that vessel'.

'Whatever for? The dal's hardly done yet'.

'Just take it down!' Temper didn't ring in his voice but what rang was nothing mild either.

Seeing his mood Mother held the vessel with the ends of a dishcloth and brought it down. Father turned, filled the bucket at the hand pump and poured down a thick jet of water on the fire. The flames died. The *choolah* slumped under the black slurry of ash and soot.

'Now listen. And pay attention...those people have come. At the head of the lane they are now. Hurry and look sharp. We must go this minute'.

'Where?'

'To the camp. The D.A.V College camp. The government holds out no safety to those sticking it out in houses. We will have to stay there for now. Hurry. Just shove in some clothes...'

Into a long canvas bag he was squeezing in a blanket.

His unmistakable fluster now had its effect on Mother. Scared, she said, 'Clothes, yes. But upstairs all the windows and doors are wide open'.

'O forget about doors and windows, woman. Get out double quick. Have you no idea...' He leaned across to whisper into her ear.

'Wait, Father. I'll go close the doors and windows ...'

He darted towards the staircase, but where did he have his wits around to close the doors and windows of the middle floor? His sole attention was on Nikkee, on warning her, reaching the terrace where he had his hush-hush trysts with her.

Living a house away from his, every time Nikkee's face appeared from the grill of his roof he knew had to go up. Up to the terrace. By any means. Go up and gratify her naughty demands. Standing in the closed stairway down the back of the house, Nikkee would be waiting for him. He had to go to her and squeeze her in his arms. Squeeze her so hard, so hard, that...

He remembered how once, under the pressure of his maddened muscles, a scream escaped her. In a panic that her, brother Kirpal would be somewhere around he clamped his hand on her mouth. So hard that she backed away and tumbled down a couple of steps. Her back bruised, of course, but her knee got injured too. A swelling came up on the joint.

'Roshan, you've gone crazy for sure today. What'll I tell them below?' She was scared.

'O come on. Tell them anything. Excellent fibber that you are ...'

That evening he learnt from his mother that Nikkee – Chawla Saheb's daughter – had had a fall in the school. That her back had bruised, that a mute pain in the knee had set in. A mute pain, his mother said was nasty, goes on and on. He also learnt that later in the evening his mother would be going to Nikkee's to ask how she was.

His generous offer to close the doors and windows, he clean forgot on the very first step. He wanted to clear the steps in one single leap. And alert Nikkee of what he'd heard his father say about the *balvais* –rioters. Alert her. His mind drummed Nikkee ... Nikkee ... Nikkee ... Nikkee wouldn't half know the things his father knew ... that they had come in, were breaking into houses.

Butchering the men folk, hauling them out and tying them to trees. And under their very eyes, stripping their women ... uphphphph. His breath choked.

The moment he set foot on the terrace he fell into stark terror. From down below rushed up a torrent of screams and pleas. Perhaps they had come up to Nikkee's house. A *balvai* stood guard on the, top step of the stairway from Nikkee's terrace. He still remembers the eyes of that brute – like live, burning coals, and the tight black band round his jaw...

As Roshan advanced, a crashing voice went up. 'You there! Twerp! Freeze up ... I'll take care of you, else ...' Without moving he aimed the glinting tip of his javelin at Roshan.

He does not now remember when his father came up to the terrace in search of him. When he gave him a kick on his back with the flat of his sole. When he dragged him all the way down the stairs. He remembers his father's hard, vise-like grip round his wrist, and ringing in his ears, Nikkee's wounded, rising scream. A scream like that of an animal not yet dead, through whose flesh a maniac draws out a serrated knife. Draws it out. Keeps drawing...

Pain floods him. Forty plus nineteen years later. He breaks down. Falls apart. Drilling the hard crust of massed ice he cried. Sobbed. Sobbed without let as if a scream condensed in the breast of time had suddenly started melting. Melting steadily, drop by drop.

All this happening now. After all these years. To an old man of nineteen and forty years who had resolved then, this is a war for freedom. Over this none of us is ever to cry. For any loss. Any time.

# Looking for the Other

*Joya Mitra*

I have a problem. I have had it for a couple of days now and I need to find a solution, fast. I know, of course, that everyone has problems, there is always something or the other to disturb a man's peace of mind. But then, those are usually problems one is familiar with. Sickness, maybe, one's own or one's wife's or one's son's, or maybe one's parents'. Maybe a sickness as serious as cancer. Worries about a son's career, children's schooling, a daughter's marriage or maybe an affair, even loss of trust between husband and wife, quarrels, accusations, bitterness. All the problems that sometimes come singly, sometimes several together, and in the end people find solutions for them, or maybe they don't and the problem stays with them for life. People like us, nondescript pen-pushers in city offices, what else can we expect from life?

Problems change, too, they change with time. I still remember, for example, how my father and his brothers came

---

This story was first published in 1993 in the autumn number of a Bengali journal, *Prabaha Tista Torsa*.

away from Khulna, came away with their families. Of course, my memory is fuzzy, no clear outlines, but there was this dark night when we left home. There was a boat ride, my mother carrying me in her arms, wrapped in a shawl. One or two lights forming flickering tapes on the dark river, like the zari threads they used to decorate Durga. And then a crowded train, a hazy impression of my father fetching us a papaya to eat, cut in the shape of a boat, a yellow boat! That's all. In Barasat, we went to school, and we lived in a shanty. In two years, there were little red and pink flowers growing around our door when the Pujas came around. After that, there was the house in Park Circus. A lovely house, better even than our old home in Daulatpur. Still, Buli and I missed those red and pink flowers. Now I know that my parents must have found it hard to meet the expenses on my father's meagre salary – he had a new job. But we never caught our parents squabbling about money. There were times when my grandmother moaned the absence of milk and fish in our meals – 'in our own land,' she would wail, but my parents always stopped her. 'All that is past, it's gone for ever, what's the use of talking about it to the children?' And my grandmother would stop complaining, only a mumbled excuse slipping her lips – no, no, it's only that the memories come back sometimes. Dada was doing well in school, and Buli of course was a good student from the beginning. We really had no choice in the matter, because we knew that if we didn't do well in school it would make our parents sad, and that was something we could not bear to contemplate. Sometimes in the evening, or even in the morning, my father would sit on the bed and read out poetry. *Lakkha bakkha chire, jhake jhake praan pakkhi saman chute jeno nij nire* or *Engraj sena chute paschate sheshe bahu dure bane niralate sakhyat holo jhashirani sathe bishal nadir tire.* On such days, the three of us forgot about our homework, mesmerised by the recitations. And so was our mother. We were just beginning to grow up then, my brother and I. We loved those evenings, when my mother would stand half-hidden behind the kitchen door, and we could make out that she was oblivious to everything around her then. She was overcome by shyness if she caught our eye, hurrying back inside the kitchen. And sometimes, late in the night, we would lie in bed listening to our father playing the flute. We knew he was playing for her. Yet our daily life was ordinary, humdrum, like everyone else's. But we could not bear to think of doing anything that might hurt our parents.

But then, so many things happen in our lives without our thinking about them. Those poems that my father read out to us, the rhythm of that poetry of courage and sacrifice, enveloped me in a kind of daze. Later, during my City College days, I somehow got thrown together with the Communist Party. Stranger still, a fair girl with her hair tied in plaits, whom I spotted staring at me in every debate or recitation session in college, suddenly became very special to me. My heart beat faster when I was with her, and also when I was not. I did not really consciously notice how the two involvements started to take shape. As for the first, I know now why it happened – there was something in the air of those times, 1965 and 1966. The atmosphere was fiery. Actually, the mercury had started to rise earlier, during 1962–64. Around 1964, my father's health started failing, but then maybe my grandmother's death had broken him some three years before that. I wrote my school-leaving examination in the year she died. The country was celebrating Rabindranath's 100th birthday. It was not clear what was wrong with her. She stopped eating and hardly spoke. Her face and limbs were swollen, she ran a slight temperature. When she talked, it was only about our old home in Daulatpur. My father sat with her every evening after he came back from work, sat by her bed till she fell asleep. In those last days, our grandmother seemed to have become completely unaware of her surroundings, and the few words she sometimes muttered were about our garden in Daulatpur, our jackfruit tree, the boy who grazed our cattle. Sometimes she would softly ask my mother, '*Nayan-bou*, have you shut the rear gate? Take out the clothes from the wooden trunk in the small room and put them out in the sun.' It made my mother cry.

Faizuddin Sahib, with whom we had exchanged houses, had a son-in-law in the BSF. It could be this that made it possible, but he would visit us every two years. He called my grandmother *Amma*. When he came, she always had lots of questions about the house at Daulatpur, the garden, even the shelves in the rooms. That embarrassed my father, but Faizuddin Sahib – whom our father taught us to call *Chachajan* – did not mind. He would tell my father, 'We keep our mouths shut, brother, we follow the social rules, we can't express what goes on in our hearts. But you mustn't stop people who can talk about their feelings. Like *Ammajan* here, your *bhabi* there sheds tears for this house – such a lot of space in your house, there's the garden, fruit trees, the pond, still she weeps for this house. And in their tears, we cry too.'

My father would ask after his sons. By the early sixties, *Chachajan*'s eldest son was in college, the same college that my father had gone to. And *Chachajan* would always take a stroll in the Park Circus Maidan, even if he had to do it in the afternoon sun.

That year, this quiet, introverted man wept when he saw how ill my grandmother was. In all the years that he visited us, that was the only time when he stayed the night. He sat down to eat with us after she fell asleep. 'I would take *Ammajan* to her house if I could, even if it was for a day,' he told us. 'It's the people who live inside four walls, *Bhaijan*, who make a home in them. I know what it is like to leave one's home behind...'

I think that was the only occasion when I heard our father say anything on the matter. 'Some people cut up the country to suit their own interests, and hundreds of thousands of lives were destroyed. We were happy together in our own land, even if we did fight sometimes, none of us wanted to leave home to settle down in a strange place, among strange people. Those people fanned the fire to roast their chicken, and we were destroyed, and you too. The leaders sat down to talk to each other before they split the country, did they ask any of us even once?'

We had never heard him talking like that. 'Let that be, let's not talk about it now,' Ma said softly.

Grandmother died about a month after Faizuddin Sahib left. After that he came only once. He sat alone on the terrace stairs for a long time, quietly, holding his head in his hands. He had brought a lot of pictures with him this time, pictures of the house in Daulatpur, the streets, the college, the chemist's shop at a crossing near the house. He left them all with my mother. He said he would come again, but he never did. Vigil on the border became stricter after the war, or so we heard. On the streets, they talked of Pakistani soldiers. People suddenly became fiercely patriotic, like once before during the Indo-Chinese war. One could not even mention Chinese ink or 'chine-badam' without being suspected of treachery. I have always noticed that people become curiously belligerent when they go through these patriotic phases. In '64 too, enthusiastic young men waylaid tramps on the road and harassed them, in Bombay Johnny Walker almost lost his living.

Then came the food movement of '66. I was out of college by then, but my heart was still with the Students' Front. Dada had a job with Senralley, he had moved to his quarters with his wife. Tanima was insisting that I tell my parents about our relationship, she wanted to tell her own parents because they were trying to arrange a match for her. She had told them that she would not meet prospective grooms if they came to see her. So of course now she wanted to tell them about us too.

In the middle of all this, there was the first United Front ministry in '66. Oh, the excitement of those days! It seemed as if all problems were about to end, Calcutta looked like Red Square to us! Then of course, within months, the dreams broke down amid the infighting. A fresh set of problems again, we could not decide what was right and what was wrong. The leaders who had condemned certain actions for so long in meetings, rallies, processions, were now doing exactly the same things themselves, and getting away with it too, the protests slowly got muted and finally died away. It was all quite confusing. But of course that was also the time when I was gradually moving away from my political involvement, getting more and more tied down by the demands of my personal life. Also, I was desperate for a job.

It was not as if they needed me to start working immediately at home. My mother's brains and her hard work had seen to that, and in addition there was the rent from the two shop spaces that we had let out on the ground floor of the house. But then, there was no way Tanima and I could tell our families that we wanted to marry, unless I had a job. Afterwards, it was all fairly smooth once I landed a job with the LIC. Tanima belonged to the same caste that we did. Her family was better off than mine, but her father had four daughters. I was not an unsuitable match for her, and I had refused to accept dowry. My mother was with me in this, though my father raised some faint protests. Would we have to fund the reception ourselves? Well, my mother was very clear about that – 'We have always provided our son with everything he needed, now are we supposed to ask the bride's father to pay for the reception?' Of course, in those days, a lot of our friends thought like that. Marrying for dowry was thought to be old-fashioned. There were some who accepted dowry on the sly, but they were careful to keep it secret, dowry was not something to boast about to friends. How did things change so much in just twenty/twenty-five years? The young boys at the office – when one of them gets married they all sit together to decide which brand of scooter would be most fuel-efficient, or which brand of steel cupboard has an extra locker. The dowry amount is 'for parents to decide'. And most of the time people seem so irritable, always criticising someone or the other, either their wives or their daughters-in-law, always talking about 'us', 'our times', about 'when we were young'. They don't seem to realise how much they too have changed, and they are not always pleased if you point it out to them. Like my old friend, Rathin. We went to college together, we started seeing our girlfriends around the same time, we started our working lives together. But he got married later than I did. Rathin's family were upper caste Brahmins, whereas Seema's were Sonar Bene. You cannot keep such things in mind when you fall in love, can you? Well, Rathin's parents were not willing to accept it. Rathin became something of a hero for us, taking a stand against prejudices of caste and class. And now, would you believe it, it was the same Rathin who rejected a groom for his daughter because the horoscopes did not match, at the behest of his 'guru'. So I asked him what horoscopes he had matched before his own wedding. He was furious, he accused me of trying to scoop out his family scandal. Scandal! Well, maybe. I went home and complained to Tanu, but she blamed me.

'He's right. Do you think everyone is like you? You are getting on in years, but just look at you, you have no respect for religion, or for social norms.'

Tanu has changed also, and haven't I too? Still, I can understand why she has changed. The pain of childlessness still gnaws away at her heart somewhere. In the first restless years of despair, she took to amulets, to numerous pleas and supplications to her gods, topped up with promises of offerings if her wish came true. Once or twice I tried reasoning with her. 'Why these promises, Tanu? Does your god take bribes, then?' It only made her angry. Well, those difficult times are behind us now. Still, there is an empty space in her heart. The wound is only hidden, it has not healed. My mother never said anything, but my brother's wife sometimes said unkind words to her. That strained her relations with my brother's family, and also mine. I find that the older I get, I move closer and closer to Tanu, away from friends, from relatives. At least in my marriage I have a partner with whom I have worked out some sort of an understanding, with whom I share some sort of a relationship, even love.

So I try to make light of her words. 'Why Tanu, when do I ever disobey the rules of your household? Aren't they social norms too?'

'That's different, but why won't you do the things that everyone else does? Why do you always have to be different?'

'So what do you want me to do? Should I come home every evening and watch TV, instead of talking to you? Isn't that what everyone does?'

That made Tanu laugh in spite of herself, but she didn't yield an inch. 'Come off it. Everyone asks me why we don't go to a guru and take a *mantra*. It is not nice at all. Really, why can't we do it?'

'Tanu, we have discussed this before. I have told that if you think that the person you accept as your guru is a better human being than anyone you know, if you think that will take you closer to your god, if you feel that you need someone to whom you want to unburden yourself, then go ahead. I do not have these needs, so I do not need a guru. And I won't do this just because everyone else is doing it. That sort of thing should only be kept for the latest fashions in sarees or film stars.'

Tanu got up and left in a huff. Like many times before.

But now there is a different problem. It's about some of those youngsters that I feel drawn to, though I don't understand them. It started in a very ordinary way. A few of us were sitting around in the ground floor canteen a little after lunch. Akhil's daughter lives in Asansol with her husband. There was news of curfew in Asansol last month, the Army had been called in. All of us had been a little worried. Akhil's son-in-law is a building contractor and spends a lot of time out of door, meets all sorts of people. But Akhil's daughter has come to visit him now and she says there was nothing much the matter really, police had taken control of the situation fairly well, the curfew was only a precautionary measure. The convorsation turned to the role of police, and from that to the

Bombay riots. The newspapers had reported how policemen stood and watched slums being torched. The police, it seems, followed instructions from their political bosses, not the administration. Nothing is going to change in this country, too much politics everywhere. Comments like this, loosely bandied about, and it was time to go. At the table next to ours, there were some young men from the billing section's computer room. I didn't really know them, but I was familiar with their faces. One of them suddenly got and came over to our table. 'It has become a habit with you people to blame your own community. Look at the other communities, how they stand by each other, they accept whatever their leaders tell them. And look at us, we have no love for our country, no respect for our own religion. Why, the people you were talking about, what harm have they done?' There was only Akhil and I at our table, the others had sneaked away. Those young boys are our colleagues, we've brushed past each other so many times on the office premises, but how strange they seemed now, how unfamiliar. I had never imagined they could have spoken so rudely to a colleague some 25 years older than them. But no one else seemed to take any notice, no one so much as turned to look. Most of the tables were empty now, only some people from the new business section were sipping tea at two tables near the counter. They went on talking nonchalantly, as if nothing had happened. 'I'm off to the section, then…' I heard Akhil muttering behind my back. He was leaving too. I looked at the boys more closely now. Expensive clothes. One or two of them had their shirt buttons open, and I could see small blue lockets peeping out, linked to silver chains. One of them had a bead of rosaries. There were five of them crowding around me now, their expressions hostile. I felt threatened, really, frozen by the fear that they might suddenly attack me. Also, I was angry.

'What happened? Why don't you say anything?'

One of them said, 'What is there to say? It's such a trendsetter for the country …'

'But in a land where so many communities live side by side, have always lived, is it good to start a riot and destroy lives of poor people?'

'Poor people! Oh! So they are poor people for you! And in other countries these poor people are razing places of worship to dust, how is it that people like you never have anything to say about that?'

'If that has happened, certainly that's very wrong, but it is also true that a lot of rumours fly about during riots. And then, is it right to punish some people for what someone else has done?'

'Of course, it is right! They are real men, those who are doing it.'

I wanted to leave now. Chitresh and the rest had finished their tea and gone. I was alone in the canteen with these boys. I saw Satya looking our way from the counter, for a moment I locked eyes with him. I drew myself together and stood up straight.

'Look, I don't think it is possible to discuss these things like this. In my opinion, religion is a private thing, killing for faith is ... anyway, we can discuss that later, I have to get back to work now, the lunch break has been over a long time.'

I did not wait for a reply. Just as I was going out of the door, I heard someone say – 'Son of a bitch! The quisling!'

I felt my blood rushing to my face. Should I turn back and face them? But I was also scared. Maybe that was what they wanted? An excuse to hit me?

I was restless in my seat. I felt people staring at me in a strange way. Do they all know what happened in the canteen? But there was no question from anyone. And if I happened to look into someone's eyes, they immediately started peering into their files. An hour passed and I hardly did anything. Then I got up and went to the union room. I found Bipul and Chitresh there. Chitresh is our branch secretary, he's a member of the divisional committee and the party's district committee. I buttonholed him.

'What is going on here? Has the office become a place for religious bonding? These young men, how dare they behave like that with a senior colleague?' My voice shook now, not out of fear, but anger.

Chitresh said, 'Sit down, sit down, why are you so excited? What's happened?'

'What's happened! Didn't you see how those boys spoke to me? The language they used?'

'Oh, no, I think you are taking it a little too seriously. I was there, I saw you talking to Sourangshu and his friends, none of them looked hostile to me.'

'They were defending the rioters of Bombay, they were using foul language.'

'No, no, Bijoy*da* '– Chitresh was now shaking his head – 'you are a senior colleague, why did you start a discussion on communal issues at a sensitive time like this? I did not expect this from you. You know that such talk only increases ill feeling on our own side, it only strengthens the enemy.'

Bipul had been sitting quietly. Now suddenly he said, 'Who supports which party, that's a personal thing, it isn't right to interfere about that.' Bipul was waving his hand as he spoke, I noticed he had gem stones on three of his fingers.

'And then Bijoy*da*, you are close to your retirement now, aren't you? Why do you get into arguments with these young people? Let them do what they like. As for their language, well, it's bound to seem shocking to you – these are the new generation, computer type!'

Chitresh and Bipul were now laughing at their own joke. I left the room, slowly.

This was the union room we had struggled so hard to get. And before that, there had been a strike for the right to form a union. There was a pen-down, fifteen to twenty people were show-caused, I was one of them.

I did not feel like taking the lift. I chose the stairs, climbing slowly. There was a time when one could look out at a lot of trees from the windows on the landings. They are gone now; when did they go? There is a supermarket being built, there is a Maruti showroom right in front. Has it been a long time since I last took the stairs? Climbing gets me out of breath these days, so I take the lift – it's been so many years now! I stopped at the second-floor landing, clutching the railing. There was a small crowd around the water cooler in the inner passage. Were they the boys who spoke to me at the canteen? I wasn't sure, but yes, they were, and some others too. A couple of them came forward. No, they did not approach me, they went and stood at the window and looked out. Then they walked down the stairs. They were talking loudly, their voice carried quite clear.

'The old idiot – amazing, doesn't feel any hatred for them, I swear!'

'A small crack on the head, and the brains will be out'...

Now they were laughing in mirth. I felt empty inside. I shouldn't have taken the stairs, now I had trouble breathing.

All this happened day before yesterday. I haven't told Tanu. She was chanting the *Laxmi Panchali* that evening, she turned to look at me when she felt my presence. I knew she was embarrassed. I picked up the newspaper and crossed over to the easy chair on the other side of the room. I could make out the words she was chanting, some lines came back to me too, I had so often heard my mother reciting same words in the past. Is Tanu a Hindu? Why then, did it only contain prayers for the good of the world, why did it say nothing about the enemies? Yesterday I did not step out of my section at the office, only slipped out for tea once and came back quickly, took the lift. Still, I was uneasy, as if someone was watching me. Today was the same.

The others in the section were unperturbed, as if nothing had happened, chatting away comfortably. The other day they said something about a crack on the head – was it me they were talking about? Come on, it is not that easy! Aren't there people on the streets? But then, there were people in the canteen that day too, in the beginning. What if they hit me that day? Maybe there are more like them in the streets, in neighbourhoods like mine. You come across these whole-night chanting sessions, they make a marquee in the middle of a street and carry on through the night, for three nights in a row – why, no one raises a finger in protest! Who goes to these programmes? Who organises them? And where do the funds come from? All that noise through the night, and think of all the children, students, sick and old people ...... yet there are no objections from any of the families. Are they all scared? The police, too, do nothing, though everyone knows there is a ban on loudspeakers after nine. But why did they talk about me like that? Everyone knows that I am not affiliated to any party. And what power do I have anyway? I have lived through fifty-six years without bothering about religion, no one ever raised any questions. I know nothing about religion, actually. My parents worshipped separately, Tanu worships in her own way. It takes all kinds to make a world – there are so many Hindus who do not accept divisions of caste, so many Muslims who don't have four wives. How do people hate on the basis of religion?

Well, that is my problem. It seems that to be safe one must hate people of a particular country or group. But who do I hate? Before I start hating, I must know why I must hate. I don't even know people of other countries, other communities, other groups! The few names I can think of, why, they are household names, cricketers, singers, painters. How then do I hate strangers, people I do not know? I am so lonely. Will even Tanu understand that I am looking for someone to hate? I need someone to hate if I must be safe, is it? But who? I don't know. I am doing my best, but so far I haven't found one known face that I can hate.

Translated by **Sarbari Sinha**

# Between Ego and Non-Ego: The Gandhian Struggle

*Jasbir Jain*

Modernity has privileged the individual through its architecture, space-structures, psychological and philosophical studies. Each one of the above stresses the elements of choice, will and freedom. The democratic framework likewise constructs itself on fundamental rights such as the right to move freely in one's own country, to employment, to practice one's religion, to purchase and own property and above all the right to equality before the law. Despite this privileging and the political support, societies move simultaneously in two opposite directions. Just as the individual is able to exercise choices with the aid of modern-day living and medical sciences, the complex social networking pushes the subject into public and political space. What then is personal? – Is it the right to protect one's privacy, the working of one's mind, to consider categories like caste, gender religion and colour as 'given' and thus beyond political or social interference and to go ahead and make personal choices? But this does not happen; or is it that it is simply not viable?

From one point of view, the 'self' in itself as it emerges from its cocoon, comes into being through interaction with socio-political realities on one hand and with traditional value-structures on the other. Values such as truth and conscience find their manifestation in an outward context, often a political context. The present paper proposes to explore the relationship between the personal and the political through Gandhi's experimentation with the making of his self through two literary texts – Partap Sharma's *Sammy* (2005) and Nand Kishore Acharya's *Bapu* (2005).

Between them, the two plays provide the beginning and the end. In Sharma's play it is the personal humiliation that a young man experienced and the realisation of how the racial 'other' viewed him came home to him with a shock, and alongside the realisation that this was inequality. This political reality challenged and dislocated his world, disrupting the world of inherited values, a disruption which changed the whole course of his life. Gandhi became conscious of collectivities such as the nation which was larger than the self, the home and the family, collectivities which were formed of people of different faiths but had similar political concerns. Acharya's play locates Gandhi at the end of his life – face to face with his sense of failure and recognition of the moments of betrayal. The latter play moves into an interrogation of the relationship between the personal and the political – whether or not the chiselling of the ego renders the personal a suitable instrument of connection with the political.

Gandhi's life did not allow for any gap between truth and justice and transparency was, for him, a suitable value for both. Just as the outer world moulded and governed his personal lifestyle the inner world had to extend its boundaries. There was always a contestation going on between the two as each pushed the other. The evolution of Gandhian strategies and principles such as satyagraha, non-violence, selective co-operation and total non-cooperation, his avoidance of compromises and conspiracies, his sense of theatre and, above all, his ability to shock through the slippages in his character resulted in a redefinition of 'resistance'. All along he resisted injustice, oppression, violence and yet he avoided the models of leadership prevalent amongst his predecessors, contemporaries and successors. Unlike both Tilak and Gokhale, worlds apart from Vivekanand and Aurobindo, the exact opposite of Jinnah and Ambedkar, Gandhi with all his follies and lapses was constantly engaged with the negotiations between the personal and the political, between personal power and political power, and between soul force and physical force.

Gandhi has to be placed in multiple contexts in order to get through to the constant erasures and re-inscriptions that were taking place in him. Within the overwhelming presence of a patriarchal set-up, the notion of the personal was a limited one. All that it amounted to was defiance, stealth and indulgence. The forces that pushed him to the recognition of the personal as well as the political were, ironically, the same. It was the stepping into the wide world of employment of success and failure that brought home to him the clash between accepted practices and public recognition. The personal is the point from where we begin, a place signified by biological, social and cultural locations, and the political is the relationship with the other or others. Family bridges the two worlds with its inbuilt hierarchies and control.

Partap Sharma dramatises the negotiation between the two worlds by creating two Gandhis – one Mohan and other the Mahatma. The two dialogue, contest, reprimand, extract confessions and mock at each other. Mohan is dislocated firstly by the attack on his headgear, a sartorial accessory of his personal self, secondly by being thrown out of the first class carriage on account of his colour, origin and colonial location and thirdly by a discrimination between the Arab and the Coolie, on grounds not only of race and religion but also of wealth and a social position. What does he do then? Not sulk, not change but instead carry the personal right into the political by testing it before in the dispute between Abdullah Sheth and his cousin and working out a fair, open negotiation between the two contestants. Then he pushes people to recognise that sameness is more important than difference – Indianness above other categories of definition – he persuades them to forget these minor differences in order to fight the larger discrimination. Next comes the third move, to bring home to everyone the commonality in their stakes.

Was Gandhi moved by idealism or practical considerations? Was it a considered strategy or an inspired response to the needs of survival? Why did the man not succumb to the ill-treatment? How did it matter that he like hundred others was pushed into subservience and pushed off pedestrian walks?

As the Mahatma and Mohan comment upon these events of Gandhi's early experience the Mahatma says – 'I was looking for – salvation. But life diverted me into the search for human dignity'. This was Gandhi's conversion from the personal into political, his moment of Enlightenment (16). The introduction of the 'conscience' into the political field, not merely in support of pacifism but in support of resistance to injustice, was in itself another introduction of the personal into the political. Conscience as part of political life called for an openness and a dialogue hitherto absent in political life. Conscience, more than a moral principle involving law and justice, was an ethical principle calling for bridging all gaps between the personal and political. Sharma's play takes up the 'split self' and questions the very notion of an integrated 'self', pointing out that the self is never fully self-contained self-sufficient or without gaps and contradictions. In this, Sharma goes beyond the Freudian concept of a layered consciousness and reaches out to the Lacanian model of the mirror image. Gandhi's journey demanded a double shift: one from the individual to the collective and the other from the spiritual to a political collectivity concerned with human dignity. This journey also marked an erasure of his masculine self and a conscious move towards the cultivation of feminine virtues. Ashis Nandy has elaborated upon this in his work *The Intimate Enemy*, where he creates a middle androgynous space and redefines the basis of resistance (Nandy 52–53). Who then is the shadow figure? Mohan or Mahatma? Or both? Combine the shadow and the real?

In his political struggle, Gandhi, despite his use of religious terms and prayer congregations in later life, began with the idea of placing nation over religious identity. He set himself the task of weaning away people from the influence of religious heads. The pursuit of personal salvation, so dear to a Hindu, and motivated by self-centredness was substituted in his own case by a desire for swaraj. As Mohan and Mahatma debate the issue in Partap Sharma's play, Mahatma tells Mohan, 'I was in search of God and stumbled upon man' (16).

*Hind Swaraj* was written mid-way between Gandhi's South African experience and his growing Indian involvement as also midway between England and South Africa. By 1909 the principles of transparency, suffering, persistence, and non-co-operation had emerged as had the principles of sharing, brahmacharya and asceticism. The last two – brahmacharya and asceticism – were the induction of political requirements of equality and social equity into personal life. Brahmacharya was a traditional motif wherewithal the erotic-libido was transformed into an ego-ideal (in Freudian terms). *Hind Swaraj* uses the term soul force as opposed to political power. Soul force, adherence to truth (satyagraha) and conscience all are rooted in the individual. The graph of Gandhi's political life, is in itself, a series of confrontations: with Gen Smuts and his policies of immigration, permits and employment, with the British in Chauri-Chaura, Salt March and fast against separate electorates, boycott of the Cripps' Mission, with his fellow countrymen in Noakhali and his final fast in Delhi. The confrontations were marked by the desire to extract, they were personal to the extent, for each time it was his self, his body, and his life that was offered, extractive as to the demands and coercive with effect to the closure of the options. The goals were always set high, often not humanly achievable and very often the concessions and pledges still left something to be desired.

In Partap Sharma's play, Mahatma is the conscience, the finer self, while Mohan is the disciple working his way towards the status of a Mahatma. In this inner voice, Mohan finds both the moment of inspiration as well as a direction to follow. Mohan wonders 'Is conscience a social phenomenon? Or is it innate in man, a gift of nature, a genetic configuration, an insistence of the spirit, the voice of Truth, a reflection of God?' (67).

Psychologists may well spend sometime over three issues – was Gandhi enamoured by the saviour myth, the service of the people? (*Sammy* 71), a man who could not take up the medical profession due to caste inhibitions? One needs also explore the nature of his confession in *My Experiments with Truth*: what was it? – a psycho-analytic exercise conducted on the self or an act of transparency, a preparation for the re-invention of the self, or does it mark the moment of merger of the personal with the political? Or above it all is it also an opening out of the inner self to others, a public acknowledgement of guilt: the part in himself he found hard to forgive, the realisation that his self-denial involved other selves and their involuntary denial like that of his wife and children (124). It is an admission of the one-sidedness of life: when the personal is totally submerged in the political, something is denied, something is lost and the death-wish begins to overtake one. Gandhi's actions and speeches from 1944–1948 are all marked by this wish. Gandhi is on record for undertaking unconditional fasts unto death, specially the Calcutta fast. On Jan 13, 1948 Gandhi undertook his last fast – an all-in all fast directed to the conscience of all: yet a fast with the political intent of bringing about an end to violence. As his health deteriorated he lay like an embryo; with his knees pulled up toward his stomach and his fists under his chest as Louis Fischer has remarked, as if in preparation for a new birth.

It is this death-wish that looms large over Nand Kishore Acharya's *Bapu,* a play about his last years when he felt that Maulana Kabul Azad, Jawahar Lal Nehru, Sardar Patel, Mohammed Ali Jinnah and Subhash Chander Bose, each of one of them had in someway misunderstood him, moved away from his beliefs and had separated the man from his political ideas. It was this split between the world of moral values and that of political action which was a separation unacceptable to Gandhi who viewed life as an integrated whole. The notion of transparency did not allow for any gap between the two – the felt emotion and the acted reality on one hand and the expressed communication and acknowledgment of it on the other. Gandhian perception of both relationships and history, is in *Bapu,* located within the psyche of one man, a man very human and in whose relationships with others, paternal and filial patterns of behaviour are perceptible; a man who locates himself at the centre as the perceiving 'eye' and opens out his own feelings to himself. The Indian political world constitutes the stage where history is being enacted. Gandhi, in this last phase, is no longer a forceful character in the external world. All others – Azad, Nehru, Jinnah, Patel and Bose – are participants and have been guiding the political moves in this power game. Lelyveld, in his recent biography of Gandhi, while commenting on this phase, writes 'In that hour of decision they had no use for Gandhi' (Lelyveld 292). Lelyveld also refers to Gandhi's comment to Louis Fischer, 'I know India is not with me, I have not convinced enough Indians of the wisdom of non-violence' (ibid.). Absent figures in the play, the ghost presence of the other leaders, marks the man's failures. Acharya succeeds in drawing attention to the conflicts which beset Gandhi in the final years of his life. Yogesh Chadha in his work *Rediscovering Gandhi,* has pointed out to the ideological differences which underlay the political differences. Even Nehru and Patel did not agree with each other or with Gandhi. And the difference was shaped by their different views on religion. Gandhi's attempt to reconcile these differences did not succeed in effect, even if occasionally short term agreements were reached (448–460). History tells us very clearly that those who wished to hold the nation together, even after the partition had taken place, were overpowered by the hostile forces.

*Bapu* works at multiple levels and can be read and enacted in different ways. The only performance that I have had occasion to see (Bhanu Bharti's production in Jaipur) failed to bring out both the complexity and the anguish of the play. It acquired a strange, flat monotone and turned Gandhi into a man with a strong ego, moved more by his own failure than by the fate of India. This Gandhi appeared to be a self-centred man with divisions and fractures in his mind with 'mine' and 'yours' sharply etched on his consciousness. Language acquires meaning through stress and emphasis. Is the use of pronouns of possession and alienation by the writer intended to problematise a sense of belonging? Is the familial pattern meant to draw lines? Is it that there was a clash between Gandhi's need to be inclusive and the political forces of exclusion and division? If so, it becomes a portrayal of the inability to transcend the claims of emotional ties.

*Bapu* as history compels us to look at the human aspect in politics and reopen the link between personal emotions and political action. It also draws attention to the processes of history and ideology. None of the two is a 'given'. They are the products of human intervention, involvement, motives. The play, once again, centralises the paradoxical issue of leadership, which on one hand demands hierarchy and obedience and on the other attempts to introduce equality and voluntariness in political acts. But in a collective political action, personal value-structures may often act as disruptive forces: the notions of truth, morality, right or wrong may differ. To compromise or not to compromise represent individual choices. From this perspective, Gandhi in *Bapu* becomes the portrayal of a frustrated leader whose reflections upon the past become an analysis of the deviations from his prescribed norms. *Sammy* and *Bapu* represent the two ends – the entry of Gandhi into political life and a near-exit soaked in a deep sense of failure. How personal is political frustration? While the man and his ideas are woven into one integrated whole, the gap between a personal value system and political manoeuvres remains and fails to work at a collective level.

It is not possible to read these plays as narratives of an individual life; it is also not possible to read them as mere history. They can best be read as the tenuous yet compulsive relationship between the personal and the political, especially when we move into the connection between the subject, authorial perspectives and the context of 2005. I refer here to Bhabha's view of the literary act, 'meaning is simply not mimetic or transparent' (Bhabha 36). Continuing in the same vein, he writes that the third space of enunciation 'destroys the mirror of representation in which cultural knowledge is customarily revealed as an integrated, open, expanding code.' It challenges our sense of historical identity and of culture as a homogenising force (ibid., 37). The year 2005 or the couple of years before that had thrown up a lot of violence in the country, during and after the Gujarat genocide. Sharma's play looks at Gandhi's inner transformation, in the context of colonial history and has been published in association with the Gandhi Smarak. Acharya has been actively associated with the Mahatma Gandhi University at Wardha and has been an intensive scholar of Gandhian thought, ideology and philosophy. Keeping these in mind, we realise that Gandhi's ideas are being looked at afresh in the context of a third trajectory, that of the contemporary destructive violence on the national scene. Against this it is important to remember our early fracturing, then the integration brought about by the Gandhian revolution, which was an intervention which lasted for barely two decades, the years from 1919 to 1942, before divisionary forces raised their heads. History is both a warning and a reminder. The plays move outside their visual and verbal limits as they move retrospectively over the events of the past, to interrogate the choices the nation has made, the roads it has taken and not taken.

In *Sammy*, the Mahatma is a product of the moment of articulation, what Bhabha refers to as a moment of 'enunciation', in effect a product of this intervening time-space, when outside the country's territorial boundaries, the linkage between personal dignity and nationhood dawned on him. (Giriraj Kishore in his novel *Pahla Girmitiya* has recorded this very movingly by his constant use of words like 'humwatani', i.e., compatriot, belonging to the same country). This is an active phase of deconstructing inherited cultural norms and selectively adopting some while rejecting others. It is also a period of reinterpretation of cultural values and using them for political ends. The play works dialogically and it is the interaction of the two figures that the ego-ideal is born. *Bapu* works out its theme through monologues and internal dialogues which move to and fro in time but stay fixed in space. The isolated places can well be imagined where the setting sun's rays are falling and correspondingly, Gandhi realises his isolation but is still unable to abandon his paternal role. *Sammy* is about the conquest of the spiritual self by a more acceptable political ethicality, while *Bapu* stands confronted by the gap between personal ethics and practical politics. Each moves the reader in its own way and gives rise to a great a deal of introspection even as each points out to the difficult relationship of the personal to the political.

## References


Acharya, Nand Kishore. *Bapu* (Hindi). My references are to the unpublished manuscript.

Bhabha, Homi K. *The Location of Culture.* London and New York: Routledge, 1994.

Chadha, Yogesh. *Rediscovering Gandhi.* London: Arrow Books, 1997, 448–460.

Gandhi, M.K. *An Autobiography: My Experiments with Truth* (1927). Ahmedabad: Navajiwan Mudranalya, 1997.

——. *Hind Swaraj and Other Writings.* Ed. Anthony J. Parel (1997). New Delhi: Foundation Books, 2000.

Kishore, Giriraj. *Pahla Girimitya.* New Delhi: Bhartiya Gyanpeeth, 1999.

Lelyveld, Joseph. *Great Soul: Mahatma Gandhi and His struggle with India.* New Delhi: Harper Collins, 2011.

Nandy, Ashis. *The Intimate Enemy: Loss and Recovery of Self under Colonialism.* New Delhi: Oxford University Press, (1983), 1989.

Sharma, Partap. *Sammy: the Word That Broke the Empire.* Mumbai: Rupa and Co in association with the Gandhi Smarak Nidhi. 2005.

# B.R. Ambedkar: From Resistance to Legislation

*Charu Mathur*

Dr B.R. Ambedkar's life was a great saga of suffering, sacrifice and struggle. His *Dalit* background gave him a bitter taste of caste tyranny, obscurantism and oppression. The painful experiences motivated the dynamics of social purpose and he waged a relentless struggle against social discrimination and upper caste despotism. The committed social reformer put up a persistent ideological and political resistance combating a society that was under the grip of caste-based divisiveness. In the century gone by both the ideology and organisation of the traditional caste system have vastly eroded. Such erosion has taken place to a much greater extent and degree in the urban areas and at the macro-system level of social stratification. The local hierarchies of caste in the rural areas are also progressively disrupting. But, though it is true that the traditional social relationships are being redefined in economic terms, the system is now thickly overlaid by new power equations created by caste loyalties and identity politics. As a result, even after almost six decades of post-independence initiative, an equitable social order and establishment of a classless society remains a far cry and the future stares into our eyes with still greater and more severe challenges than ever before due to this continuing social imbalance.

The scope of this paper is to map out how Ambedkar's agonising experiences transformed him into a social revolutionary one who fought against the pernicious and inhuman facets of Hindu society. The paper also traces the legislative measures taken by Ambedkar to fight apartheid in India and subsequently explores the various political and socio-cultural dimensions that to a great extent frustrate these efforts. This is because when resistance translates in terms of legislation the outcome often goes tangent to the desired goal.

Born in the Mahar community of 'untouchables', Ambedkar grew up with sore experiences of being socially despised and ostracised. The pollution-purity syndrome of the caste Hindus inflicted a social disability by virtue of which the life opportunities to the so-called untouchables were denied. In a reminiscent piece which was penned in his own handwriting and that was later published as a booklet under the title *Waiting for a Visa* (1990), Ambedkar recounts a number of incidents from his life that reveal the social discrimination and personal humiliation he was subjected to. As a little boy in school, he describes how he could not sit with his classmates but had to sit all by himself in the corner of the room. He had to bring a separate piece of gunny cloth to squat on in the classroom. Even the servant employed to clean the school would not touch the gunny cloth used by him and Ambedkar had to take it home every evening to bring it back the next day. When thirsty, he could not go to the water tap to quench his thirst like the other students. In his case the permission of the teacher was not enough. The presence of the school peon was necessary to pour water. If the peon was not available, he had to go without water. Ambedkar sums up the situation in a statement: 'No peon, No water'. At home no washerwoman was willing to wash the clothes of the 'untouchables' and no barber agreed to cut their hair or shave them.

Ambedkar also narrates an incident when as a child while travelling with his brother and cousin to Koregaon to meet his father, no cartman was willing to carry them for fear of being polluted, even though they were ready to pay double the fare.

When one finally agreed, he refused to sit with them so they had to take the reins while the cartman walked by their side. During the long journey, although they carried a food packet, they had to sleep without food because as 'untouchables' they could not get water anywhere.

Even Ambedkar's five years of education in Europe and America did not change his status of an object of caste based social ostracism in India. He returned to his country in 1916 after studying in Columbia University in New York and then at the School of Economics of the University of London. He was appointed as the Military Secretary of the Gaikwad of Baroda but his prestigious position could not ensure even the basic requirement of a roof over his head. He had to quit the job because more than a dozen Parsis menacingly armed with sticks forced him to quit the humble Parsi inn he had managed to lodge in. It was then that he realised that a person who is an 'untouchable' for a Hindu is also an 'untouchable' for a Parsi.

Having undergone the affliction of untouchability, Ambedkar resolved to fight against it. He endeavoured to bring about a radical transformation of the consciousness of the underprivileged class. However, he was not merely interested in bringing about reforms within the predominant Hindu hierarchical caste structure. His point of departure was to completely reject the ascribed status of the depressed classes and create conditions wherein they could assert their rights for their resurgence. His protestant approach with regards to the scriptures not only helped in making the depressed class conscious of its dehumanised position but also quickened the forces for wider reforms in the stratified Hindu fold. Ambedkar was not merely a caste politician but a patriot and a philosopher who recognised the fact that religion is the foundation of a society and as a social force it cannot be ignored. The practice of untouchability, according to him, was the tyranny of exploitation through religion. He applied the test of justice and the test of utility to judge the philosophy of Hinduism and found them wanting in these tenets since the Hindu social organisation is based on caste system. *Varna* is the parent of caste and both uphold the principle of gradation and rank, in other words inequality.

Symbolising in himself the sufferings and indignities heaped on the untouchables for many centuries, he assumed a political stand and mobilised people against this dehumanising practice by striking at the roots of their religious beliefs. On March 20, 1927 he led the 'Sweet Water Tank Satyagraha' at Mahad when more than ten thousand men marched to the Chowdar tank to assert their right of drinking water from the Municipal reservoir. On December 25th, the same year a resolution was passed condemning the *Manu Smriti* and a copy of the same was ceremoniously burnt. Ambedkar launched another Satyagraha on March 3, 1930, just ten days before Gandhi's Dandi March. He organised a temple entry by the untouchables at Nasik before the Kalaram temple. The way to uplift the untouchables lay in the social elevation and not in the act of temple entry itself.

The timing of this movement was not a sheer coincidence but a part of a well thought strategy of Ambedkar to bring the issue of social justice for Dalits at the centre stage of the freedom struggle. Like Gandhi wanted to challenge the political hegemony of colonial rulers and to establish the rights of Indians to make salt, Ambedkar wanted to challenge the social hegemony of caste Hindus and to establish the social and political rights of Dalits in the society. Ambedkar vehemently refuted the claim that the problem of the depressed classes is merely a social problem and not a political one and therefore he sought for them political power that would lead to social and political upliftment. While Gandhi and other national leaders were taking a religio-political approach to the problem, Ambedkar sought a solution mainly through the instrumentality of politics. He participated in the first Round Table Conference held in London in November 1930. His denunciation of the loathsome condition of the untouchables in India brought the position of this oppressed class into sharp focus in the world body.

The most controversial aspect of Ambedkar's mission was his demand for separate Dalit electorates in the second Round Table Conference in 1931. He endeavoured to get recognition for the claims of the untouchables to be treated as a political minority so that they could get safeguards in the constitutional arrangement. Ambedkar's contention was that Muslims as a minority grew from strength to strength because of the protection under the system of separate electorates. The untouchables though forming a part of the Hindu religion should also be accorded such a special protection in view of the severe social, economic and political disabilities they had undergone. This however was strongly opposed by Gandhi who felt that special electoral protection to the Dalits would mean a deep wedge between the Hindu religion and society. The Mahatma was for the upliftment of the untouchables within the framework of religion. Whereas Ambedkar held that the emancipation and elevation of untouchables was a matter of right, upheld by law and statute and not through derivative concessions. The resultant Poona Pact between Ambedkar and Gandhi frustrated Ambedkar's avowed policies and programmes. Gandhi's 'fast unto death' compelled the Dalit leader to cancel the communal award and accept joint electorates and reservation of seats as the only alternative to solve the constitutional deadlock.

Ambedkar nevertheless continued his efforts in mobilising public opinion in favour of the political rights of backward castes. A bill for the removal of untouchability was moved by Sardar Patel in the House which declared on 29 April 1949 that untouchability in any form is abolished and the imposition of any disability on that account shall be an offence. As the first Law Minister of independent India, and then, as a chief architect of the Indian Constitution he strove to secure the interests of his community. The safeguards that he succeeded in procuring for the untouchables, as listed by Chitkara, are – representation in legislature (Article 330), representation in services (Article 336) and grants for educational benefits (Article 337). He was instrumental in providing reservation for backward communities, scheduled castes and scheduled tribes, in services, central as well as state legislatures under Special Provisions Related to Certain Classes (91). These were supposed to be for a stipulated period of ten years. The purpose behind these safeguards was to make it possible for the underprivileged class to participate in the political power of the country. He had longed to see the 'untouchables' cast off their centuries old blemish and join the mainstream of national life. But, as the Constitution finally emerged, he came to realise that, after all, it was not possible to achieve the objective fully. He knew that a political arrangement and solution devoid of economic and social content was not going to bring his excluded community anywhere near the goal he had envisaged.

It is for this reason that the privileged provision made in the Constitution to usher in a casteless society does not meet the expectations of the Scheduled Castes even after almost six decades of enforcement. On the contrary, they pose other complications that are evident from the formulations of the Mandal Commission. The Commission was formed to consider the question of seat reservation, and its report in 1980 that recommended stronger affirmative practice under Indian law, became a source of great controversy. Its partial implementation in 1990 became the ultimate cause of the then Prime Minister V.P. Singh's resignation. The penetration of the problem in the present can be seen in the sparking off of an intense political debate about the recent proposal for a bill to provide reservation for the backward classes in the central educational institutions and deemed universities maintained by the Centre. Still, in spite of political resolutions and constitutional guarantees, the levelling that Ambedkar hoped for continues to be elusive. Instead, the system of reservation of legislative seats has strengthened caste politics. It has created vested interests and made the protected community more conscious of its separate existence. This consciousness coupled with the resentment felt by non-reserved castes, stands in the way of assimilation. Continued atrocities on Dalits, caste conflicts and brain-drain are logical conclusions of this politicised special constitutional provision. Caste politics has defeated the very purpose of this constitutional provision. The present reservation system cannot bring about social justice because, in the words of Chetakar Jha, 'the policy of reservation has been adopted ostensibly to protect them from what is called "unfair competition" from others. This is in effect a policy of reverse discrimination, i.e., discrimination against the traditionally privileged to favour a weaker and deprived group. Hence, the epithet "new Brahmins" is occasionally hurled at the Dalits by opponents of reservation' (29–30). Thus efforts to compensate them for historical injustices, in turn threaten to accentuate social cleavages and perpetuate the Dalit's indelible status.

The problem has its origin in communal politics at the time of the British rule. It is argued that the British saw the problem of plural society such as that of India as essentially a problem of the identification of natural groups and their natural conciliation and thought that the only solution lay in group representation (Kothari 66). However, the obvious primary motivation behind the reservation was to emasculate the strength of the nationalist forces that were posing a threat to the imperial dominance. The British knew that the counterforce can be stationed against the nationalists by creating group reservation and spurring caste and communal feelings among Indians. As part of their usual colonial policy of 'divide and rule' they fanned hostilities and encouraged parochial feelings between the Hindus and the Muslims at the horizontal level by making wide use of the system of special electorate. Then by reserving 28 seats for non-Brahmins in 1920 constitutional reforms they sought an institutionalised vertical division between Brahmin and non-Brahmin communities which also provided a counterweight to the Brahmin oriented Congress.

The British colonial politics in India had fizzled out the possibility of the emergence of organic national politics by exploiting the politically divisive and explosive potentialities of the culturally fragmented and economically stratified Indian social structure. The reservation policy acted as a double-edged sword. On the one hand it was used to crush the nationalist forces and on the other, it helped the minority communities to develop political consciousness. This political consciousness was created at the cost of killing their revolutionary potentials. 'Legal measures and institutional rearrangements with welfarism', as Shah points out, 'are not substitutes for struggle. They may provide temporary respite. Reservation too is one such measure. It has very limited potential for transformation of society' (409).

It is true, that the past fifty years have seen a gradual but consistent rise in the economic and social status of the Dalits. However, parochial preoccupation of the reservation beneficiaries has resulted in the elite formulation from respective communities. There has been little or no organised attempt between the elites and the general masses of the community to fight for common causes. This creates a kind of particularistic politics which completes the division between elite culture and mass culture within a caste. With the introduction of adult franchise and competitive politics these Scheduled Caste and Scheduled Tribe elites specially the political elites have been successfully subservient to the causes of the ruling party. And the ruling parties with their time tested minorities welfare programme have left no stone unturned to mobilise the numerical and legislative strength of these communities for their own sectional interest. The reservation policy has not helped the underprivileged class to improve their lot but on the contrary helped to create a micro-group amongst them which is playing into the hands of the patrons. Politicians instead use both the elite and the masses as a vote bank to further their own interests and that of their party.

The conflict is not just limited to the backward castes and the upper castes, but the very logic of reservation divided the Scheduled Castes in various factions as there is an increasing competition between them to win the positions of power. This has resulted in infighting and hatred among the already heterogeneous Scheduled Caste structure. The privileged among the underprivileged class continue to reap the advantages which gives rise to the formulation of a creamy layer that misuses the system. In such a situation the discrimination is not between one caste and another but between the haves and have-nots. Reservations, therefore should no longer be based on class criteria alone, as suggested by the Kaka Kalelkar Committee, but linked to the factor of economic backwardness. But, since there is no uniform yardstick to measure backwardness, some of the most vociferous and influential sections like the Kurmis and Yadavs in Bihar, who own large tracts of land, have also entered the reserved list.

It is evident, therefore, that the reservation policy fails to gauge the ground realities. Reservations are provided at higher levels but the basic prerequisites in order to bring about a levelling are not bothered about. Jobs are reserved but the ladder of basic education is not strengthened to make them reach that level. Shah imaginatively describes the situation: 'It is like allotting a pent house to a physically challenged in an elevator less building' (409).

Ambedkar while drafting the Constitution hoped that the forced intermingling of the communities would first blur, and then completely erase the caste lines from the Indian psyche. But the reservation policy ended up achieving just the opposite. Not only did caste lines harden but even a generation that was born without the venom of caste hostility soon caught on the vicious attitude. Instead of blurring the Dalit identity, there is enforcement and as long as this identity is maintained equality and assimilation will remain far fetched dreams. Subharao rightly states in this connection: 'There is an element of self-perpetuating discrimination in the doctrine of preferential opportunities' (qtd. in Kothari 236). Thus, even if reservation is one of the methods of state intervention to provide a helping hand to those who have been traditionally deprived in the caste structure, it is not enough. Ambedkar's opinion that political democracy without social democracy does not work holds good even in the present day context. He felt it necessary to establish a correlation between the political constitution and social institutions of India if democracy was to become real and meaningful. Political democracy presupposes equality but if the social structure is hierarchical, then that cuts at the roots of political democracy.

Therefore, besides a legislative reorientation of the reservation policy, what is required is a notional change, for 'caste' is a notion; it is a state of mind. The behaviour of the people is merely the outcome of their beliefs inculcated through religion. Since religion provides a basis of social organisation, should not humanism and rationalism govern these religious beliefs and the resultant social attitudes? The solution lies in providing a new doctrinal basis to religious ideology – a basis that is in consonance with the trinity of liberty, equality and fraternity, i.e., with democracy.

Social backwardness is not insurmountable. Though the factors responsible for it change with change in the economic structure, they do not get eradicated automatically. This requires intervention in the sociocultural milieu supported by a change in the economic and political structure. For rights cannot be protected by law alone. It is the social and moral conscience of the society that is accountable in ascertaining a change in the caste based iniquity.

## References

Ambedkar, B.R. *Waiting for a Visa*. New Delhi: People's Education Society, 1990.

Chitkara, M.G. *Dr Ambedkar and Social Justice*. New Delhi: APH Publishing, 2002.

Jha, Chetakar S and Satish K. Singh. *Indian Government and Politics: A Political Commentary*. New Delhi: Research India Press, 2008.

Kothari, Rajni., ed. *Caste in Indian Politics*. Hyderabad: Orient Longman, 1995.

Shah, Ghanshyam. 'Social Backwardness and the Politics of Reservations.' *Caste and Democratic Politics in India*. Ed. Ghanshyam Shah. Delhi: Permanent Black, 2002, 388–412.

# The Bifocal Vision of Home: The Personal and the Political in the Select Works of Uma Parameswaran

*Nidhi Singh*

The line dividing the personal and the political has worn thin with human consciousness constantly negotiating it in a progressively politicised ethos. Home too has become a contested site with the political making inroads into the jealously guarded sanctity of this personal space. The process is best observed the world over in the growing community of diaspora with geographical dislocation not only making them review their perception of home and homeland, but also making it imperative for them to view the alternative as at par with the native. The concept of home gets problematised since it exceeds the limited geographical and physical association and it also connotes political, social, cultural and emotional territories that are often transgressed and reconstituted by the diaspora.

Uma Parameswaran, the diasporic writer from Canada, in her work addresses the bifocal visioning of home where the personal and the political interpenetrate. The title of Parameswaran's first novel *Mangoes on the Maple Tree* (2002) is indicative of the grafting that accompanies the move from one country to the other, and the collection of essays *Writing the Diaspora: Essays on Culture and Identity* (2007) theorises the process of grafting wherein the concept of 'home' brings into sharp focus the tension between the personal and the political. The aforementioned works by the writer explore the creative impetus and the theoretical fall off of the diasporic sensibility. The geographical dislocation leads not only to reviewing of the relation with home, but also makes it imperative for the diaspora to come to grips with the alternative political, cultural and social milieu across the boundaries.

The political and the geographical demarcations of territory are reflected in the invisible boundaries dividing the earth into nations and continents, and larger territorial manifestations like North, South, East and West. Edward Said quotes Hugo of St. Victor in *Culture and Imperialism* describing the ideal state where the imperial, national, and provincial boundaries are transcended:

> The person who finds his home land sweet is still a tender beginner; he to whom every soil is as his native one is already strong; but he is perfect to whom the entire world is as a foreign place. (407)

The diasporic sensibility traverses a gamut of emotions ranging from nostalgia for the home left behind to bonding with the home of adoption and even attempts to transcend it through transnationalism. There is a movement away from local to global with the divisive boundaries becoming progressively porous. With identity markers like nation and culture losing their rigid definitive contours owing to superimposition of one world over the other, the margins of identity and the idea of home too have become fluid.

The territorial demarcations are at times reinforced and at others undermined by diasporic writers. Uma Parameswaran in 'Writing the Diaspora' refers to the dilemma of the Indo-Canadians and says, 'as a Canadian, I believe in borders but as a Diaspora member I can see that strength lies in the erasure of borders' (316). There is an interweaving of preoccupation with geographical territories and the emotional response to it. Landscape and mindscape coalesce, giving rise to interesting configurations. What emerges as the arena of conflict as well as celebration is the dual yet simultaneous points of reference that the diasporic consciousness negotiates: the ancestral home with associated political and socio-cultural identity, and the adopted land with a new set of political and socio-cultural affiliations.

Tracing the meaning of the word 'diaspora' takes us back to the Jewish experience of dispersal. In time it came to be associated with migratory movements initiated due to varied reasons: historical, political, economic or religious. Vijay Mishra in 'Diasporas and the Art of Impossible Mourning' refers to two kinds of diaspora. The old diaspora comprising of slave and indentured labourers, the product of 'classic capitalism' and the new diaspora made up of economic migrants and refugees, product of 'late capitalism' (26). While old diaspora broke contact with India but kept it alive imaginatively through memory and exclusion, the new diaspora was economically more secure and had easy access to the homeland. Uma Parameswaran in the article 'Literature of the Indian Diaspora in Canada: An Overview' (1996: 3–30) referring to Indo-Canadian diasporic experience points out that Canada does not have a history of indentured labourers from India. Instead, early twentieth century saw the influx of farmers from Punjab. However, dislocation when forced, and relocation when out of free choice, both result in a sense of alienation arising from being positioned between two cultures and two nations.

Dislocation followed by relocation involves negotiating both cultural and political constructs and the binary pull of longing and belonging. Longing for the home left behind is countered by the necessity to belong to the lived reality of the new home. Parameswaran in *Writing the Diaspora* holds, 'People who move away from their native countries occupy (not only inherit but also bequeath to subsequent generations, actually) a liminality, an uneasy pull between two cultures' (316).

Uma Parameswaran works out the dilemma of the binary pull in her novel *Mangoes on the Maple Tree*. How does a South-Asian Indo-Canadian diaspora negotiate the bifocal vision of home and the dualities and multiplicities arising there of? What are the shifting nuances of diasporic approach to nation state and culture? The oft repeated and clichéd refrain 'Home is where the heart is' encapsulates the dilemma of diasporic community as it strives to decipher where it is that it belongs. These are the questions that need to be interrogated. In an attempt to counterbalance divided loyalty with dual loyalty, the Indo-Canadian writer seeks to strike a fine balance between the threat of assimilation and hence loss of ethnic identity on one hand, and separatism which might lead to regressive ghettoisation on the other.

Parameswaran comes up with her 'thesis' of 'Ganga *in* the Assiniboine' as opposed to 'Ganga *as* Assiniboine or Assiniboine *as* Ganga'. Ganga *in* Assiniboine she holds 'implies a flowing into, a merger that enriches the river'. She refers to two literary streams coming together and maintaining their individuality till further down they become indistinguishable as 'distinctions blur and fade away' (2007: 71). The question that troubles one is, who merges in whom? Flowing into and merging *is* assimilation and loss of identity that the diaspora aim to safeguard. R. Radhakrishnan, in his article 'Ethnicity in Age of Diaspora', refers to a similar dilemma faced by the American diaspora and enquires, 'If the Asian is to be Americanized, will the American submit to Asianisation?' (127). Of the two identities flanking the hyphen, is it justified for one to be subsumed by the other?

Canada, a nation with the professed policy of multiculturalism is marked with racist sensibility, a theme taken up consistently by diasporic writers. The mainstream is still predominantly west-centred and the ethnic 'visible-minorities' jostle for a foothold in a milieu which privileges one over others. The 'othering' of diasporic community is a lived reality which invariably results in reinforcing the nostalgic invocation of 'home' and invention of what Rushdie refers to as 'imaginary homelands' (10) in literature produced. Uma Parameswaran envisages four phases of immigrant settlement in Canada in the essay 'Writing the Diaspora'. From nostalgia for the old home and fear of the new, to adjustment and establishing oneself in the new. Next step is the involvement in ethno-cultural issues and community. Finally, there is participation in larger political and national issues. All the four phases have a strong undercurrent of the need to belong cutting across time and generations (2007: 304–307). Though diasporic position is undeniably that of a 'Trishanku' (1988: 66) as presented by Uma Parameswaran in the collection of poems so titled, yet the bicultural vision can enrich and empower its unique positioning. The flip side of the diasporic consciousness is that it renders the boundaries of the 'liminal' space it occupies porous, thus facilitating easy accessibility to two cultures and two homes.

Makarand Paranjape in the article titled 'One Foot in Canada and a Couple of Toes in India' argues, 'the main thrust of South Asian Canadian Writers is away from India and towards Canada' (161). Similarly Uma Parameswaran, in her collection of essays *Writing the Diaspora,* emphasises the need for Indo-Canadian writers to stop mourning the loss of old home and be celebratory in their depiction Indo-Canadian diasporic experience in all its authenticity. The first generation diaspora invariably use India as a 'safe space' (2007: 323) to write about. Parameswaran points at the need to write about the 'here and now', instead of 'there and then'. Radhakrishnan makes a distinction between information about and knowledge of India in the second generation, and the emotional investment which was present in the first. However, one cannot overlook the fact that for the diaspora, India was frozen at the point of time they left the country. In spite of the emotional investment, the recreation of an India based on memory, is as much an invention as one the based on information and knowledge. Parameswaran in 'Dispelling the Spells of Memory' expresses the view that 'both writers and critics of the Indian diaspora need to shift their focus from original homeland to the present homeland' (2007: 323).

Uma Parameswaran's *Mangoes on the Maple Tree* is an actualisation and affirmation of her views about Indo-Canadian writings as reflected in her many essays on related issues. The work is based in Winnipeg and tells the story of twenty days in the life of an Indo-Canadian family. Individual crisis of the Bhave family and friends are framed within the national crisis of the 'flood of the century' of 1997. In the collection of essays Parameswaran points out that 'Nature as common enemy unified the settlers and made origins irrelevant to social interaction' (2007: 60). In the novel, Jayant the son of the family involves himself in the community work of putting up sand bags against the rising flood. He is able to embrace and become a part of the larger Canadian community in the moment of national crisis. Most vocal in his support of here and now, like his aunt Veejala, he is impatient of his father Sharad's constant nostalgic reference to India. He blurts out, 'Dad there's no our people, no old country for anyone in the world anymore, least of all us. *This* is our land and here we shall stay' (31). But his father who is a first generation immigrant still feels at a loss in the world he has relocated himself in.

Parameswaran brings out the generational gap in the response to the land of adoption. While the first generation immigrants' relationship with the adopted home is hampered by the need to hold on to the past which defined them, the second generation youth try to blend in to prevent being differentiated against. Nonetheless they too are haunted by the fear of assimilation resulting in the loss of individual identity due to the submergence in the larger Canadian identity. The longing to be accepted on one's own terms comes across strongly through Veejla's decision to return to India. What is at stake is not just cultural identity but also national and political identities. Her son Vithal believes in confrontation, not retreat. He emphasises the need to stay together as a community and hit back actively at the discriminatory racist approach. 'We have to stay separate from them and stay together, and we have got to show them we have as much right to be here as all those pissed-off whites who have bullied their way into this country these last three hundred years' (81). The concept of a community here is based more on exclusion that on inclusion. There is awareness that this could lead to ghettoisation and Rajen, Jayant's friend, chips in with the tongue in cheek observation, 'But that's called multiculturalism here. Each group stays within a closed charmed circle never bothering about others' (81). Vithal challenges the greater claim and domination of 'Founding Nations' as the British, Scots and French are referred to, emphasising the need to stand up for one's right of self-determination in multicultural Canada.

Parameswaran in her essay 'Ganga in the Assiniboine: prospects of Indo-Canadian Literature' holds, 'In the immigrant imagination there is the intermingling of imagery drawn from the landscape of one's memory with the actual landscape around us' (2007: 79). *Mangoes on the Maple Tree* not only incorporates Canadian reality of day-to-day activities of an average Indo-Canadian family, but also enriches the same by interweaving it with Indian myths, personal histories related to old home land, cultural markers in the form of dress, food, mores, language and even names and nick-names. Krishna becomes Krish, Savitri becomes Savit, Veejala becomes Vee. The cultural reverberations of the names cannot be missed. Savitri is as comfortable in her work-dress of skirt, blouse and coat as she is in the sari she dons when at home. Use of 'beta' as a form of address for her sons sounds as natural as her children calling her 'mom'. References to Indian dishes crop up as frequently as the words 'beta' and 'bahu'. Jyoti's memory of religious service where ancestors are called upon to ensure healthy continuity of family is juxtaposed to Jayant's feverish preparations prior to 'leaving home' and striking out with his friends.

The superimposition of one culture over the other as the diasporic sensibility comes to terms with its bicultural vision is highlighted. Uma Parameswaran holds, 'Given the diversity of ethnic streams Canadian literature will, we hope, extend its frontiers and expand its vocabulary in order to accommodate the diversity of our multicultural reality' (2007: 71). The inclusion of the story of Panchali and Durvasa in the novel is an interesting re-rendering by Parameswaran. The oral rendition is enacted as children join in with inflections which are contemporaneous and personal. The explosive temper of Durvasa in the novel is equated with the Nuclear bomb and with Vithal. The grain of cooked rice is consciously substituted by spinach. Interspersed with the bickering of the two children that emphasises their westernised speech and a loaded comment like 'Aw, all girls are soppy' (38), the story comes to an interesting conclusion with discussion about 'burping' after a meal which is considered a sign of appreciation and satisfaction in Indian culture, but is 'bad manners' in Canada. Along with the dilemma arising from the divided self, the awareness of the possibility of more than one approach to shared experience and reality enriches the perception of the diaspora.

Parameswaran refers to the Komagata Maru incident (1914) as well as crash of Kanishka (1985) which earmark the shifts in diasporic experience of Indians in Canada. The historical incidents and their political implications find place in her works and she is unsparing in her criticism of the Canadian stance towards India. She is also scathing about the celebrations of annual Folklorma which is referred to as 'three-ring circus' (81). Jyoti, the daughter, instinctively resists the racist aggression perpetrated against immigrants through greater aggression. The challenge of separatism is countered either by negation or through affirmative response. Vithal, in spite of his strong plea for community bonding amongst immigrants to counter racism, is reconciled and reunited with his white girl friend. Jyoti too is able to acknowledge the dual pull of her love for Pierre and the attraction she experiences for Sridhar. She emerges a stronger person better equipped to deal with the question of marriage. Jayant decides to stay home and help the family cope with the crisis resulting from Veejala's decision to leave her family and return to India. The novel ends on a note of affirmation as family and friends come together to celebrate by putting up a Christmas tree in the backyard.

Parameswaran makes a distinction between home and homeland in the essay 'Home is Where Your Feet are, and may Your Heart be There Too'. Home is Canada and homeland is India that is kept alive through the memories of older generation. For the diaspora, home is where one decides to go and the heart follows the feet. India is an inheritance to be treasured while Canada is a home to be loved and lived in. Parameswaran, in the essay 'Driving into the New Millennium on a Trans-Canada Highway that has only Entry Ramps', cites her preference by declaring, 'I choose writers who introduce and establish archetypes and culture allusions out of the historical experiences of their ethno-cultural, and make it a part of the, national literary and cultural arena' (2007: 367). Inclusion of events that are specifically Indo-Canadian diasporic experience is an attempt to inscribe them into the mainstream sensibility and conscience of the nation. The personal and the political converge and diverge, interfusing and moulding the consciousness into new configuration pregnant with possibilities where the diaspora can look forward to growing '... mangoes on maples, and *jamuns* on birches, and *bilvas* on spruces' (221).

## References

Mishra, Vijay. 'Diasporas and the Art of Impossible Mourning' in *In Diaspora: Theories, Histories, Texts*. Ed. Makarand Paranjape. New Delhi: Indialog Publications, 2001, 24–47.

Paranjape, Makarand. 'One Foot in Canada and a Couple of Toes in India: Diasporas and Homelands in South Asian Canadian

Experience' in *In Diaspora: Theories, Histories, Texts*. Ed. Makarand Paranjape. New Delhi: Indialog Publications, 2001, 161–170.

Parameswaran, Uma. *Trishanku*. Toronto: TSAR Books, 1988, 66.

——. 'Ganga in the Assiniboine: Prospects of Indo-Canadian Literature' *Writing the Diaspora*. Jaipur: Rawat Publications, 2007, 70–83.

——. 'Dispelling the Spells of Memory', *Writing the Diaspora*. 311–328.

——. 'Driving into the New Millennium', *Writing the Diaspora*. 359–380.

——. 'Home is Where Your Feet are, and May Your Heart be There Too', *Writing the Diaspora*. 208–217.

——. *Mangoes on the Maple Tree*. Frederiction: Broken Jaw Press, 2002.

——. *Writing the Diaspora: Essays on Culture and Identity*. Jaipur: Rawat Publications, 2007.

——. 'Literature of the Indian Diaspora in Canada: An Overview'. SACLIT: *An Introduction to South Asian Canadian Literature*, Madras: East West Books, 1996, 3–30.

Radhakrishnan, R. 'Ethnicity in an Age of Diaspora' in *Theorizing Diaspora: A Reader*. Eds. Jana Evans, Braziel and Anita Mannur. USA: Blackwell, 2003, 119–131.

Rushdie, Salman. *Imaginary Homelands: Essays and Criticism 1981–1991*. London: Granta Books in Association with Viking Penguin, 1991.

Said, Edward. *Culture and Imperialism*. New Delhi: Penguin, 1994.

# III

# Community Narratives

## Shifting Community Spaces

Doors that open on the countryside seem to confer freedom behind the world's back.

Ramon Gomez de la Serna, Enchantillons

*Gaston Bachelard quotes the above lines in his Poetics of Space (1958; 1964: 224). They can be interpreted in different ways but the truth of the fact remains that the rural, the countryside and the pastoral allow a greater degree of freedom cannot be denied, despite whatever other compulsions and discriminations that may be there.*

*This section begins with an exploration of two folk narratives and their delinking from a particular time or space, and then proceeds to look at Steinbeck and Marquez as the authors – Rama Rani Lall and Madhuri Chatterjee – proceed to work with histories where individuals were voluntarily subsumed into larger constructs. The relocation of community life in urban space through the creation of a tenement or chawl is explored as is the consequent fragmentation of this space through walls, apartments and personal pursuits by Jasbir Jain. The creation of a reading community in a personal space to free the mind from political impositions and to allow explorations of freedom through narratives is the subject of the essay by Nishevita Murthy and Sudha Sastri.*

*An imaginative pursuit of cooking opens out a whole discourse of recipe-exchange and cultural preservation through this pursuit in Nidhi Singh's study of cooking as a factor which binds people together while Charu Mathur's fine analysis of the manner in which violence and death tear people apart, touches a raw nerve in the contemporary times of violence. But violence again has another tale to tell when communities come together in grief and sorrow.*

*In the community narrative, the individual voice is muted. The movement is centripetal and the narrative voice is either decentred or omniscient.*

# Reading Culture Through Folklore: A Study of an Assamese Folktale and an Oriya Folktale

*Bharat Bhushan Mohanty*

William R. Bascom, in his paper 'Folklore and Anthropology' (1965), talks about the significance of folklore in cultural anthropology. He is of the view that folklore belongs to one of the branches of anthropology, namely, cultural anthropology, where it has a vital role to play in the making of the culture of any given people. No known culture can have its existence without having a folklore of its own. Bascom comments: 'Folklore is studied in anthropology because it is part of man's learned traditions and customs, and a part of his social heritage' (28). To make his stance more credible he offers the methodology of examining folklore data ... to use folklore data to test theories or hypothesis about culture a whole and conversely, the accepted theories of culture.

Bronislaw Malinowski in his book *Myth in Primitive Psychology* (1926) has studied the Malanesian culture by making a survey on the opinions, traditions and behaviour of the Malanesian native people. There is a conspicuous attempt in that book to explore the extent of control and influence that myths enjoy in the real life of the native people. He finds that several sacred traditions, ritual and myths, enter deeply into the pursuits of the native people and they control strongly their moral and social behaviour. He is of the opinion that 'an intimate connection exists between the word, mythos, the sacred tales of the tribe on the one hand, and their ritual acts, and even their practical activities on the other' (11).

Similarly, a report of a discussion from the Indo-American week-long seminar on Indian Folklore, held in Mysore in August 1980, emphasises the greater significance of folklore in the real life of the people. Beyond the level of fun and amusement, beauty and flexibility of oral presentation, and the urgency of preserving remote primitive heritage, it has a day-to-day relevance to the understanding of the social as well as the moral values of our society. Folklore is an instrument that serves to express life values and offers metaphors for the shared understanding of life. In addition to that it preserves the past of those areas where there are no historical records. It provides an alternative history, which is by nature, democratic. It is democratic because every member of the society has rightful access to that community memory and has got the authority to construct the historical reality in his own way (*Indian Folklore* 2).

An Oriya folktale 'Tapoee' and an Assamese folktale 'Tejimola' have been taken up for discussion here. Both the folk items are orally transmitted and they share a noteworthy similarity. An attempt has been made to examine these folktales in the light of relationship between folklore and culture studies. The present study also highlights the mechanism and the process of codification of cultural values and ideas in the folktales, which are generally sacrificed for narrative exigency and for immediate spatio-temporal reasons.

The story of 'Tejimola' moves round the character of Tejimloa who is the loving and beautiful daughter of a wealthy merchant in Assam. While still a child, she had lost her mother and her stepmother had brought her up. Once when the merchant leaves on a trading venture to a far off place entrusting his second wife to take every care of Tejimola, the stepmother subjects the girl to various kinds of hardships and finally brutally kills Tejimola by pounding her hands, legs and head with the help of a paddy-husking pedal. Then she proceeded to dig a pit in the ground just below the eaves of the house and buried Tejimola there. After some days a bottle-gourd plant grew luxuriantly and bore a rich harvest. A beggar woman while passing that way was tempted by the rich yield and tried to pluck the gourds. At this the plant wailed and narrated the story of her brutal murder by her stepmother in the form of a song. Then the merchant's wicked wife cut the plant with a knife and threw away the plant in the backyard. After a few days, a plant bearing citrus fruits began to grow in that spot. Some cowherds, noticing that, tried to pluck some fruits. But the tree again began wailing and narrated the same story again. Then the merchant's wife cut the plant and threw it into the river. In the river the plant turned into a lotus and blossomed. Tejimola's father while returning by that river route in his boat saw the lotus flower and came to know about the death of his loving daughter from the creeper. The merchant then asks the plant to become a mynah bird and so it happens. The story ends with Tejimola regaining her human form and the wicked stepmother is given punishment and driven out of that locality.

The story of 'Tapoee' does have an identical narrative feature. Tapoee is the beautiful and loving daughter of a wealthy merchant in Orissa. She has seven extremely caring and affectionate brothers and seven sister-in-laws. Once on a full moon night, being a pampered child, Tapoee demands her old parents to give her a moon so that she can play with that. A famous goldsmith of that locality takes the responsibility of making a moon-like object, made of various precious metals. But before the completion of the task, Tapoee's parents pass away and her seven brothers leave for distant lands for purposes of trade. At the time of departure all the seven brothers instruct their wives to take every care of Tapoee and provide her all comforts in their absence. An elderly woman, who is envious of Tapoee's good fortune, instigates the seven sister-in-laws to put her to various household works. Six of the seven sister-in-laws act accordingly but not the youngest one. The youngest sister-in-law secretly helps her. Tapoee looks after a flock of goats in the forest and regularly collects firewood. Yet despite her hard work, she does not get proper food and cloth. One day one of the goats, called Gharamani, is lost in the deep forest. The six wicked sister-in-laws come to know about that and throw her out of the house telling her not to return home without the lost goat. Tapoee is left hungry, tired, helpless and lonely in the deep wild forest at night to find out the goat. She comes across a shrine of a goddess called Khudurunkini (goddess hungry for broken rice) while desperately crying for help in that forest. She prays to the goddess to help her trace the missing goat and to bring back her seven brothers safely from their trading mission. She narrates the whole story of her life before the goddess when all her brothers are coincidentally present near the shrine. The seven brothers along with Tapoee punish the six sister-in-laws by mutilating their noses. The youngest one is spared because of her good deeds.

Structurally, these two tales share an identical pattern. Both Tejimola and Tapoee come from rich merchant family background and both are extremely pampered and very well looked after by their respective guardians. The male counterparts in both cases entrust the womenfolk to take every possible care in their absence. The womenfolk in both the tales create various troubles and physically torture the girls once the male members are away. As a result of that Tejimola dies and Tapoee is banished into the dense forest to be killed by wild animals. The male members of the family give exemplary punishment to the erring women for their crime. Both the tales end with a strong sense of justice as Tejimola regains her human form and Tapoee gets back her seven brothers and lost happiness.

Beyond the structural pattern there are some other identical areas where the codification of cultural ideas and values in the tales are noticeable. Bascom offers a perspective on the deeper meaning of folklore in his discussions on the functions of folklore. He is of the view that folklore is not mere a form of amusement though amusement is one the functions of folklore. It is imperative to decode the encoded deeper meaning of folklore beneath the cover of humour (290). He firmly believes folklore is a credible mirror of culture, which 'incorporates descriptions of the details of ceremonies, institutions and technology, as well as the expression of beliefs and attitudes' (284). Talking about the role of myth in primitive society Malinowski echoes a similar concern. He emphasises the function of myths by illustrating how it 'expresses, enhances, codifies belief' and 'safeguards and enforces morality' (19).

There is a subtle reference to an authoritative presence of patriarchal system in both the tales. The system functions at two different levels. First, male members in the tales enjoy absolute authority and they seem to have unquestionable nobility and socio-economic responsibilities and values. They are the protectors and the guardians of all the female members in the tales. They have the authority to impose moral as well as ethical standards upon their female counterparts and in case of violation they have the power to take adequate punitive measures for restoring normalcy.

Second, the women characters in the tales, in the absence of their respective male counterparts, reinforce a similar system of coercion and control over the comparatively weaker female characters, such as Tejimola and Tapoee. In these two concerned societies – Orissa and Assam, the tales are suggestive of the presence a strict system of retribution. Compliance to the system is so indispensable that in case of any form of violation can cause serious punishment. In this context Bascom's observations are noteworthy. He says: 'Folklore is an important mechanism for maintaining the stability of culture. It is used to inculcate the customs and ethical standards in the young, and as an adult to reward him with praise when he conforms, to punish with ridicule or criticism when he deviates' (298). In addition to that, to focus on deviation as recurrent theme in the folklore and as a potential area for the codification of cultural taboos, is to emphasise one of the chief functions of folklore. In Bascom's view, the characters in folktales and myths act in a manner which is likely to be regarded as shocking in daily life (33). He considers this performance of deviation in a folktale becomes an ideal ground where social pressure and social control can be applied effectively (294).

Such kind of deviations can be associated with the character of Tapoee. Her obstinate persistence in desiring the impossible, like a demand for the moon, seems to have invited unparalleled adversity in her life. I have heard from the ordinary people in Orissa that Tapoee's demand for a moon is a bad omen and a case of violation of convention. Thus she has to undergo all those sufferings for the cause of purification. Similar kind of violations can be located in Tejimola. After the departure of her father she insisted on attending the marriage ceremony of her friend. This act of Tejimola was against her father's wish. Her stepmother got the opportunity to hatch a conspiracy to kill her with all her cruel ideas.

There are a good number of incongruities and differences at the level of construction of plots, characters and narrative movement. In Tapoee's case the relationship between the seven brothers and their sister has assumed prominence. The society she lives in is a society that upholds such a relationship with reverence and dignity. On the other hand in 'Tejimola' we notice a different kind of socio-cultural ordering. The father plays an important role in all kinds of affairs. When Tejimola's father saw the lotus flower in the river he took a chewed mixture of areca-nut from his mouth in his left hand and sweet meat in his right hand and said 'if you are my Tejimola, then you would surely become a mynah bird and choose between the two'. The lotus becomes a mynah and flows to him and takes the chewed mixture to prove the sacrosanct bond.

From the point of view of description of myths and performance of rituals and ceremonies these two folk tales have remarkable differences. In case of Tapoee, when she is thrown out of her house the weather is hostile; she is hungry and helpless in the forest with all kinds of wild animals around. This is as good as being killed. She suddenly discovers the shrine of the goddess Khudrunkini. She has nothing to offer to the goddess to please her. She collects petals of lily and prepares a kind of libation mixing lily roots with a little broken rice and offers that to the goddess. As a result of that worship Tapoee gets back her seven brothers, her missing goat and her lost happiness. There is a clear reference to the performance of a specific ritual in the story. Tapoee's performance of the rituals has guaranteed security, prosperity and happiness. This legitimises and validates the practicing of such rituals. This ritual is still in practice in Orissa, mostly in the remote villages of Orissa. In the month of Bhadra (September/October) the village girls gather near a pond. They collect mud from the pond and make two round shaped lumps on the edge of pond and decorates them with fresh petals of lily from the pond. They offer puja to the goddess khudurunkini praying for the well-being and prosperity of theirs brothers and for their own future. In this context, Bascom's observations on the functions of folklore are quite interesting. He states, 'folklore validates culture by justifying rituals and institutions to those who perform and observe them' (292).

In 'Tejimola', on the contrary, we don't find any reference to performance of rituals. We don't come across the presence of any external agent like the goddess Khudurunkini in 'Tapoee' to ensure justice for Tejimola. Nature is found to have played the role of the external agent. When Tejimola dies her body does not perish away. She undergoes a kind of metamorphosis and regains her life in the form of a bottle-gourd plant. When the plant is destroyed and thrown in the backyard it reappears in the form a citrus plant and when the citrus plant is destroyed and thrown into the river it regains life in the form a lotus flower. It is quite clear that the stepmother has destroyed Tejimola's human body but her re-emergence in the forms of bottle-gourd, citrus, lotus and mynah is suggestive of certain cultural codes. The primitive society's belief on the continuation of life through nature after the death of the physical body as nature is the only source of endless life on earth, may have been incorporated into this story of Tejimola. This is also suggestive of the immortality of the soul and the transience of the human body. There is another way of looking at this particular phenomenon of reappearance. The folktale may have made an attempt to accommodate the age-old myth of the cycle of birth and death, which is a never-ending process. The condition of continuation of life through natural objects reveals the truth about Tejimola's unfortunate death and establishes justice and balance, which has been jeopardised through the violation of social laws by her stepmother. The convention of personification of nature and the juxtaposition of man with nature are still a living and colourful tradition of Assam. The distinction between human body and nature disappears and they get inter-mingled, unified and become one. The most colourful festival of Assam –'Bohag Bihu', upholds a similar kind of belief. Bohag Bihu which is also called Rongali Bihu is celebrated every year in the month of April. This is essentially a celebration of fertility and regeneration in both man and nature.

These two tales, discussed here, clearly indicate a pattern in the Indian folklore tradition. There is a clear suggestion of folktales travelling from one region to another. In that process of trans-mission a good number of society-specific and culture-specific ideas get incorporated into the apparent narrative flexibility that every oral transmission naturally demands. It is quite likely that folktales and other forms of folklore can be studied to formulate genuine cultural meanings and its formation of a particular society simultaneously showing its subtle differences, present in specific geo-cultural and ethno-linguistic societies in India.

## References

Anonymous. *Khudurunkini Osha* (Oriya). Kesharpur, Cuttack: Rimi Prakashani. n.d.

Bascom, William R. 'Folklore And Anthropology,' *The Study of Folklore*. Ed. Alan Dundes. N.J.: Prentice Hall, Inc. 1965, 25–33.

——. 'Four Functions of Folklore'. *The Study of Folklore*. 1965, 279–298.

Bezbaua, Laxminath. compiled. *Grandma's Tale*. Trans. Pallavi Barua. Hornbill Publication: Guwahati, 2006.

Dash, Kunjabihari. 'Tapoee Katha'. *Kunjabihari Granthabali*. Odisha Book Store: Cuttack, 1986. p. 393–398.

Malinowski, Bronislaw. *Myth in Primitive Psychology*. W.W. Norton & Company, Inc. 1926.

Pattnayak, D.P. and P.J. Claus., ed. *Indian Folklore*. CIIL, Mysore: 1981.

# John Steinbeck: Community Consciousness and the Eternal Migrant in *The Grapes of Wrath*

*Rama Rani Lall*

Steinbeck published his novel *The Grapes of Wrath* in April 1939. Though more than seventy years have passed it has not lost its popularity and relevance and it continues to move millions of readers all over the world. If all writing is a dialogue between a writer and a reader, Bakhtin's concept of 'dialogic tension' helps to interpret this novel. Steinbeck attempts to give voice to the silent majority of migrant labourers and opens out his discourse to a multiplicity of voices. He projects various conflictual situations to foreground the suffering of dislocated farmers in the affluent community of America.

To contextualise the text of the novel we have to turn to its historical and sociological background. During the 1930s, a severe drought led to massive agricultural failure in many parts of the southern great plains of America, chiefly throughout Oklahoma, Arkanas, Texas and other neighbouring states. In the absence of rains, crops withered and died. The topsoil, no longer anchored by growing roots, was picked up by strong winds. Huge dust storms blew over the area. The affected region came to be known as the 'Dust Bowl' of America. Steinbeck has described this natural calamity and the despair of the farmers in the opening chapter of the novel which ends with a graphic picture of the men standing by their fences and looking at the ruined corn, 'The men were silent and they did not move often'. Sometimes 'The men sat in the doorways of their houses; their hands were busy with sticks and little rocks. The men sat still – thinking – figuring' (*GOW* 5–6).

By the early 1930s, the drought had crippled countless farm families and with the crash of the stock market America had fallen into the great gloom of the Great Depression. Many small farmers had to mortgage their land for the purposes of survival. Fontenrose summarises the situation and says, 'Dust storms and erosion exhausted the land and completed what economic depression had begun. The banks and the agricultural corporations (creatures of the banks) found it more profitable to foreclose mortgages and terminate tenancies, combine many farms into one plantation, and put it all to cotton' (67). The banks knew that one man with a tractor could do much more than hundreds of human hands as the tractor could work a whole plantation and the driver willing to work for wages as low as three dollars a day. Keeping their own interest above all human considerations, the banks evicted the farmers and their families from their homes, rendering them homeless. Thousands of unfortunate farmers travelled to California, in the hope of finding employment there. They had heard or read the handbills that announced that men were needed to pick the crops of oranges and grapes. *The Grapes of Wrath* chronicles the hardships and suffering of these migrant farmers.

Steinbeck made several trips to the migrant camps to study the conditions under which they lived. He wrote a number of newspaper articles to make America know what was happening in California. Many times he joined the migrants on their journey and later picked cotton or peaches with them. Thus he gained a first hand knowledge of their struggles. He became familiar with their speech patterns, reactions and experiences directly from them. He did not go into the field to substantiate a readymade theory but with the intention to understand the human condition. He admits in a letter, 'I'm probably making a mistake in simply listening to men talk and watching them act; hoping that the projection of the microcosm will define the outlines of the macrocosm' (qtd. by Lisca 76). Steinbeck was well aware that general statements and theoretical descriptions easily merge into vague abstractions. He wanted to shock his readers into an awareness of the appalling conditions under which the migrant farmers were forced to live. To channelise his genuine sympathy and anger he fixed his gaze on one fictional family of Joads.

Migration from one geographical location to another is as old as human history. The Biblical substructure of *The Grapes of Wrath* adds to its mythical and epic dimensions. The migration of dust bowl farmers has many similarities to the exodus of thousands of Hebrews from Egypt. Gladstein admits that though the story of the novel describes, 'a quintessential American experience' (134), its appeal is worldwide with migration having become an international phenomenon today for, 'People move, boundaries change, economic and political problems create migrations. The Oklahomans in California are like the Chinese in Malaysia, the Indians in South Africa, the Turkish in Germany, or the Algerians in France' (134). In India, the memory of millions crossing from India to Pakistan and vice versa is still fresh in our minds. Hundreds of unfortunate victims of war and economic exploitation also move from one place to another. *The Grapes of Wrath* chronicles this tragedy of homelessness and subsequent loss of identity. It gives us a new insight into this perennial human problem and perhaps makes us more humane and considerate towards them.

Gladstein has tried to identify certain common experiences of all migrant communities and shows that what the Joads suffered in the novel is very similar to what millions of others have suffered and are still suffering. Taking the Joad family as an archetype of all migrant experience, she shows how most migrants begin their journey with high expectations of a better life at their journey's end. The Joads' vision of California is of a place which is never cold, where people 'the oranges represent more than gold; they represent luxury and nourishment of the Promised Land.' (Gladstein 137). The 'ingroup' in California like all other insiders have a tendency to use derogatory terms to label the 'outgroup' of the new arrivals. In *The Grapes of Wrath* the word 'Okies' is used for all outsiders. It becomes synonymous with the phrase 'a beaten down loser.' This negative stereotyping has a soul withering effect on the migrants. Even Tom and Ma Joad were shocked and felt humiliated when they heard the word for the first time.

The Joads were not beggars and hated to accept charity. They were normal hardworking farmers who had undertaken the hazardous journey to California to find some honest work. They were prepared to dig, to plant, to pick, to pull, or to do any hard work, to survive with dignity. They found that it was not easy to find suitable employment in California as the residents and policemen were hostile to them. Like other migrant groups the Joads were paid lower wages and had to endure poorer working conditions in the new state. They were often described as sub-human. One gas salesman had the audacity to compare them to 'gorillas' because they looked so dirty and miserable. Perhaps poverty, humiliation and suffering are the fate of all migrants. According to Gladstein, 'Because of their powerlessness and because they are seen as less than human, immigrants are often housed apart and in dehumanising facilities .... This "segregation" or "ghettoisation" is called "spatial segregation in contemporary sociological studies" (142). The Joads are also subjected to this 'spatial segregation' and had to live in temporary camps or shacks. They are gradually devastated by death, desertion and floods.

*The Grapes of Wrath* has thirty chapters out of which only fourteen carry the Joad story which constitutes the major portion of the novel. The other sixteen chapters are often called the inter-chapters or intercalary chapters and take little more than one sixth of the whole book. According to Fontenrose, they are 'either expository essays or sketches of typical situations in the great migration. They present the social, economic and historical background, telling the story of all the migrants' (69). Usually, the general experiences described in the inter-chapters are followed by the narration of the actual experiences of the Joad family. To a great extent the narrative section of the novel illustrates the descriptive part of the interchapters. The artistic blending of the descriptive and narrative sections of the book gives us a better view of the whole problem. Through the interchapters, Steinbeck was able to bridge the 'dialogic tension' between universality and particularity.

The twelve members of the Joad family start their journey with only a few of their possessions and a little bit of money. They had to sell their household goods and farming tools at outrageously low prices. They travelled in an old Hudson Car which was converted into a truck. Their journey to California on Highway 66 took several days and they saw thousands of other cars traveling in the same direction, with similar farm families. Both Granpa and Granma Joad died on the way. Noah, their mentally retarded son, leaves them and their son-in-law Connie Rivers deserts his pregnant wife Rose of Sharon without any explanation. From their day of entry into California they experienced the hostility of the California policemen and residents. Camping at the temporary camp of Hooverville, they were witnesses to the misery and hunger of the migrant workers as well as the arrogance and cruelty of deputy sheriffs. When they no longer had money or food or work they travelled northwards and found work picking peaches at Hooper Ranch, which provided miserable lodgings and low wages. Jim Casy, the preacher friend, was arrested and later killed while trying to help Tom Joad, the elder son of the family. In turn Tom killed the attacker and is compelled to become a fugitive. Before leaving he told his mother that he was going to carry on Casy's work for the union of farm labourers to demand social justice. After cotton-picking there was no work for three months and the camp was flooded by the heavy winter rains. The Joads took shelter in an old barn on a higher ground after their daughter Rose of Sharon gave birth to a stillborn child. In the barn they found a starving man dying of hunger. Ma Joad and Rose of Sharon exchanged glances and understood each other well. Rose of Sharon fed the dying man with her breast milk to save his life. Many readers have objected to this closing scene but it contains a very profound human reality and is representative of a religious feeling. Perceptive critics like Fontenrose find it to be a comprehensive image to highlight the chief message of the novel. He says, 'for Steinbeck it is an oracular image, forecasting in a moment of defeat and despair the final triumph of the people – a contingent forecast, for only if the people nourish and sustain one another will they achieve their ends' (69). He continues, 'The Joads intense feelings of family loyalty have been transcended. They have expanded to embrace all men. Another image could have symbolised this universality, but, for Steinbeck, perhaps no other could have done it so effectively' (69).

In the beginning Tom was concerned only with his own needs. Later living with the Christ-like Casy, he gains a deeper understanding of the migrant's situation, which marks the Joads' progress from 'an exclusive concern for family interests to a broader vision of co-operation with all oppressed people' (Fontenrose 70). Lisca points out that in addition to the supporting Biblical structure and context, 'there are interwoven two opposing themes which make up the book's plot' (96). The negative movement concerns itself with the decline of the Joad family's financial and moral strength. In the beginning they have some money, some food, a truck and their good health. As the novel progresses, they become more and more impoverished. At the end, they have become total destitutes without food, money or goods, 'This economic decline is paralleled by a similar decline in the family's morale' (96). But it is from these depths that Rose lifts the family by acting the saviour for the man in the shed.

Also as the family unit becomes weaker, the social group becomes stronger. When the Joads meet the Wilsons on the highway at the critical moment of Granpa's death, mutual help and support revives their morale. They share their anxiety, their money and their food. This brings about a gradual change in the attitude of the migrants towards their own suffering. This change is often designated as the 'education' and 'conversion' of the Joads. Birje Patil says, 'the shared experiences compels the Joad family to think in terms of the communal "we" instead of the individual "I" and enables them to integrate with the larger camping community' (172).

Steinbeck has vividly described the birth of this community consciousness in some of the inter-chapters. Showing how during the daytime the migrants continued on their journey but as the evening came they wanted to camp near a spring. One by one a number of families put up their tents at one place. And then a strange thing happened, 'The twenty families became one family, the children were the children of all. The loss of home became one loss, and the golden time in the west was one dream' (*GOW* 227). Gradually, Ma Joad recognises that the power of the people lies in their unity, for when thousands fight against the system, no one can stop them.

In one of the earlier chapters of the novel Steinbeck describes a turtle's indomitable progress over land and across a highway, where a cruel truck driver tries to crush it. Surviving somehow the turtle reaches the other side of the road and the seeds caught in his shell are inadvertently planted into the soil. This episode symbolises the journey of the 'Okies', and their determined moving forward and final survival in a hostile land. *The Grapes of Wrath* is not only concerned about highlighting the heroic struggle of one family but shows how collective action can bring about social change and give birth to hope.

## References

Fontenrose, Joseph. *John Steinbeck.* New York: Holt, Rinehart and Winston, Inc., 1963. 67–83.

Gladstein, Mimi Reisel. '*The Grapes of Wrath*: Steinbeck and the Eternal Immigrant.' In *John Steinbeck*: *The Years of Greatness 1936–1939.* Ed. Tetsumaro Hayashi, Tuscaloosaz London: The University of Alabama Press, 1993. 132–144.

Lisca, Peter, '*The Grapes of Wrath*'. in *Twentieth Century Views: Steinbeck*: *A Collection of Critical Essays*. Ed. Qobert Murray Davis. Englewood Cliff, N.J., Prentice-Hall, Inc. 1972. 75–121.

Patil, J. Birje. 'Steinbeck's: *The Grapes of Wrath*' in *Indian Response to Steinbeck.* Ed. R.K. Sharma. New Delhi: Rachna Prakashan, 1984. 168–183.

Steinbeck, John. *The Grapes of Wrath,* 1939, London: Penguin, 1969.

# Heterotopic Spaces and Community Narratives from *Katha* to *Metro*

*Jasbir Jain*

In this paper, I propose to explore the manner in which heterotopic spaces interact with the temporal flow of time to create meaning as well as a community narrative. For this purpose I travel from Sai Paranjpe's 1982 film *Katha* through Gloria Naylor's novel of different narratives, *The Women of Brewster Place* (1982) to Anurag Basu's *Life in a Metro* (2007) in order to trace the shifting parameters of the community narrative as it interacts with modernity and postmodernity and their representation in two different mediums.

*Katha*, as the title announces, works through the construct of a fable and provides a double frame for the inner narrative. First it is a grandmother, narrating a story to a grandchild who is the listener; second the story itself is a fable of the 'hare and the tortoise', a story found across cultures with its archetypal character contrasts with the simple yet honest person, tentative in his behaviour and limited in his goals and the sharper, street smart counterpart who talks big, does not hesitate either to flatter or exploit, and steamrolls over others in his way to his goals. The first incorporates the characteristics of a simpleton, the second of the trickster. But predictably it is the slow reacting tortoise that wins the race with the hare having to search for other pastures. The centre space is the *chawl,* the low-middle-class tenement in an urban space but still cherishing and nurturing a rural lifestyle with its lack of privacy, sharing of resources with neighbours and multi-generational presence within this community. There are several dreams contesting for space and there are several spaces contesting for meaning as cultural contexts are uncovered in the larger scenario. Space is expanded through memories, fears, ambitions, hopes and fabrications – Rajaram Purshottam Joshi's village home, his neighbour's flat with its refrigerator, TV and a son in the US, and Basu the newcomer's, fabricated memories – all move out of the chawl into cattleyards, technology, restaurants and beaches. A counterpoint to the chawl is Joshi's office and his golf-playing boss. Within these two main spaces, the story moves as a shuttlecock but there are other mini spaces like the cupboard in which Rajaram keeps his money, his clothes, his letters, the files which have a certain anonymity and can be passed on, and the nude pictures which contest for space with the photograph of his parents. These spaces create cultural and moral meaning and are like little moves in a game of chess which is being played between opposing value structures. Within this narrative, several questions are posed and answered in different ways: What is success? Who makes a good son and a good husband? How do women choose life partners? And how much of deviation can one condone?

We, as viewers (or listeners), sympathise with Rajaram, even as we resent his inability to cope with his opponents. His gentle smile, his controlled anger, his tolerance, all invite exploitation. Whereas Basu's defeat is no defeat at all, it is in keeping with his policy of moving from one lie to another. The note he leaves behind is his only piece of honesty. The mini spaces form a semiotic pattern just as colours, clothes and flowers do. When sugar, milk and samosas are sent across from one house to the other and children and women run these errands, and when Rajaram desists from disturbing the honeymooning couple … all these events form a pattern of communication and language. Later we have the young groom reciprocate Rajaram's gesture when the latter gets married thus entering into a relational dialogue.

Through the semiotics of these mini spaces, a heterotopic community comes into being as divisions and opposition between public and private, family and social circle, leisure and work are blurred, erased and broken down. Yet not altogether destroyed. Under the surface blurring a hidden resistance to encroachments and a struggle for preserving the moral values meaningful for the individual psyche are also constantly discernible. Sites and counter sites shift as the children's ball is bowled into a woman's home, one who cuts the ball into bits before throwing it back – revenge, loneliness, disappointment, frustration – all cluster together in the act. The distance between the self and the other is muted – as people living in close proximity in a community whose resemblance to a family is outward and thin and which does not cater for sharing of dreams, come to look upon the 'other' both as an extension of the self and an 'other' they do not wish to become.

Foucault in 'Of Other Spaces' (3), talks of crisis heterotopias.[1] In *Katha* because of the simple straightforward lines, the chawl serves a multiple purpose – home, transient home, nursing home, marital home – as both stability and temporariness occupy the same space and different heterochronies also inhabit it. It is both a comfort and a crisis zone. At any given time, at least four generations are there. As the chawl neighbourhood shares its failures, disappointments and joys a community narrative comes into view in a very elemental way: lack of individual space and privacy, a meeting of the 'self' and the 'other' as roles interchange rapidly and the trickster approach begins to appropriate the subconscious desires of the morally correct. Contesting the limits both of physical and moral space, the narrative frame begins to evolve.

*Katha* uses the tradition of a moral tale, but Gloria Naylor's *Women of Brewster Place*, written contemporaneously, uses a capitalistic society's indifference as the basis of constructing a heterotopic community of blacks in a block of four double-units walled in a closed space. The traits of a community narrative are incorporated into a postmodernist space, which in effect is a crisis heterotopia. The frames here are however different: instead of the grandmother and the fable, the frames are created by class and race, and the dominant metaphor is one of legitimacy versus illegitimacy in that context. The language emphasis this: 'Brewster Place was the *bastard* child of several *clandestine* meetings between the alderman of the sixth district and the managing director of UNICO, Realty Company ...' (emphasis mine). And these corrupt forces together were responsible for this conception. Its initial inhabitants, the Irish, give way to the Mediterranean people who gradually move up and Brewster place becomes a black community; as the neighbourhood develops, this auxiliary street is walled off and it literally becomes a 'dead-end' street (Naylor 2) and then it acquires Ben as a janitor. Ben and the wall are its two limits and the ending of the narrative links them through death and dismantling. Together they carry a mixed symbol of freedom and exclusion, of protection and control.

Using the space of a tenement, like *Katha*, Gloria Naylor extends this space not as much through dreams as through memory and the presence of the past. The people who come here are strays, refugees, lonely people who have either been abandoned or are fugitives moving towards this centre in a centrifugal way. In this sense it is a crisis heterotopia and the issues here are also those of morality – of the socially acceptable and not acceptable. There are characters that interlink these stories and act as support systems, characters who step into the shoes of their predecessors, as kindness and compassion are handed out to the needy ones. Eva is one such figure, who takes in Mattie and Mattie fulfils this role for others when Eva is no more. Eva's grandchild Ciel is another interlinking character as is Kiswana who has left her middle class black home as a gesture of protest and as an open acknowledgement of her black status.

In someway or the other, all of them – Mattie, Eva, Etta Mae, Kiswana Browne, Luciella Louisa Turner, Cora Lee, Lorraine and Theresa – are different, yet they are not individualised. Their weaknesses are common enough – Mattie who was seduced and later refuses to see her son's weaknesses, Etta Mae who is still in pursuit of a man, despite having been repeatedly used, Luceilla who like Mattie goes on making concessions for her temperamental lover, Lorraine and Theresa who are lesbians, Cora Lee who stunted in her doll-playing role loves having babies and is not bothered about men as such. In some measure they all step away from the so-called 'norms' and are women on the periphery. But between themselves they form a community, concerned and caring. Brewster Place brings them together as they watch over each others' movements, betrayals, obsessions and problems and all divisions into public and private space are erased. When Lorraine is brutally gang-raped by the neighbourhood boys and sees Ben sitting outside and drinking, she crawls along the alley and finding a loose brick, hammers Ben to death with it. And then it rains, the rains go on for a week, obliterating the difference between night and day as if the floods had come. Dreams turn into nightmares. And even as it begins to rain, the women begin to remove the blood-stained bricks. It is almost a riot as the police sirens are heard. And then the sun emerges.

The final chapter is titled 'Dusk' just as the first is titled 'Dawn'. It begins with the sentence. 'No one cries when a street dies'. And Brewster was no exception – 'The last generation of children were torn away from it by court orders and eviction notices … . The water pipes froze … . Hallways were blind holes' (191). The building is abandoned as rats breed in it, leaving behind a haunting image of the rat-infested Harlem buildings, reminders of their rat eaten lives. The novel is an account of a community, bound together by its blackness and the exploitation of this blackness and defined by space. The work measures time through the lives of Eva, Mattie and Ciel, through the births of Cora Lee's children, through the deaths of Eva and Ben, and through broken marriages and relationships and through rain and sun. And all are defined by blackness. The most powerful dialogue is between Cora Lee and her son Sammy: 'Mama', Sammy pulled on her arm, 'Shakespeare's black?' 'Not yet', she said softly …. (127).

Using multiple narratives that interlink with each other, Anurag Basu, creates a postmodernist community narrative in *Life in a Metro*. Here space works in two different ways – first, the larger, unencompassable area of a metropolis where life is anonymous and upwardly mobile and moves at a fast pace where buses, trains and cars compete with each other for speed, and second the defined spaces within it. There is Rahul's flat, which is less his than of his seniors who borrow it for their liaisons;

there is the office space where Rahul works as does Neha, the girl he is interested in; then there are homes – Shikha's home, her sister Shruti's shared flat, and Shivani's home and last of all there is the railway platform signifying a transient relationship with all who come and go.

These different spaces are interlinked: Shivani and Shikha use the railway platform to wait for their lovers; Shikha's husband Ranjeet is Rahul's boss, Rahul's girl is Shruti's roommate and Ranjeet's mistress, Shruti is Shikha's sister. If we attempt to map these different places and draw the lines of connection, the peripheries are occupied by the transient space of the railway platform where Shivani waits for Amol and where he arrives to catch up with the past; and where Shikha and Akash wait for each other. At the centre is Rahul's flat from which he is perpetually ousted and which is occupied temporarily by a host of different people whose relationships are exploitative, secret and clandestine. The other living spaces like Shikha's home, Shruti's flat, Shivani's house and the office space come together in a quadrangle as members from one migrate to the other. Shivani lives next to a rehearsal space and has hardly any privacy; her relationship with Amol is also put under the scanner; Rahul's neighbours are aware of the migrant population of his flat; Shikha's flat represents frustration and tension where the feeling of being a restful home is absent. Rahul's flat, Shikha's and Shruti's living spaces in fact work in opposition to their defined role. Nowhere do we locate signs of any past, any memories, any photographs or sacred spaces; nowhere does one trace any sense of belonging or nesting, except in Shivani's home where food is cooked, shared and enjoyed, letters are read out and relationships worked at. Is it because Shivani and Amol represent a different generation?

In *Metro* the various characters move outside the limits of their space, transgress all kinds of values, live life purely in the present, even as they seek fulfillment of some personal goal. Shruti's search for a prospective husband, Rahul's unexpressed attraction for an office mate are pursuits that are sketchily portrayed until at one point the occupation with the present is punctured by reference to values as hidden dreams are unveiled. Rahul's flat-lending is not in pursuit of promotion or wealth, but a pursuit towards the fulfilment of his father's dream; Shruti realises she loves Monty; Shikha and Akash attracted towards each other are unable to take the final decision. Rahul tells Neha that money does not matter, Shruti realises that realisation of possibilities is in relationships not in dreams. Amol who, like a fish, had come home to die finds his lifelong love breathing her last in his arms. What the *Metro* cannot control is death. It also cannot control desire, but it does segment human lives, it creates a gap between the real and the perceived, it encourages almost everyone to put on a mask. The 'metro' community is made up of segments, it does not have a cohesive narrative instead it works through juxtapositions and variations on the same theme – relationships, their meaning and their opposition to the pull of contemporariness. There is a constant tension between the external and the internal and there is no attempt at linearity. In this Basu's dependence on modern technology is more than obvious as the scenes rush past one with amazing speed and moving trains, buses or cars become the space of togetherness.

*Katha* had worked with a fable and within it with linearity and community imagination. People placed in such close vicinity, creating surrogate families work within the dynamics of love and marriage. The stairs that connect the two floors, the courtyard in the centre and the corridor above are the spaces where things happen. In *Women of Brewster Place* community is created by race and economics, and also through transgressions. They are the dropouts of society shut in a blind alley. It is Mattie's window which provides her with an observation post through which she reaches out. The tension is constantly between desire and the thwarting of desire. Sexual deviancy doesn't pass muster even in this fugitive community where all else – drunkenness, whoring, illicit relationships are tolerated. *Metro* nearly twenty-five years later does away with the sense of a single focal point and goes on instead to work with multiple locations and relationships playing on the theme of waiting and relating. Listeners are either absent or singular, interventions by others are again muted, judgements are internally gauged not expressed. No longer is it the question what next, or as Deleuze has phrased it 'what will happen', but instead on 'something has happened but what?'[2] – the audience is called in to put the various segments together to carve out the meaning of this community narrative which lacks orality and is based on a technological, fast-moving environment, the atmosphere of BPOs and frustrated, broken relationships, representing almost a battleground.

Environmental influences dominate the cultural narrative, which does however surface through Amol-Shivani relationship, Ranjeet's relationship with his daughter and Rahul's with his father's dream. But in other respects the affairs, the tentative groping for fulfilment transforms the Self-Other relationship dramatically. In *Katha* the other is a mirror in which one sees the self or the potential self, in *Brewster Place* the 'other' is the hostile element – whites, men who abandon, and the sexually different. The early trickster image of the oral narrative present in *Katha* is abandoned here. Working through remembered pasts, a transient community inhabits a fixed space and moves towards the demolition of the barrier. In *Brewster Place* the community narrative has become a socio-economic narrative of an unequal society. In *Metro*, the capitalistic economy and morality have supplanted both the moral tale and linearity as multiplicity, juxtapositions and segments of the present simultaneously isolate and connect this wandering population. They are constantly recreating their communities. The meanings of commune, community and communicate emphasise the acts of interaction and sharing; community narratives downplay individual lives and when we define communities through the category of space, the social production of this space becomes significant. Both the chawl and the four double unit block are created by the more prosperous to ward off the margins. But in *Metro* the upwardly mobile shift away from enclosed spaces, a shifting which leads to the segmenting of space and the disruption of a linear movement. Moving towards a future, the 'self' like the 'community' is constantly re-forming itself in the postmodern narrative. The observer-frame status present in *Katha* is absent in both *Brewster Place* and *Metro*. In *Brewster Place* meaning is created through death and dismantling but in *Metro* the meaning is also fragmented. If Shivani's death triggers off the sudden realisation for love, then it is only the viewer who is conscious of this link not the individual characters involved.

Shruti and Monty, Rahul and Neha learn from their own mistakes. And Shika who is the only one connected with Shivani, chooses the harder option of surrendering desire. In this community narrative connectivity works through disruptions and marginal figures, and the capitalist culture takes over as spaces and meanings both are fragmented and presented through scattered images. The postmodernist narrative stresses the role of images and through this of space. With its multiplicity and fragmentariness, it goes on to create heterotopias where home zones become prisons and synchronicity becomes important. The defining principle of separation (of space) ceases to work in this context. It is here that the Bakhtinian concept of a chronotope intersects with the Foucauldian heteretopia, where space intersects with time (and its pace).[3] In *Metro*, places are re-purposed; they dislocate, impose and govern. Open spaces are few and when they impact the viewer, they may often be a garbage dump or a bloodstained wall.

## Notes

1. See Michel Foucault, "Of Other Spaces" (1967), Heteretopias (trans. Jay Miskowiec, Internet Source http://foucault.info/documents/heterotopia/Foucault.heterotopia.en.html.) 2, 'There are oppositions that we regard as simple givens: for example between private space and public space, between family space and social space, between cultural space and useful space, between the space of leisure and that of work. All these are still nurtured by the hidden presence of the sacred.'
2. See Deleuze and Guattari, *A Thousand Plateaus*, especially chapter 8 '1874: Three Novellas or What Happened?' 212–228. The main distinction between the tale and the novella is the question the reader is obsessed with. In the tale one asks 'what is going to happen? But in the novella the question is something has happened, but what?' The novel absorbs both these questions. (213).
3. See Jay L. Lemke's "Learning Across Multiple Places and their Chronotopes", 1–3. (Internet source)

## References

Deleuze, Gilles and Felix Guattari. *A Thousand Plateaus: Capitalism and Schizophrenia* (1980). Trans. Brian Massumi London: Continuum, 1988, 2004.

Foucault, Michel. "Of Other Spaces" (1967). Trans. Jay Miskowiec. Internet source. http://Foucault.info/documents/heterotopia/foucault.heterotopia.en.html. accessed 7 May 2011.

*Katha*: Dir: Sai Paranjpe. Perf: Naseerudin Shah, Farooque Shaikh, Deepti Naval, Mallika Sarabhai Leela Mishra, Winnie Paranjpye – Joglekar. 1982.

Lemke, Jay L. 'Learning Across Multiple Places and their Chronotopes', Symposium: Spaces and Boundaries of learning. San Diego 2004? Internet source http://www.personal.umich.edu/jaylemke/papers/area_2004 htm. Accessed 7 May 2011

*Life in a Metro*. Dir: Anurag Basu. Perf. Shilpa Shetty, Kay Kay Menon, Shiny Ahuja, Konkana Sen Sharma, Kangana Ranaut, Irfan Khan. 2007.

Naylor, Gloria. The *Women of Brewster Place*. (1983) London: Sphere Books, 1984.

Wegner, Phillip E. 'Spatial Criticism', *Introducing Criticism at the 21st Century*. Ed. Julian Wolfreys. Edinburgh: Edinburgh University Press, 2002.

# The Mimetic Eden of Marquez: *One Hundred Years of Solitude*

*Madhuri Chatterjee*

*One Hundred Years of Solitude* is Gabriel Garcia Marquez's masterpiece, first published in Spanish in 1967. It metaphorically encompasses the history of Columbia and Latin America and chronicles a family's struggle, and the history of their fictional town Macondo, for hundred years. Marquez acknowledges in his autobiography *Living to Tell the Tale* that Macondo was based on the town Aracataca where he spent his childhood. *One Hundred Years* is a novel which contains everything – the grand and the insignificant, the absurd and the transcendent and in the process it crosses genres. So in this sense the novel is mimetic, as it imitates real life and life includes seemingly infinite number of voices and wide array of emotions and qualities. The novel gets its epic scope from its attempt to include everything that life includes.

Mimesis according to Halliwell is a linguistic, philosophical or cosmic phenomenon or an 'eternal model' of the world of language, thought and material things respectively (121). In *One Hundred Years* this attempt at mimesis, is one reason for its confused timeline and tendency to jump from story to story without obvious transition. Marquez believes that modern life is entropic – chaotic, tending towards eventual dissolution – thus he refuses to impose a rigid structure on the novel, choosing instead to allow the novel to meander digressingly and at times unraveling, towards the eventual apocalypse at its close. In defining magical realism Jean-Pierre Durix argues that 'the magic realist aims at a basis of mimetic illusion while destroying it regularly with a strange treatment of time, space, characters or what many people [...] take as the basic rules of the physical world' (146). Magic realists usually have a definite idea of their social role and pose political problems which beset the country described. This trend is also synonymous with Latin American literature during the 'Boom' period which Swanson argues as 'an exemplification of the sense of 'break with tradition' (321) that has come to be associated with the new world. In this sense, the novel justifies itself as a kind of modern Latin American fiction that rejects the premises and structures of conventional realism.

The language of the novel also tends towards metaphoric and euphemistic rather than literal and precise. He avoids graphic and realistic use of language throughout the novel in his description of sex and violence and substitutes euphemisms for a realistic depiction of events (Remedios). Throughout the novel, language also functions as a barrier between humans, a dilemma inspired by the biblical Eden. Jose Buendia and Ursula speak gibberish, while Rebecca and Amaranda and Col. Aureliano recede into their own quiet world. The narrative technique, in which the novel assumes the voice of a character without openly indicating that it is switching perspectives, is part of the indirect discourse. The epic and community feel of the novel can be accounted for by its multiplicity of voices, its desire to see things from different perspective, and its description of events in the subjective terms used by different characters.

Another interesting feature of the novel is that it does not adopt a straightforward approach to telling its version of history. The progression of time from the founding of the town to its decline, from the origins of the Buendia clan to their destruction, provides a rough structure for the novel. Marquez does not necessarily narrate the events chronologically but flits forward and backward in time and creates the mythic feel and informality of a meandering oral history. Although the first extended episode of the novel tells of the gypsies who came to Macondo bearing technological innovations that seemed miraculous to the citizens of the isolated village, the first sentence of the novel refers to an episode far in the future – the planned execution of Colonel Aureliano Buendia. The novel begins with a memory of a future past when Aureliano Buendia, in front of a firing squad, recalls the day he was taken by his father to get the feel of ice for the first time. The whole chapter becomes a parenthetic description of the initial founding of a village in the middle of a remote tropical jungle. The reader is also aware that Aureliano's story is but one instance of a much larger, collective tale of the rise and fall of an idealistic community. The story of the gypsies leading up to the moment when Jose Arcadio Buendia sees ice for the first time is cast as Colonel Aureliano's recollection. So immediately in the novel there is a chronological disjunction.

The indefinite time framework blurs the distinction between memory, history and fiction. In the beginning, we are not sure of the historical setting and as Marquez writes about the founding of Macondo 'the world was so recent that many things lacked names' (1) but we also learn that Ursula's (the Biblical Eve) great grand-mother was alive when Sir Francis Drake attacked Riohacha, an actual event that took place in 1568 and obviously Sir Francis Drake lived long after the world grew old enough for every object to have a name. Memory is given the same authority as history and history is subject to the same emotional colourings and flights of fancy as memory. The remarkable feature of this novel is the working throughout of two senses of time – linear and circular.

The novel is the history of the founding, development and death of human settlement Macondo and the community set by Buendia and in the process we are confronted with a picture of how at a particular movement in human civilisation, a unique group of people organised its life (like *Odyssey*) and parallel to the myths of Latin American history. The novel is organised around the symbolic movement from Genesis to Eden and through to the Apocalypse.

Interestingly, the two senses of time create some of the novel's most important effects. The linear history of the town falls into four sections (a) Utopian innocence and social harmony, in which Macondo exists like an early Eden, its inhabitants so innocent that no one has yet died and they don't even have name for things, 'the world was so new.... It was essential to point' (11). This section takes up five chapters of the book. The story then moves on the military struggle in the various civil wars and revolutions (chapters 6 to 9) and then into a period of economic prosperity and spiritual decline (chapters 10 to 15) and finally to decadence and physical destruction (chapters 16 to 20).

The narrative for the most part follows this linear story where various 'invasions' also occur. Macondo's evolution becomes a parable of the typical arc of human societal progress and the community a microcosm for all human civilisation, 'At that time, Macondo was a village of twenty adobe houses, built on the bank of a river of clear water that ran along a bed of polished stones, which were white and enormous, like prehistoric eggs'. These lines from the first page of the novel establish Macondo as a kind of Eden, recalling the biblical tale of Adam and Eve and this parallel to Old Testament is present throughout the book. The prehistoric eggs also perhaps refer to evolution. The novel is structured to trace an epic narrative of biblical proportions expressed through the struggles of Jose Arcadio Buendia – the archetypal man and his descendants. In the Bible, Adam's job is to name the animals, exercising his power over them and cataloging them to conform to his vision of the world. In establishing Macondo, Jose Arcadio does the same thing. He and his wife Ursula represent the Biblical Adam and Eve (Macondo Eden is founded accidentally when Buendia expedition decides to stop in the middle of number of natural barriers), who were expelled from Eden for eating from the Tree of Knowledge. The name Macondo itself appears in Jose Arcadio Buendia's dream on the night that he and other founders decide to choose the location of their own A vivid image of a town looms large in this dream, 'He asked what city it was and they answered him with a name that he had never heard, that had no meaning at all, but that had a supernatural echo in his dream: Macondo' (24).

Jose Arcadio Buendia's relentless pursuit for knowledge, drives him to insanity and in his madness he is tied to a tree (the tree of knowledge). Macondo is an expression of the imaginative desire of Jose Arcadio who flees his past but is incapable of creating a political future for his community because of his over heated imagination. Even the village Macondo, after a time, begins its long decline from the blissful innocence of earlier years. Fernando del Caprio, the wife of Aureliano Segundo, tries to change things as she comes from an old historic town, presumably Bogota itself, where the domination of colonial culture has made itself strongly felt. The space also expands to include outsiders who arrive bringing the latest in technology or bureaucracy – gypsies, government officials, priests, various military forces, the lawyers, the railway, the American capitalists, the Europeans with bicycles and passion for planes and so on. Macondo is a microcosm, in which various sources of interventions and forces play their role in determining the course of the town, not unlike the birth and evolution of a nation like Columbia itself, especially when taking into account colonial and neo-colonial impositions upon its establishment at large. This interplay between microcosms and macrocosms is suggested by Homi K. Bhabha 'redrawing the domestic space as the space of the normalising, pastoralising and individuating techniques of modern power and police: the personal -is -the political; the world- in- the home' (11). The clash between Macondo's old fashioned Edenic simplicity with modern world echoes in the women's expression who see and describe the train as 'a kitchen dragging a village behind it,' and Ursula in her commonsense wisdom realises 'The world is slowly coming to an end and these things (flying carpets and tragic gypsies) don't happen here anymore' (351).The people gradually lose their sense of the miraculous and dreamy wonder, and the replacement of this with modern technology shatters them. Other motifs like the five-year flood parallels the Biblical flood and its function as a cleansing act. This also introduces the comic element – as Fernando de Caprio and other priests appear foolish because of their catholic principles whereas Remedios represents the innocence of Eden and Macondo which is lost after she floats upwards to heaven. It hints at the Buendias' inability to laugh at themselves. This also points to a constant in the world of Macondo – the powerlessness of the people to take charge of the invasions which arise from outside. As Browitt has observed, 'Garcia Marquez's way around classical realist mimesis is simply to situate his story telling at the level of popular culture, focalising events through the consciousness of the towns people, who through their selective memory re-animate the past. Moreover, instead of problematising the language of representation itself, allows the magical and superstitious world of oral folk culture to represent itself' (19).

The linear sense of time is also reflected in the Buendia family lineage as they form a series of figures who are representing their community the particular historical period of which they are a part. The patriarch Jose Arcadio is in some sense a renaissance man of many interests with pioneering ambitions and energies; his son Aureliano becomes a great military leader and then he is succeeded by a bourgeois farmer entrepreneur and family man Aureliano Segurdo and by the twin Jose Arcadio who works for the American capitalist and becomes the radical labour organiser. And so the story moves from generation to generation, with a strong linear force marking the socio economic transitions.

However, the response of the people to Macondo of the Buendia family creates a second sense of time – history as almost obsessively circular as their personalities, they constantly repeat the experience of earlier generations. There is also a sense of fate in this – as the person's life is determined by the name conferred on him and the legacy the man carries working almost as a predestination. Commenting on this Ursula observes that while the Aurelianos were withdrawn they had lucid minds, the Jose Arcadios were impulsive and enterprising but they were marked with a tragic sign. Even their deaths are pre-ordained. The Jose suffer as victims of murder or disease, the three Aurelianos die with their mental powers intact. And they all succumb to self-imposed exile in solitude which lasts for decades.

Interestingly, their comic energies are undercut by a sense of irony for 'There was no mystery in the heart of a Buendia that was impenetrable for [Pillar Terena] because a century of cards and experience had taught her that the history of the family was a machine with unavoidable repetitions, a turning wheel that would have gone on spiraling into eternity were it not for the progressive and irremediable wearing of the axle' (402). Time is cyclical and it is as easy to look into the future as to remember the past. Time here does not function as finite but rather moves forward again and again.

Finally, as a community narrative, the novel also shares the burden of social and cultural responsibility. The theme is worked up into a narrative of progressive social decay, symbolised by natural decay and the creation of a ruined landscape. The eventual solution to failure in the quest for community is to banish all and sundry beyond history in a biblical holocaust that engulfs both the guilty and the innocent. Marquez's experiences and memories are also incorporated into the narrative as are his political beliefs. The political parties and uprisings in the novel are fictionalised accounts of the political struggles in Marquez's native Columbia and the dictators who had ruled over Cuba and Nicaragua. The banana company in Macondo hints at the history of western imperialism in Latin America and depicts it as voracious and harmful to the inhabitants of Macondo. Together with capitalism and imperialism the country's conservative government further brings brutality and corruption to Macondo. The unreality and in-authenticity imposed by five hundred years of colonialism makes life a permanent living nightmare. Most of the actions which at first work like the structure of the novel as a whole, are circular as Gerald Martin has observed: 'They are living out their lives in the name of someone else's values. Hence the solitude is the central theme of Latin American history. Cornered by Spain in the sixteenth century, the characters awaken in the late eighteenth century enlightenment but are unable to bring themselves into focus settling always in an uncertain territory ....' (Martin 103).

The community collapses and the fated destruction of the family happens together as 'Aureliano saw the epigraph of the parchment perfectly paced ... in such a way that they co-existed in one instant ... and he already understood that he would never leave ... that races condemned to hundred years of solitude did not have a second opportunity on earth' (422). Malequides had not put events in the order of man's conventional time, but had concentrated a century of daily episodes in such a way that they coexisted in one moment. Timothy Brennan believes that 'the use of deep, sacred origins...instead of furthering unquestioning, ritualistic reaffirmations of a people [...] becomes a contemporary, practical means of *creating* a people' (59). In this reading past/present and future all happen at once as the Buendias move makes the past, present and future identical. Suddenly there is not a single linear progression of events – instead it is an infinite number of progressions all happening simultaneously. In deciphering the manuscript, the community is fated to end as they do not have what is required in order to continue. Their solitude, commitment, withdrawal, fantasy, subjective desire dooms them. The possibility of forgetting the past threatens the coherence of society and relationship. They also lack an ability to orient themselves with the underdeveloped world and take control of their historical destiny. They turn in upon themselves incestuously, alienated from the outside world. To analyse Macando as a nation and community in this light can thus be compared to a journey back through time, to the time when a nation first came to exist, develop, and encounter extraneous influences, both benign and malign not unlike the emergence of Columbia.

Malequiade's vision of a city with walls of glass comes true – Macondo is a city made of glass and mirrors reflect the reality of the author's world and Aurendiano's role in reading and interpreting a story – makes reading an action, destroying and erasing both memory and town and collapsing time in the process. What survives is a testimony to the community life that lived and a story which remains a guide to the construction of a better civilisation. However, Morton P. Levitt argues that, while this view of subjective time is a phenomenon of the individual psyche alone (Virginia Woolf) or the community at large (James Joyce), in Garcia Marquez this challenge 'seems still broader, more inclusive, more Jungian, than Freudian (or Bergsonian or Proustian), connected intimately to nature myth' (88). History is however always coloured by people and community.

## References

Bhabha, Homi K. *The Location of Culture*, London and New York: Routledge, 1994.

Brennan, Timothy.'The National Longing for Form' *Nation and Narration*. Ed. Homi K Bhabha. London and New York: Routledge, 1990. 44–70.

Browitt, Jeff. 'Tropics of Tragedy: The Caribbean in Gabriel Garcia Marquez's *One Hundred Years of Solitude*', Shibboleths: *Journal of Comparative Theory*, 2007. 16–33.

Durix, Jean-Pierre. *Mimesis, Genres and Postcolonial Discourse: Deconstructing Magic Realism*, London: Macmillan, 1998.

Levitt, Morton P. 'From Realism to Magic Realism: The Meticulous Modernist Fictions of Gabriel Garcia Marquez' in *Critical Perspectives on Gabriel Garcia Marquez*. Eds. Bradley A. Shaw and Nora Vera-Godwin, Nebraska: Society of Spanish and Spanish-American Studies, 1986. 73–89.

Halliwell, S. *Aristotle's Poetics*, London: Duckworth:1998.

Marquez, Gabriel Garcia. *One Hundred Years of Solitude* (1967). New Delhi, Penguin: 1996.

——. *Living to tell the tale*. Trans. Edith Grossman, Columbia: Atlanta Books, 2002.

Martin, Gerald. *Journeys Through the Labyrinth: Latin American Fiction in the Twentieth Century*, London and New York: Verso, 1989.

Swanson, Philip. *The New Novel in Latin America: Politics and Popular Culture after the Boom*. Manchester, Manchester University Press, 1995.

# Food for Thought: The Dynamics of Community and Culinary

*Nidhi Singh*

Sociologists Ogburn and Nimkoff hold: '*A community is the total organised social life of a locality*' (247). Community is indicative of not only a collectivity living together within a shared geographical location but also common socio-cultural, religious, economic and political intents amongst others. Community formation generally gets associated with affiliation to a nation, culture, faith, race, caste, gender, profession and even hobbies, to name a few. It cannot be monolithic as there is an ample scope for varied communities to exist within a community. For example, a geographic community can have a number of ethnic communities within it. The character of the community and the role of an individual in it depend largely on the territorial placement, strength of members, existent social and political configurations, as well as economic pursuits of the community at large.

At its best, community provides a sense of physical and psychological well-being arising from the 'belongingness' experienced by the members. However, the flip side of it is the probability of ghettoisation into closed ethnic groups: the support system and the ethical impulse underlying community being replaced by a narrow fundamentalism and communalism. Yogendra Singh in his book *Culture Change in India: Identity and Globalization* refers to the paradox of progressive decline of traditional communities and the rise of ethnic groups in the post-industrial modern society. In the case of immigrants, he relates it to their minority status and an acute sense of alienation leading to heightened consciousness of beleaguered identity and ethno-cultural self-awareness. Similar strain can be found in marginalised groups like dalits and tribals within India itself. He holds:

> This feeling which is rooted essentially in existential deprivation of ethnic groups in relation to dominant communities is sharpened by projection of deprivation into symbolic idiom of politics. (212)

While ethnicity becomes problematic due to its politicisation, the concepts of home and nation too emerge as oft contested sites for immigrant communities. Ogburn and Nimkoff in *A Handbook of Sociology* emphasise the relevance of residential tie to an area for a community. Paradoxically, dislocation is instrumental in the formation of a progressively expanding community of diaspora. The dislocation is both physical and psychological. Crossing of geographical and national boundaries generally entails coping with cultural shifts as well.

The creative sensibility of the diaspora occupies the unique but unenviable position of straddling two cultures. When it is a writer from the 'third world' giving voice to the immigrant experience in the 'first', it becomes a more complex and challenging enterprise. There is a need to negotiate diametrically opposed cultures of East and West. Torn between the two worlds, the identity crisis experienced by the immigrants results in what has also been termed as a 'fractured self'. Stripped of the identity that defined them in their homeland, it becomes imperative for an immigrant to reconstitute an identity so as to counter the alienation experienced in the new land. Diasporic writing addresses itself to identity reconstitution within historical, social, cultural and political frameworks in relation to both the old world and the new. Memory, remembering, and even forgetting are tools used to reconstruct the self that had become psychologically as much as physically, unmoored. Dislocation and relocation open up issues related to the construction of the self.

The immigrant community charters its way through day-to-day experiences. In the process, the personal histories along with that of the community get overlaid by the lived experiences, as it progressively restructures its socio-cultural identity. Community emerges as the refuge from the threat of assimilation into dominant culture. Resisting assimilation results in a sense of displacement and alienation leading to the need to belong that is met to a great extent by community bonding. The cross-cultural contact and resultant friction is inevitable. Despite the constant association which is unavoidable, the gap persists between what has been referred to by Jasbir Jain as "home" – the culture of origin; and "world" – the culture of adoption (13). The presence of the two opposed yet simultaneous points of reference can be both a bane and a blessing for the immigrants. A bane, if it leads to assimilation where there is absorption of one into the other, generally of the marginalised and the weaker section into the mainstream and the dominant one. A blessing, if it is enriched through acculturation where there is a mutual exchange and internalisation of cultural features, exchange being the keyword. However, it is important to be conscious of the thin line dividing assimilation that might lead to loss of identity, and acculturation resulting in a cultural mosaic.

The relocation into a new culture and consequently locating oneself anew in relation to the old, leads to a socio-cultural reorientation culminating in hybridity. There is a need for immigrant communities to establish continuity, with the two cultures not seen as substitutes but as 'correlative'. The old world inevitably shapes the response to the new world inhabited and vice versa. The there and then is very much a part of and continues to influence the here and now. The immigrant community hence tends to define homeland through absence: absence of the sights, the sounds, the smells, and the flavours that possess the power to evoke not only the physical and the sensual, but also the social and cultural connotations of the world left behind.

The impulse to reclaim one's culture through different strategies is effected: cooking being one of them. Food, and the way it is cooked, emerges as one of the most prominent cultural markers of immigrant communities. How does the immigrant community recreate itself through culinary skills? How does food that is largely free of cultural associations in its raw form gets appropriated when cooked in a specific way? What is the role of food in reconstruction and deconstruction of diasporic community? Can food cooked in a particular way embody a culture and yet emerge as the contact zone for the host nation and the immigrants? Like 'gendered memory', can the art of cooking too become gendered? This article shall attempt to explore these questions in the context of Diana Abu Jaber's food memoir *The Language of Baklava* that delves into the writer's Arab-American experience of growing up with the immigrant father who loves cooking, and the novel *Crescent*, a love story of an exile from war torn Iraq and an Arab-American cook by profession who shares with the writer the experience of being a hybrid.

The use of the expression Arab-American immigrant community may be construed as homogenisation and an erasure of intra-Arabic differences. As a plea in defence of the usage, it is necessary to be aware of the presence of certain issues and experiences that cut across distances and unite the immigrants from different parts of Middle East residing in America. Marginalisation, racism, discrimination, alienation, dislocation, stereotyping, nostalgia for the old world, fear of assimilation, divided loyalty, split vision, strong ties of community and family are common not only among Arab-Americans but also other immigrant communities. The affiliations within the Arab community are forged largely through shared culture and faith. However, Amartya Sen in *Identity and Violence: The Illusion of Destiny* refers to the nature of community and cautions: 'The adversity of exclusion can be made to go hand in hand with the gifts of inclusion' (3). Cultural artifacts, be it music, dance, dress or food, may be used to the same effect. Sudha Rai in the article titled 'The Discourse of Food and the Matrilineages in Contemporary Women's Writings' holds:

> The belief systems that surround the topic of food, stabilise cultural and national identities. While contributing to bonding within a community, food is also a marker of the 'other' and can divide races and nations as also religions, caste and class groups within traditional societies. (133)

The 'stabilising' of cultural identity through food in Diana Abu-Jaber's works is affected by cooking culture-specific dishes and the rituals associated with the consumption of that food. Arab community, like that of the Indians (and most Asian societies), looks at family, kith and kin, cousins and friends with affection and good-humoured tolerance. Keeping an open house for guests and relatives, whether expected or unexpected, features in both the works under consideration. Food secures the ties between relatives and friends as the ambience of Arab homeland is recreated through specific smells and flavours, music and language. In the Foreword of the food memoir *The Language of Baklava,* Abu-Jaber confesses: 'Lives don't usually correspond to narrative arcs, but all of these stories spring out of real people, memories, and joyously gathered and prepared meals.'

The food memoir intertwines the autobiographical elements of personal history of the immigrant experience of the writer's father and her own growth into an adult. The ritual of cooking of meals is dominated by her father's fierce determination to make his daughters, especially the author, a 'good Arabian girl'. The dilemma of the immigrant father as he struggles to hold on to his Arab identity and bestow it to his family is heightened by the inherent unreliability and subjectivity of the memories of the past he relies on. The dislocation from Jordan is followed by relocation in America. Always nostalgic about the old home, he decides to again locate the family in Jordan. Abu-Jaber who looked at America as home, is dislocated and has to learn to recreate herself at the age of seven in Jordan. The father, unable to adjust, decides to return to America repeating the cycle of dislocation and relocation. For immigrants, every time they move it involves 'unbecoming or rebecoming' (58).

Similar experience of unbecoming and rebecoming is experienced by Hanif in *Crescent.* A political exile from war-torn Iraq, the dislocation is more intensely and poignantly experienced due to his inability to return to his country. His stealthy return to Iraq is followed by imprisonment and a final escape away from the old world to America, he now learns to refer as 'home'. There is self-alienation arising from an alienation from the place of residence. The first generation immigrant sensibility as well as that of an exile, construct and deconstruct the notion of 'home' in their restless search for the perfect haven. The inability to make any place a home, torn by dual-loyalties, developing a split vision, they are never at ease, be it Iraq or America. Dislocated by choice or circumstances, both the immigrant and the exile find themselves displaced from their roots, their antecedents, their centre. They become imbued with dualities and multiplicities which emphasise their alienation. The writer's father seeks to counter the split within by attempting to create a microcosm of an Arabic home by cooking food that will teach his growing daughters about Arabic culture and affiliations. For Hanif in *Crescent*, his study and teaching of Arabic culture and visits to the cafe that serves Arabic food, helps. Both works are marked by a vivid portrayal of the Arab community in America where paradoxically it is the American characters who are marginalised, almost swept away in the surge of warmth and passion for living that gets associated with the Arab characters.

Abu-Jaber recalls the various phases of her growing up: from a doting daughter helping her father cook, to a rebellions teenager rejecting Arabic food, and later to an adult who finds comfort in smells of Arabic cooking. Abu-Jaber inherits the legacy of rootlessness and divided loyalty of an immigrant consciousness. One can trace the movement from the childhood perplexity, through teenage rebellion, to mature acceptance of hybrid identity. Food is the thread that strings memories together. Abu-Jaber ends the Foreword to the memoir by asserting, 'Memories give our lives their fullest shape, and eating together helps us to remember'. Anecdotes from past are intimately intertwined with food. Every happening is marked by cooking of a dish and followed by recipes with names like 'Eat it now' Shish Kabob. They are evocative of people, places and specific events. The dishes that remind the Arabs of 'who they used to be' (19) and link them to their past as well as their community, also highlight who they no longer are, thus encapsulating their immigrant status.

Inclusion into community through food is affected at Nadia's Cafe in *Crescent* where homesick and lonely students of Arab descent congregate to find consolation in each other's company and also in the Arabic dishes cooked by Sirine, the hybrid Arab-American cook. However, food can also be used as a tool of exclusion. In the memoir Abu-Jaber's American grandmother serves ham to the Muslim suitor of her daughter, when he came courting. Food here is used for airing her disapproval and highlighting the religio-cultural barriers lined against the inter-religious relationship. Munira, the maid from Jordan, is as skeptical of American food as the grandmother is of Arabic cooking. Bennett, an English boy whom Abu-Jaber befriends in Jordan declares, 'I never eat native food. Neither should you' (42). Food here is used to exclude on lines of race and nationality.

In spite of suspicion and prejudices based on the unknown and the unexplored 'other', food can build bridges too and provide a meeting ground for the possibility of acceptance and even appreciation. Though initially suspicious and critical, Munira and other Arab women are able to appreciate the pancakes cooked by Abu-Jaber's American mother and ask for its recipe. Sirine in *Crescent* promises to learn to cook Iranian dish, creating good-will and dispelling to some degree the tension created by Iran-Iraq war in the interpersonal relationships of the immigrants who visit the cafe. She cooks an all Arabic Thanksgiving dinner as a gesture of friendliness. For her, cooking is like praying, both being acts of devotion and love.

Another interesting usage of food being used to subvert and deconstruct the stereotypes of Arabic femininity, is in Aya, the paternal aunt of Abu-Jaber. She echoes the American grandmother's stance that cooking imprisons women and calls it, 'trapping the women inside like slaves' (186), and yet goes ahead to bake cakes instead of having babies. Rana, a character in *Crescent,* cooks to escape from an unhappy marriage and the home which is like a prison hence subverting the disclaimer that cooking imprisons women. Immigrant experience also allows for role-reversal where, at times, the mother maybe the one with a regular job and father stays at home, more comfortable in the kitchen space traditionally allocated to women. There is a destabilising of the stereotype of Arab women as passive, helpless victims, exploited by patriarchal system.

The constructive role of food and women in establishing universal harmony is emphasised time and again. Herself an excellent cook, Aya holds that offering food till it is accepted is the way to establish world peace: the language of war to be countered by language of food, of baklava. Sustenance, support and reaching out are alternatives to war that perpetrates violence. Aya's questioning of the claims made to the origin of dishes undermines the cultural hegemony as practiced by Arabs themselves. She calls it 'food robbery' as she points out how the dish of Baklava is claimed by Arabs, Greeks as well as Turks. The choice of calling it by its Greek name 'baklava' instead of Arabic 'baklawa' points at the hybridity inherent in food which represents culture. The concept of cultural purity is questioned. Manarelli, an Italian neighbour, in the memoir makes a statement, a kind of protest which is also an act of self-assertion by having food in the frontyard, something 'not done' in America. Assertion of the difference is a demand for acceptance of the same.

The two works *Language of Baklava* and *Crescent* have characters who revel in cooking. In one, there is a Jordanian male cook who cooks on weekends for the family, and in the other is a female professional cook who is part Arab and part American working in a cafe owned by a Lebanese. It is interesting to note the convergences and divergences in their approach to the culinary art. Both enjoy cooking and excel in Arabic dishes. Both innovate and experiment and both contribute to the forging of community bonds through cooking. The similarities seem to taper off and one can observe a kind of exhibitionism in Bud, Abu-Jaber's father, that is not there in Sirine. The movements and activities of Bud as he cooks are vigorous and exaggerated while that of Sirine are described in terms of almost dance-like motion. Sweeping gestures like chopping the lamb meat as he 'whomps' the cleaver down accompanied with loud music and singing are in stark contrast to the silent efficiency of Sirine as she slices, cuts, tucks, folds and cooks. While Bud is very conscious of the cultural statement he is making through food, Sirine concentrates on the act of cooking and evolves a philosophy that everything is ephemeral as she watches the food being consumed. For Bud, cooking takes a form of assertion and control over people who eat the food, with Sirine it encourages meditation and a feeling of being centred in her self. As much as an expression of their individual make up, it can also be used to compare male and female response to the act of cooking and towards food. One is projected outwards and becomes an act of assertion and the other encourages movement inwards and emerges as an act of love and nurturance.

Diana Abu-Jaber, both in her memoir and her novel, achieves a delicate balance between the cultural traditions of her community and the life and opportunities provided by America. These works successfully project representation of community and culinary combination with literary accomplishment. Her work debunks the stereotypes of the American view of the Oriental while simultaneously countering the Arab fundamentalist one by projecting role reversals and community relationships. The essentialisation of ethnic identities is interrogated. Dichotomy of 'us' and 'them' which divides people is rejected in favour of accepting the other by going across and meeting them halfway. The dynamics of community and culinary emerge as a powerful means of connecting not only events, both of the past and the present, but also as an arena of resistance, redefinition and articulation of difference. These work towards bridging different cultures while also knitting the community together in the interests of cultural traditions.

## References

Abu-Jaber, Diana. *Crescent*. New York: W.W. Norton and Company, 2003.

——. *The Language of Baklava*. New York: Anchor Books, 2006.

Jain, Jasbir. Introduction. *Writers of Indian Diaspora: Theory and Practice*. Ed. Jasbir Jain. Jaipur: Rawat Publications, (1998), 2007. 11–19.

Ogburn, William F. and Meyer F. Nimkoff. *A Handbook of Sociology*. New Delhi: Eurasia Publishing House (Pvt.) Ltd., 1979.

Rai, Sudha. 'The Discourse of Food and Matrilineages in Contemporary Women's Writings' in *Rethinking Modernity*. Eds. Santosh Gupta, Prafulla C. Kar and Parul Dave Mukherji. Delhi: Pencraft International, 2005. 133–143.

Sen, Amartya. *Identity and Violence: The Illusion of Destiny*. New Delhi: Allen Lane an imprint of Penguin Books, 2006.

Singh, Yogendra. *Culture Change in India: Identity and Globalization*. New Delhi: Rawat Publications, 2000.

# Narrative of a Disrupted Community: Paro Anand's *No Guns At My Son's Funeral*

*Charu Mathur*

Community living involves perceptions of social structures. It seeks to understand how community members articulate their lives in ways that allow each other to reflect on the make up of the overall community and how they represent their community needs to others. There is an experience of shared history or a co-dependence – links which are not merely passive ties but allow the individual to actively occupy a role within the larger community. Role taking, therefore, becomes a means by which the social order and culture gets incorporated into the self. There is formation of personal and cultural values as well as an understanding of group dynamics. The dialogic interplay, where the community influences its members and vice-versa, results in an integration and fulfilment of needs for the individual and leads to a shared emotional connection at the level of collectivity that can be very empowering.

Gusfield identifies two dimensions of a community and describes them as territorial and relational (128). While the former is circumscribed by spatial proximity or shared territory, the latter is concerned with the nature and quality of interpersonal relationships. Shared territory cannot, by itself, constitute a community; for the latter to come into being the relational element is essential. When the two come together it results in the formation of a stable, resilient and cohesive local community which can be enriching, enabling and forward-looking for both the individual and the larger society. Place can also be used in an essentialising way and this happens in most multi-ethnic local communities where religion plays an important role in bonding people of a community together through the creation of a common consciousness and facilitating togetherness in places of worship. This provides a sense of solidarity through mutual understanding.

However, there is a dismantling of these structures when the community experiences the destabilising impact of violence. New identities emerge with the formation of new communities and the changed equations give rise to changed relationships that, in turn, lead to further violence. Paro Anand's novel, *No Guns At My Son's Funeral* (2005) is a narrative set against the background of militancy in Kashmir. With reference to Anand's novel, I propose to show the disruptive impact of violence on the health of a community. The novel's protagonist Aftab is a young Kashmiri boy who leads a double life. A bubbly teenager, interested in fishing and cricket by day, he sneaks away at night to confabulate with Akram and his fledging group of tear-away terrorists. His sister Shazia's submissive involvement in household chores is a façade that conceals her secret liaison with the Afghan militant, her brother idealises. Anand's enterprise in tracing the fate of Aftab and Shazia is an attempt to explore the grim reality of young impressionable teenagers getting drawn towards the path of terror without comprehending the implications of such an involvement, either for themselves as individuals or for others as members of a community.

The Kashmiris enjoy significant ethnic, cultural and religious diversity and have a history of ethno-national and social consciousness of Kashmiriyat which is characterised by religious and cultural harmony that has been strongly influenced by

Shaivism, Buddhism, Sikhism and Sufism. Kashmir was also influenced by Akbar's syncretic philosophy of Din-i-illahi that emphasised the blending of Hindu and Muslim ideals. Kashmir's strength had been its inclusive culture and that both the Muslim majority and the Hindu minority contributed to the social and cultural ethos and each respected and honoured the other community's religious festivals and practices. They shared a Kashmiri identity which created a bond stronger than the differences of faith and belief. 'There was a time when we were just Kashmiris', Aftab's mother recalls, 'Religion did not matter, you just leaned on the nearest shoulder, wept on it, if you needed to. We had brothers around us all the time, to help us, protect us' (*No Guns* 17).

The infiltration of Afghan separatists posing as 'freedom fighters' significantly changes the situation. Freedom in the Kashmiri psyche became synonymous with the fanatic element of that agency and violence became an ingredient of life in Kashmir. People belonging to the same peaceful territorial community underwent a drastic relational change. In this connection, Newman's observation that the sense of community is inevitably linked with the sense of identity and identity is the most essential and personal characteristic that is constituted by our memberships of various social groups like race, ethnicity, religion and gender, is relevant. Therefore, our identity, according to him, locates us in the social world, thoroughly affecting everything we do, feel, say and think in our lives (134–140). The inter-ethnic violence in Kashmir was a precipitation of a shift from the local Kashmiri identity to the stereotypic religious one. The collectivist Kashmiri subjectivity gave way to a personal religious sense of selfhood, leading to friction. Without relational binding, the territorial community crumbled. In a passionate letter to Aftab, his childhood friend Laxman Kachru writes, 'You and I, we've never thought that I am a Kashmiri Pandit and you're a Muslim or that Angu's a Sikh .... We never thought of our differences.... But they, Afti, they're making us think like that' (*No Guns* 121). Kashmiriyat as an expression of solidarity, resilience and patriotism got deeply affected. The frustrated people of Kashmir surrendered Kashmiriyat to the requirements of law and polity, even if it meant living in a polarised society. 'The gun had entered the valley' writes Meena Nayak, 'its first victim: Kashmiriyat'. The gun is a symbol of destruction and it is an abhorrence of this destructive element that the title of the novel evokes. Violence has not only caused destruction of life and property but also a total disruption of an embracing co-existence.

The onset of militancy in Kashmir in the past two decades has led to the exodus of more than one lakh Hindus from the state and the violent attacks against the remaining communities of Hindus and Sikhs, further erodes the fabric of Kashmiriyat. Descendents of Hindu priests, the Kashmiri Pandits are among the original inhabitants of the Kashmir valley with a recorded history of over five thousand years. Over the millennia, this community has been integral not only to the cultural and social life of the people of this region, but has immensely contributed to the administrative and economic development as well. But, according to K.P.S. Gill, they 'have now become the targets and victims of one of the most successful ... ethnic cleansing in the world'. Forced to leave his home Baramullah for Delhi along with his family, after Sonu mama's legs were blown off in a bomb explosion, Laxman complains in desperation, 'Abbu says we've become refugees .... Refugees? Like when India and Pakistan were separated? But there is no partition here – then why are we refugees in our own country .... And there are so many Kashmiri Pandits here. Almost everyone has lost family members and property, money, jobs. But it isn't only Kashmiri Pandits, I try to tell them, everyone, everyone has suffered but no one wants to listen' (*No Guns* 118). Among the complex reasons why the Kashmiri Pandits' suffering goes unnoticed, Gill points out, is the nature of the community itself. 'Where other campaigns of ethnic cleansing,' he argues 'have invariably provoked at least some retaliatory violence, the deep rooted tradition and culture of non-violence among the Kashmiri Pandits has made them accept the suffering in silence'. When Laxman asked his father when he could go back home, his father 'beat his fist against his head' and with an air of resignation said that 'I should forget that Kashmir was ever my home' (*No Guns* 119). 'People here' says Laxman, 'have forgotten or want to forget that they are Kashmiri too' (*No Guns* 119). In spite of repeated rejection of co-existence and pluralism, the Kashmiri Pandits have not given up their faith in these values. They choose not to reciprocate fanaticism with fanaticism and violence with violence.

The three friends Aftab, Angad and Laxman epitomise the fate of the three religious communities – Muslim, Sikh and Hindu – that they respectively belong to. Their life and friendship is ruined not because of mutual differences but due to the disrupting influence of the Afghan militant Akram – 'a firangi who wore his battle scars like medals' (3). The young impressionable Aftab who is struggling with issues of personality and independence, gets carried away by the images of 'heroism', the Afghan's mission evokes. He becomes a victim of Akram's carefully planned strategy: 'One should never wait' Akram tells Feroze 'till these new recruits are old enough to start thinking for themselves. Then they loose courage, once they know what the dangers ahead of them are. You have to use them while their dreams are bigger than their knowledge. While they are still hypnotised by its romance' (8–9).

Unaware of the potential dangers of crossing over to the militant side, Aftab and Shazia feel they have moved from the community of the fear-torn to the community of the fear-borne in an attempt to negotiate positions of power against odd images of violence they have grown up with. But a community derives its strength not from weapons but from a spirit of peace, love and mutual understanding. According to M. Scott Peck, a community is 'a laboratory of personal disarmament' wherein, the members experientially discover the rules for peace making and embrace its virtues (83). 'But, these firangis' as Aftab's mother warns, 'have no iman of their own. No religion, no roots. They come here and sever the roots. Our roots, our children's roots. Cut them so deep that we'll all fall down one day' (18).

The militant ideology, in contrast, rejects any sense of bonding even within its own community. According to Akram, 'it just doesn't pay to become too fond of each other? That's the first rule for a militant. Don't grow roots, don't develop bonds. Because then it becomes difficult to cut them and let go when the time comes' (75). So, Akram did not hesitate to get even his closest associate killed, when this man became soft-hearted and started treating the younger boys as brothers rather than jihadis in training. 'In this world of theirs, death was just another part of life and there was no love greater than the cause they lived and indeed died for' (76).

The terrorist training camps that the younger Kashmiri boys are lured into joining are totalitarian institutions, aimed at a radical re-socialisation of the individuals. Total regulation of their lives and complete isolation from the familiar outside world is targeted towards a re-construction of their identities. Indoctrinated into the militant way of thinking, Shazia tells her brother, 'remember this for now and for as long as you live. In this path you have chosen for yourself, there are no friends, or family, even. No one is to be treated with anything less than suspicion' (111). There is a de-socialisation from the known familial community and a re-socialisation into an adopted violent one. But in this adopted community, according to Goffman, 'the personal identity equipment is removed and the organiser effectively create[s] and sustain[s] a particular kind of tension between the home world and the institutional world and use[s] this persistent tension as strategic leverage in the management of men'. Unlike a social community which is protective and supportive, the militant community is exploitative. When Akram looked into Aftab's eyes, 'He likes what he saw – an honesty, an integrity. An unquestioning innocence. An innocence he could use. An innocence that was like clay in his hands' (23–24). Besides, the militant enterprise thrives by creating differences, for when people are physically and emotionally cut off from friends and family, they can be influenced, cajoled or threatened into doing virtually anything, even injuring others or taking their lives.

However, in spite of repeated ruptures into expectations about security and bonding, the Kashmiris are struggling to preserve a sense of community that allows them to share their vulnerability, and heal and protect each other. Though, Lalaji, 'the halwai' was aware of Aftab's association with the terrorist, he 'father-like' tries to shield him from the police, for he did not want the boy and his family to come to any harm (162). Aftab's Sikh friend Angad also tries to help him by warning him of the consequences of militant involvement. Their loving concern bothers Aftab, but influenced by Akram he nurtures mistrust for both as 'rumour', according to Strathern and Stewart, 'sometimes trumps "facts" because rumour can appeal more to the imagination and a desired mindset than facts may do' (14). Desperately 'trying not to be drawn into the general warm friendliness that pervaded the space', Aftab fights the urge to bo one of them (*No Guns* 163). In his passion to achieve an individualised 'heroic' self, he completely disregards the collective pull and protection of the community.

As a consequence of militancy, the peaceful co-existence of the Kashmiris is further threatened by the security forces that under the Armed Forces Special Power Act started their own reign of terror, interrogating civilians at gunpoint and torturing and killing others on mere suspicion. Even if Kashmir is not fighting a conventional war, it is a war zone for there are approximately seven lac Indian military personnel from different brigades posted in the region at all times. Trapped between the security forces and the militants, the Kashmiris are tempted to nurture misplaced loyalties towards the 'firangis'. 'These people are not outsiders here' asserts Aftab, 'It's the Indians, the army, the police. They're just puppets in the hands of the people in Delhi' (*No Guns* 18). The cause that began as a freedom movement for Kashmir turned into a fractured war against military occupation.

In both cases, whether it is militant aggression or operations of the security forces, according to Strathern and Stewart, Benedict Anderson's concept of an 'imagined community' is involved where the individual is trained to sacrifice himself or herself for the 'greater good' of this community and the sacrifice may involve the death of others (9). So, no matter which side the current of conflict may flow, it is always violence that flourishes. This spiral of 'violence' in the novel, soon sucks in the unsuspecting Aftab and a number of others who form the part of his loving, caring world, revealing the flawed human faces of all faces – the army which believes that violence can combat militancy, the militants who mercilessly pursue a self-proclaimed agenda and the family and community that cannot douse the flames of hatred in the hearts of the young.

The Kashmiri consciousness of Kashmiriyat that is believed to embody an ethos of harmony is disrupted by violence. To quote from the novel, 'Kashmir is like a bird whose wings have been torn apart. I don't know if she will ever fly again' (*No Guns* 17). For, violence takes the centre stage of action whichever side one is on and the concept of terror loses its specificity and as always, it is the community that is trapped in-between that suffers.

## References

Anand, Paro. *No Guns At My Sons Funeral.* New Delhi: Indialink, 2005.

Gusfield, J.K. *The Community: A Critical Response.* New York: Harper Colaphon, 1975.

Newman, D. *Sociology: Exploring the Architecture of Everyday Life.* New York: Pine Forge Press, 2005.

Peck, M. Scott. *The Different Drum: Community Making and Peace.* New York: Simon & Schuster, 1987.

Strathern, Andrew, Pamela J. and Stewart, Neil L. Whitehead., eds. *Terror and Violence: Imagination and the Unimaginable.* Hyderabad: Orient Longman, 2006.

## Online

Gill, K.P.S. 'The Kashmiri Pandits: An Ethnic Cleansing the World Forgot' *South Asia Terrorism Portal.* 2003. Site visited: 15 Sept. 2009 <http://www.satp.org/saporgtp/kprsgill/htm.>

Goffman, Erving. "Characteristics of Total Institutions" *Politics of Health Knowledge Network.* Site visited 24 Sept. 2009 <http://www.politicsofhealth.org/main/characterstics_of_total_institutions>

Nayak, Meera. "Kashmiriyat: An Embracing Spirit Languishes like the Dying Chinar Tree". *World View Magazine 17 Sept. 2008* <http://www.worldviewmagazine.com/issues/articles.cfm?id>

# 'Imagined worlds are more potent than real ones'[1] *Reading Lolita in Tehran*: The Reading Group as Community Narrative

*Nishevita Murthy and Sudha Shastri*

*Reading Lolita in Tehran: A Memoir in Books* (2003) recapitulates the experience of a university professor of English, Azar Nafisi, who returns from America to Iran, after the Revolution in 1979. Her experiences in the regime of Ayatollah Khomeini, however, gradually disillusion her about the nature of the Revolution, and the subsequent imposition of the veil for women prompts her to resign from her job at the University. More importantly, the growing restrictions on freedom dictated by the regime necessitate her finding a space of resistance where she can retain her individuality. She locates this in a community she creates of her erstwhile students at the university, who congregate at her house every week to read works of fiction.[2]

Nafisi's memoir has four sections: 'Lolita', 'Gatsby', 'James' and 'Austen', where 'Lolita' and 'Austen' form group readings situated in

Nafisi's home, and 'Gatsby' and 'James', classroom discussions. Nabokov's Lolita and Austen's heroines are at two opposing ends of the spectrum, and yet Nafisi succeeds in making them both meaningful to the experiences of her group, showing the way imagination can make variable entry points into their lives.

The section on Austen begins with the sentence, 'It is a truth universally acknowledged that a Muslim man, regardless of his fortune, must be in want of a nine-year-old [virgin] wife …' (*Reading Lolita in Tehran* 257). It is possible to interpret this statement as a kind of community narrative, which this paper goes on to define.

On a simplistic level, 'community narrative' can be defined as a narrative within, about and/or by a community; stories that a community tells of itself and the shared construction of the community's values, beliefs and reality. Such a narrative would focus on issues as various as the conditions of existence within a particular space and time in a community; the politics of power involved between groups; identity and self-definition of individuals; and their relationship with the world outside. *Reading Lolita in Tehran* can be read as a community narrative on all these counts, even if, by being a written memoir it challenges the traditional, received understanding of itself as oral.

A closer look at the implications of a community narrative, which involve a decentring process and the co-existence of plural voices, shows that these features are deeply entrenched in *Reading Lolita in Tehran*: a narrative of and by a community of readers who read from, with, and into novels authored by writers as diverse and culturally/historically separated as Austen and Nabokov. The texts are chosen by Nafisi to emphasise her experience of oppression, and she and her students use these fictional texts not just to counter reality but to construct a counter-reality.

Bakhtin, in *The Dialogic Imagination*, identifies the novel as a genre that is characterised by heteroglossia and polyphony, making it an open-ended form of representation. 'Community' implies dialogue, accommodation, tolerance. Bakhtin's profiling of the novel as the most democratic of genres is evident in the way the readers in *Reading Lolita in Tehran* find their voices and locate themselves within the novels in point.

*Lolita*, *Invitation to a Beheading*, *The Great Gatsby*, *Daisy Miller* and *Pride and Prejudice* are some of the novels that Nafisi and her students read, interpret and discuss. Apart from *Gatsby* and those of James', which are discussed in the classroom, all other novels are discussed by the reading group in Nafisi's house. *The Great Gatsby* becomes another kind of community narrative that is located in a classroom, during Nafisi's tenure as a university lecturer. The fact that it is structured as a trial adds a significant dimension to its interpreting community since its participants must take on roles to play, thereby determining each reader's engagement in a certain way to the rest of the community. Conversely, the space of the home is less hierarchical besides being less deterministic, where there is no judge to arbitrate matters of interpretation.

A fundamental question raised by the book is how the reading community in Nafisi's home connects with the larger community that supports Ayatollah's regime. Reading and interpreting fiction empowers the community, encouraging them to choose from competing realities arising from the texts. The rest of this paper also addresses the following questions: How does *Reading Lolita in Tehran* as a community narrative create entry points for individual readers into literary texts? (How) does the reading community arrive at a consensus within interpretation? How does the idea of 'right' or acceptable reading get challenged by this community? How persuasively does *Reading Lolita in Tehran* present the paradox of a community engendering individuality?

## The Power of Literature: Imagination and Subversion

The women who meet in Nafisi's house escape into the realm of literature, a place that can temporarily free them from the grim reality determined for them by the Iranian government. At the same time they are gradually awakened to the subversive power of literature by their mentor, Nafisi. That the world outside is also aware of this power, is something that they understand with increasing clarity through their discussions.

Khomeini's need to control literature is an implicit acknowledgement of the power of writers and the influence they wield. The increase in vigilance in Iran on every aspect of social, cultural and personal life threatens democracy; consequently, every gesture is construed as a political act.

Under such circumstances, Nafisi remarks that the 'room, for all of us, became a place of transgression. What a wonderland it was! Sitting around the large coffee table covered with bouquets of flowers, we moved in and out of the novels we read' (*Reading Lolita in Tehran* 8). Fiction comes to their rescue because of its power to create an imaginary world portraying real problems, where the individual inhabits different spatio-temporal realms from the grim Iranian reality; and learns to cope with it through observing, understanding, empathising and evaluating characters within the fictional text.

Fiction thereby empowers Nafisi's community of readers in several significant ways. Most crucially, it helps them resist a totalitarian perspective on the text/world. It also rejects a literal understanding of what is read, by bringing in the principle of the 'alternative'. This not only means that a reading community enables two readings, but also that the collective nature of this reading ensures that the readings need not be mutually exclusive.

While the texts discussed by Nafisi's community belong predominantly to the Western canon, the figure of Scheherazade from the *Arabian Nights*, raised by Nafisi at the outset as an allusion, draws attention to a significant aspect of their lives. Like Nafisi's students, Scheherazade is besieged as well, and her only refuge lies in her ability to tell stories to Shahryâr, her listener, and thus keep death at arm's length. The circumstances of these women's lives bear comparison with Scheherazade's in the way they use fiction to control their reality.

The choice of Lolita as a fictional figure for Nafisi's students to empathise with may, at first glance, seem improbable and incomprehensible. But the discussion unwinds to reveal Lolita as the ideal choice for the women's understanding of their reality.

Although critical responses to the heroine of Nabokov's eponymous novel include such phrases as 'little monster', 'shallow', 'corrupt' (*Reading Lolita in Tehran* 40), Nafisi and her community of readers reject this interpretation as limited and inaccurate. They realise that Humbert is not just a character in the story of Lolita, but he is also the narrator, the man who *represents* Lolita to them, and this changes the representation by adding a crucial dimension to their insight into Lolita's situation. In their revised version, 'Lolita belongs to a category of victims who have no defense and are never given a chance to articulate their own story. As such, she becomes a double victim: not only her life but her life story is taken from her. We told ourselves we were in that class to prevent ourselves from falling victim to this second crime' (*Reading Lolita in Tehran* 41)

'Who writes?' thus becomes the critical question that determines interpretation. When Nafisi's community of readers interprets, the temptress Lolita is seen as a puppet in the hands of a self-absorbed, self-indulgent villain. In turn this reading community demonstrates its power with a complementary question: Who *reads*? *Reading Lolita in Tehran* then projects the question, what happens to the original narrative when a community rewrites it?

## The Reading Group as Community Narrative

The reading group acts as a micro-community using imaginative writing to comment on the oppressive world of the *polis*, and through its discussions, generates a narrative on the community of Iran, alongside its own dissenting role. On the one hand, *Reading Lolita in Tehran* finds its feet rather defiantly, if covertly, within the larger Iranian community as a narrative of the beliefs of individuals, and their desire to think freely without being monitored to think in a predetermined direction. It also becomes, on the other hand, a narrative of the clash of ideas within a community, showing how fears, hopes and political affiliations shape personal faith. This conflict assumes particular significance within educational institutions where Nafisi claims that 'students and faculty were differentiated mainly by their political affiliations. Gradually I matched names to faces, and learned to read them, to know who was with whom against whom and who belonged to what group' (*Reading Lolita in Tehran* 94). For instance, the section on 'Gatsby' introduces Bahri and Nyazi, students in the University of Tehran, and later Ghomi[3], in the Allameh Tabatabai, who are all supporters of Khomeini. These men perform the role of spies, overseeing student and faculty behaviour and reporting free-speech and 'revolutionary' actions, such as unveiling by women, to the authorities. Nafisi discovers, moreover, that their literary opinions are directly informed by their political affiliations, which prevents them from accepting alternate perspectives.

In striking contrast is the competence with which Nafisi's group uses dialogue as a means to confront, if not resolve, difficult personal choices. Discussion ensures a multiplicity of perspectives, particularly when the participants of the discussion are free to differ in their respective stands. Each of the women in Nafisi's reading group is unique and different from the other. Simultaneously, they share a common space within the drawing room as part of a community characterised by resistance, and empowered by literature.

Nafisi mentions early in the book that given a choice, these women would not have interacted with each other voluntarily. There is awkwardness between them in the initial classes that stems from ideological differences and beliefs, which situate them in opposing camps. Azin and Mahshid, for instance, find themselves in disagreement with each other from the first instance of their meeting. Yet a love of literature and the shared belief that they will not submit to intellectual tyranny, bring these women together.

The reading group, qua group, acquires greater power than the individual since it allows for interaction of different worldviews that an isolated reading of a novel would not allow. Such an interaction, Nafisi suggests while discussing Austen's novels, increases tolerance and the ability to empathise with the other that, she states, is also the primary function of fiction:

> In Austen's novels, there are spaces for oppositions that do not need to eliminate each other in order to exist. There is also space – not just space but a necessity – for self-reflection and self-criticism. Such reflection is the cause of change … . It is not accidental that the most unsympathetic characters in Austen's novels are those who are incapable of genuine dialogue with others. This incapacity for dialogue implies an incapacity for tolerance, self-reflection and empathy.
>
> (*Reading Lolita in Tehran* 268)

The democratic character of the reading community is an implicit comment, developed by contrast, on the outside Iranian community that disallows dissent. Interaction also nuances issues so that absolute positions – which constitute real danger, as exemplified by the 'outside' community – are pre-empted. Therefore, at a time and place where frank expression of opinions could be severely punished, Nafisi's community discovers the value of honest communication. A case in point is Mahshid's criticism of Nafisi in the final section of the book, as the latter prepares to move out of Iran. Mahshid accuses her teacher of shirking responsibility to her land and her students by leaving Iran, pointing out to Nafisi that her action is tantamount to a betrayal. The community values fostered by the reading group provide a space for dissent and contradiction, within which Mahshid situates herself and articulates her position.

## Knowledge as Process

A sample discussion from *Reading Lolita in Tehran* helps demonstrate one of the ways through which the community arrives at an understanding of an event or idea through dialogue. Discussing Lolita, Mahshid recognises that Lolita has feelings, which makes parts of the novel painful for a reader. All that Lolita desires is to be a 'normal' girl, and live a 'normal' life, which is denied to her. Nassrin, at this juncture, notes how Nabokov makes one pity 'the loss of the most conventional forms of life' (*Reading Lolita in Tehran* 50). Nassrin is struck by the irony of Lolita's inability to achieve even the aspiration for the ordinary; it is not the unreachable or the fantastic that she craves for, after all. When Yassi wonders if Humbert changes when he sees Lolita broken in the end, it remains for Manna to raise the crucial question: What do we, as readers, see?

This is a proposition that *Reading Lolita in Tehran* offers time and again: that what we see is often a question of how we bring ourselves into what we read.

> 'Some critics seem to treat the text the same way Humbert treats Lolita: they only see themselves and what they want to see'. She turned to me and continued: 'I mean, the censors, or some of our politicized critics, don't they do the same thing, cutting up books and re-creating them in their own image?'
>
> (*Reading Lolita in Tehran* 50)

In contrast to this reading community that grows in knowledge through discussions, and sometimes through dissension as well, exists the other 'discussion group' in the book: the classroom community. Nafisi shows how the traditional centres of knowledge production and transmission, i.e., the university become steeped in ideological and political conflict. The sections on 'Gatsby' and 'James' depict the university as a site of political control and power play. Both the University of Tehran and the Allameh Tabatabai harbour political groups amongst students who act as spies to the fundamentalist parties and prevent open discussions. Freedom, creativity and imagination are suppressed, thereby preventing growth through knowledge which Nafisi suggests happens through assimilation.

In the university, the political intrudes into the personal, infusing a fear of punishment into non-conformists. An example of intolerance is evidenced in a mock-trial of *Gatsby* conducted in Nafisi's classroom at the University of Tehran. The 'trial' arises out of difference of opinion among students with respect to Fitzgerald's message in his novel *The Great Gatsby*. Nyazi condemns the novel as immoral, claiming that it encourages materialistic desires, leading to infidelity and depravity. Another group of students, headed by a young woman, Zarrin, argues that such reading negates the message of the book: that material possession is not enough to re-unite Gatsby and Daisy.

Nafisi structures these arguments in the form of a trial of the book *Gatsby*, where Nyazi plays the prosecutor, Zarrin, the defense and Nafisi, the defendant (of the book itself). The mock trial demonstrates Nyazi's inability to read novels on their own terms, preventing him from fully appreciating them.[4] *Gatsby* becomes, for Nyazi and Bahri, a representative of everything that America is, and Iran should not become. The classroom projects a situation where imagined worlds within novels become potent enough to threaten real material existence of life outside, consequently infusing fear in the Islamists. Nafisi simultaneously suggests that Nyazi and Bahri see their reality as threatened *because* they are impervious to the plurality that the novels represent. Nafisi's reading group at home, on the other hand, gains much from the very same novels because it is open to multiple perspectives.

## Reality and the Community

One of the implicit claims of *Reading Lolita in Tehran* is that reality can get threatening when constructed by a tyrant, and especially so for people who do not realise it. This is contrasted with the women in the reading community who perceive political orchestration in their lives with greater clarity. Supporting this claim, Nafisi describes an incident when the American embassy in Iran was occupied by a group of students. 'People were bused in daily from the provinces and villages who didn't even know where America was, and sometimes thought they were actually being taken to America' (*Reading Lolita in Tehran* 105). Nafisi asserts that they were characters in a story authored by someone else, and that, ironically, they were unaware of it. By contrast, Nafisi's group uses fiction to question the reality it encounters, and decide whether or not to choose it. Fiction, as stated earlier, is premised on an 'imagined world' and alternate reality; recognising this premise empowers fiction-readers in *Reading Lolita in Tehran* to consider the nature of reality given to them as provisional.

Another instructive intersection between fiction and reality for this community is located in Nafisi's discussion of *Invitation to a Beheading*. One of the injunctions on the prison cell of Cincinnatus C in this novel forbids him from dreaming, adding that if he does, he must suppress his dreams at once. This absurd command takes on an overwhelmingly nightmarish note, as the prisoner is liable to be punished for transgression in dreams, a space that is beyond his conscious control. In a frightening parallel, Nafisi recounts that her students confessed to suffering from nightmares of political transgression. Several months into the class, the women in the group realised that they were having recurring nightmares of not having worn the veil, intentionally or otherwise.

At least two significant points can be made in this context. Shared experience validates the women as one community. Fraught by restrictions, injunctions and objections, overwhelmed by guilt and fear, the community outside needs to be kept at bay by this resisting group; literature comes to its aid. The implicitly subversive nature of the texts they read equips them with a potent weapon: perspective.

The outcome of this is to make the community bond closer, and deeper. The people of this community are under threat, which makes their investment as individuals risky. Conversely, the community tests its dedication to the spirit with which it came to be formed, initially.

## Conclusion

After the publication of *Reading Lolita in Tehran*, Nafisi has come under critique on several counts. Hamid Dabashi, in his article 'Native Informers and the Making of the American Empire' claims that at a time when America was looking for hegemonic expansion across the globe, Nafisi's memoir portrays an oppressed Iranian community looking to the West for redemption. Consequently, he accuses her of giving the United States sufficient ammunition to attack Iran and justify their imperial stand. Dabashi also accuses her of anti-Iranian diatribes and misrepresentation of Iran, especially on the cover page of her book.[5] Other accusations against Nafisi include her stand on several political issues that she could afford to voice because of her influential background. She is also accused of desertion when she decides to return to America, instead of staying on in Iran to fight the women's cause, a point also raised by her student Mahshid.

Her choice of books for discussion in the reading group, most of which are western classics, is also a matter of objection and unease. Nafisi admits in an interview with Random House Reader's Circle that several students were discomfited by the choice of texts ('A Conversation with Azar Nafisi'). She however defends her decision to stay by her choice of books by stating that the texts opened their minds to alternative realities.

In 'The Veiled Threat: The Iranian Revolution's Woman Problem', Nafisi says 'Every private act or gesture in defiance of official rules is now a strong political statement.' Similarly, in a conversation with Sara O'Reilly, she contends that the reading group, by discussing 'illicit' literature in Iran, could have put the girls in grave danger. And yet, it is this existential desire to assert their rights that made the exercise political. 'Our class was not political; its subversive nature was defined by our attempt to create an atmosphere in which we retrieved what we lacked in public, open spaces and open relations. It was an assertion that life had not stopped because the state had ordered it.' (Nafisi, 'P.S. Ideas, interviews and feature…', 7) Nafisi argues that it is easier to destroy overt political groups but far more difficult to crush resistance that asserts the right to exist. Nafisi states that the community helped the girls to be themselves, and it is in such assertion of its self, this 'polyphony, that democracy of voices that becomes so very dangerous to an autocratic mindset' ('A Conversation with Azar Nafisi', an interview with Random House Reader's Circle) that its biggest strength and challenge lies.

The reading group finally makes imaginative entry points into itself as a community, retelling its life story and dynamics through dialogue and discussion. In this respect, the group becomes a trope for freedom and debate, of constant reappraisal, self-definition and renewal that characterise the community narrative, which prevails long after the seven students cease meeting in Nafisi's house.

## Notes

1. Katherine Frank. 'Women Without Men: The Feminist Novel in Africa' (1987), quoted by Kofi Owusu, 344, in 'Canons Under Seige: Blackness, Femaleness, and Ama Ata Aidoo's Our Sister Killjoy', *Callalloo* 13:2 (Spring 1990), 341–363.
2. The seven women (Mahshid, Nassrin, Sanaz, Azin, Manna, Yassi and Mitra) with whom Nafisi discusses fiction come from different backgrounds. Mahshid, for instance, chooses to wear the veil as part of her religious beliefs, devoid of political affiliations. Azin, on the other hand, is thrice married and struggling with an abusive husband. Sanaz has to deal with an overly interfering younger brother, who intrudes her privacy on the pretext of protecting her. Manna is happily married to her college sweetheart Nima. Despite the varying experiences life deals them, the women congregate at their mentor's house to discuss fiction, and its relevance to their lives.
3. It is curious that Nafisi prefixes the men's names with 'Mr' while offering no such marker to her women students. The girls are addressed throughout the memoir by their first names.
4. This is not to claim that the reading group interprets texts 'correctly'. What differentiates the reading community of

women from the fundamentalists in the classroom is its refusal to take absolute stands on the novels that are discussed. By virtue of this difference in approach, which provides an alternate perspective, the reading as well as the text is rendered richer by the experience.

5. The first edition of the memoir depicted two young girls, wearing veils, reading with their heads together. The picture, however, did not show what they were reading. Dabashi accuses Nafisi of suggesting through the cover that the girls were reading *Lolita* in Tehran. The original picture, taken from another newspaper, shows the girls reading a revolutionary journal that propagated women's rights. Dabashi suggests that such movements did exist in Iran and Nafisi has misrepresented the country in her memoir.

## References

'Native Informers and the Making of the American Empire'. *Al-Ahram Weekly Online*, Issue No. 797 (1–7 June, 2006). 29th January 2009 http://weekly.ahram.org.eg/2006/797/special.htm

Nafisi, Azar. *Reading Lolita in Tehran: A Memoir in Books*. 2003. London: Harper Perennial, 2007.

_____. 'The Veiled Threat: The Iranian Revolution's Woman Problem'. *The New Republic*, Feb 22, 1999. Quoted in *Middle East Quarterly* 10:2 Spring (2003), 3–17. http://www.meforum.org/542/reading-lolita-in-tehran#_ftn1

——. 'P.S. Ideas, interviews, features...'. *Reading Lolita in Tehran: A Memoir in Books*. 2003. London: Harper Perennial, 2007. 1–32.

——. 'A Conversation with Azar Nafisi'. Azar Nafisi: *Reading Lolita in Tehran*. http://azarnafisi.com/books/reading-lolita-in-tehran/

# IV

# Urban Spaces

## Enacting Narratives in Urban Spaces

*Cities have a life of their own, a life crowded with roads and railway tracks, with people and buildings and are capable of creating a sense of separation. Moments are fleetingly captured as one takes a train or gets on a bus; acquaintances are met on the stair of malls, in lifts or at bus stops.*

*How do urban spaces affect the art of storytelling? Do the narratives move towards a non-linearity, a fragmentation, a disjointedness? What does it do to the individual psyche, to the consciousness of identity? And what impact does it have on the relationship between time and space? These are some of the queries that demand attention, especially as multiple forces like technology, terrorism and materialism have fragmented our lives as well as accelerated its pace.*

*The essays in this section take up some of the above questions as creation of private space takes place amidst a crowd; a narrative is enacted in buses and at railway platforms or as cities trace their own histories and evolutionary lines through their monuments and congested streets; through their shift of centres and creation of new peripheries, and above all through segregating areas within the city space bringing multiple centres into existence. Does the human agency bring this about or is it space that defines boundaries for the human being? None of these questions has a simple answer. Jasbir Jain takes up several of them; the construction of space through political rulers, through the notion of respectability and wealth and through monuments, while Shaila Mahan works with the fast moving pace of the city and the inroads it makes into personal lives. Music, poetry and nostalgia provide a way out of this loss. Maheeka Nanda turns to Azar Nafisi's novel where personal space is created in order to resist the power diktats. The narratives which emerge tell their own story.*

# Flow of Urbanscapes: History, Temporality and Challenges

*Jasbir Jain*

History and temporality stand at opposite ends; the first seeks to consolidate and preserve and contests the onslaught of time; the second brings in change or erosion. The first digs in its feet through monuments and, at a second stretch, through documents, as it attempts to reach out to the future through legend, historical memory and by invading the very 'presence' of a place. The second (that is temporality) questions the objectivity and the stability of this 'presence', is inhabited by living human beings whose lives are shaped by their conflicts, faiths, temptations, actions and notions of respectability and, at another level, by inheritance, lineage and memory.

The two – history and temporality – are at odds with each other yet they exist in a simultaneity, continuing a love-hate relationship with each other. Together they evoke contradictory images of the city. Today, at this particular point of human history, technology, town planning and architecture have become visible instruments of negotiating both power and space, urbanscapes are changing very rapidly and multi-layered cities are emerging. Any consideration of urban space has to work not only vis-à-vis the village, but also vis-à-vis the earlier city. Examples of cities coming into being though shifts of power, of smaller townships coming together or expanding to create suburbs, satellite cities or newer townships, processes of mergers, relocations and de-centralisation are in abundance. Or twin cities come into being, carrying on different functions in unison – such as Delhi-New Delhi, Mhow-Indore, Pune-Kirkee, Mumbai-Navi Mumbai, Hyderabad-Secunderabad and closer home we have the shift from Amer to Jaipur, from the walled city to C-Scheme, then now a host of mergers and satellites like Mansarovar, Sanganer and Jagatpura. In colonial times, sharp divisions existed between the city and the cantonment, which persist to this day. Each space carries a different culture and fulfils a different function.

Cities inherit and create their own cultures even as each successive collectivity of immigrants such as immigrant labour, refugees or industrial houses bring their own community cultures and add to or alter the existing pattern.[1] How do these produce meaning in a fictional narrative? And does space have a role to play in shaping environments, notions of respectability and freedom? In the early phase of modernism, in the mid-nineteenth century, the city was seen as conferring anonymity, alternatively it was also seen as the place of opportunity, employment and education. In those days it was ordinarily a single gender migration to the cities, a crisis migration or, in India, a durbar migration.

No matter where one begins space plays a dominant part in cultural and environmental change, which is not always progressive or linear. The meaning of a text is governed and produced by the interaction of space with human lives. Working with Michel Foucault's idea of space and Hans Ulrich Gumbrecht's concept of presence, I propose to take up two entirely different kinds of novels, located in Delhi, for purposes of illustration – Khushwant Singh's *Delhi* (1990) and Krishna Sobti's *Dil-o-Danish* (1993). They also bring out the differences in gender perspective and in the use of language. Singh writes in English while Sobti uses the Urdu of Delhi is it was used in the 1920s. But Singh's narrative moves through nearly eight centuries and an equal number of narrative voices: Masaudi Lal, a Kayasth munshi; Jaita Rangrela, a Sikh convertee; Bahadur Shah Zafar, the last

Mughal; Alice Aldwell an English woman later converted to Islam; Nadir Shah Abdali; the poet Meer Taqi Meer, Nihal Singh, and Ram Rakha – a partition refugee – and shifts the style to suit the speaker and the period, incorporating Arabic or Persian or Urdu or Hindustani nuances, and at times Sanskrit and Hindi. There is an abundant variety of linguistic registers. There are also the many interventions by the authorial persona where his Oxonian English and liberal sexuality find free expression as well as the street language of his hermaphrodite mistress Bhagmati. *Delhi* is a history of the city's making as it is shaped by power struggles, the building of the Qutub Minar, the Sufi philosophy of Nizamuddin Auliya and the shift to Shahjehanabad, the construction of the Red Fort, the Rakabganj Gurudwara, the martyrdom of Guru Tegh Bahadur and later of the tenth Guru – Gobind Singh and his sons – leading to Lutyen's Delhi. It is a rich complex tapestry. Khushwant Singh has a personal history to contribute to its making with his grandfather Sujan Singh being one of the contractors. His narrative moves to and fro between the present and the past, from South Delhi to Mehrauli, to the inner city, back again to its outskirts as the fluctuations in power are worked out. In short, *Delhi* is a narrative built on his love for the city.[2]

In contrast Krishna Sobti's narrative is located in the old city, in an aristocratic lifestyle where mistresses were supported but encroachments into family life held strictly taboo, where the affairs of the heart were controlled by both practical economics and social norms, where youth as it yielded to age rendered men as vulnerable as women, and where the undercurrents of passion were stemmed by the legally wedded wife. Time and again, Sobti points out that it is a patriarchal society but on closer analysis it is a study also of respectability and lineage. Who can defy the norms and cross into forbidden territory? And who has the courage to stand up alone? *Dil-o-Danish* works closely with family constructs, marriage, legality, male progeny, restrictions upon women and their manipulative acts in order to countercheck male indulgence, the reliance on superstition and the whole concept of social acceptance and respectability. The narrative is also a very subtle statement of the relationship between romance and ageing. It works with a taut plot construction and projects rival claims through the scene when Raju, the Vakil Sahib's legitimate son's birthday is celebrated and the father extends an invitation to his other two children born of Mehak, to the party, the occasion becomes a site for testing the strength of relationships. Through an evening of poetry recitations, puzzles and other such enactments, good use is made of the oral tradition and the scene has a central place in the one-sided battle that Kutumb, the legal wife, launches with full determination against Mehak, the mistress.

Foucault in his essay 'Of Other Spaces' and the interviews put together in *Power/Knowledge* went on to link space and within it heterotopias with locations of power and knowledge – cultural centres, libraries, theatres, government offices – but this does not necessarily work on similar lines in every culture. In *Delhi* the power centres are palaces and forts, and secondarily prison-houses and embassies. Countering these with parallel power-structures are houses of faith and holy men such as Nizamuddin Auliya and the Sikh gurus and poets like Meer Taqi Meer. They create their heterotopias through their prayer-sessions, devotion and mushiaras where traditions are tested and reinvented. In *Dil-o-Danish* the two houses are architecturally different, just as the families inhabit different spaces marking different social status. Kripanarayan, Kutumb and their three sons, the lawyer's mother and widowed sister live in the haveli while Mehak with her two children lives in the poor quarters, crowded and noisy.

Foucault in an interview given to *Quel Corps* came very close to what Gumbrecht developed later into his theory of presence. Foucault was of the view that the social body is a product not only of a consensus but of 'a materiality of power operating on the very body of individuals' (55). Power does not deny the reality of the body. He admitted that to people with a belief in history as a lived continuity, spatial terms seem 'to have the air of an anti-history' (Interview given to *Herodote*, 'Questions of Geography') instead of compelling them to realise that spatial demarcations throw into relief the processes of power (Foucault 70). Gumbrecht's work on the materiality of presence paid a lot of attention to the body, to media, to boxing-rings and different kinds of heterotopias. In an essay on his fifty-ninth birthday 'Will my Present have a Future?' he admitted that what he longed for was 'the physicality of life' and the best way to achieve that is to emphasise, protract and expand, as best as we can, the moments of 'lived experience' ('Erlebnis') in which 'we are fully aware of what our senses perceive .... Humanities and the Arts have an aesthetic responsibility towards producing this presence' (Mendes and Rocha 342–343).[3] Both Singh and Sobti are intensely aware of space and the impact of presence and they deal with the 'body' as part of the world with all its sexuality, repressions and self-divisions (as in an hermaphrodite) and the structures of institutions. But their approaches and foci are very different from each other, and work differently.

*Dil-o-Danish* opens with the winter setting in and new quilts being delivered to the haveli, where the making of two more quilts, apparently intended for the *farashkhana*, is leaked out. As Kutumb proclaims her right to the two extra quilts, a storm literally sets in. The next delivery is to the Begum's house where the Munshi is received with traditional hospitality. The haveli is a house full of servants but Mehak is all-in-one in her small establishment. As Kripanarayan finds his way there he compares the two women in his life – one who fulfils his physical and emotional being, the other who sets her eyes on her rights. As the neighbourhood dogs bark at passing strangers, he becomes conscious of the lateness of the hour and the possible gossip around his visits. Mehak lives a lonely life as she strives to protect both her privacy and respectability by her aloofness. The crowded space, the close neighbourhood, conditions of dependence all encroach upon her freedom. Not really poor, Mehak has inherited some property and a deal of jewellery from her mother, which are all now under the care of the lawyer.

Despite his attraction towards her, he considers her a singer's daughter, a woman of pleasure but mentally compares her with the behavioural code of women from respectable families (17). Spaces mark their place in society even as men are shared. Obviously the family has its own views about this relationship. Kripanarayan's mother and sister, and his eldest son accept it, but the pull of the wife works against this illegal tie.

The young girls in the family put together a play where different kinds of 'bahus' are presented – the spendthrift, the fashionable one, obsessed with appearances, the well-behaved respectful and courteous one, the idle one and the preachy one always full of advice; out of all these the old man (the father-in-law) favours the well-behaved one. The Hindi words have nuances which cannot be conveyed through translation – *kharchili, khalifa, palita, salika*. The expected behaviour from wives is spelt out – to bear children, to share happiness and sorrow, visit the temple, perform acts of charity, look after the home – but these duties need not to be rewarded (33). This heterotopic embedding underlines the theme as it encapsulates the dynamic relationship between spaces and roles.

Like the camera-eye, and the multiple narrators of *Delhi*, the narrative voice shifts in *Dil-o-Danish* but with a difference. Here it often acquires a confessional tone, an interior dialogue, a lawyer's argument, a suppressing of the voice of conscience.

> दोनों औरतें हैं और हम औरत नहीं हैं, मर्द हैं। क्या मर्द होने से ही हम इनकी तकलीफ नहीं समझ सकते? क्या मर्द का औरत होना जरूरी है? या औरत का मर्द? सोचें तो खुद कुदरत ने उन्हें एक-सा वजूद नहीं दिया। एक दूसरे का स्वरूप धारण कर भी लें तो यह ज़िन्दगी रामलीला होकर रह जाएगी। दूसरे सब झगड़े-झमेले निपटाने के लिए कानून है लेकिन इस मामले में कानून अन्धा है। (38)

> [Both are women, I am not a woman but a man. Does the fact of maleness lead to a non-comprehension of their pain? Is it necessary for a man to be a woman? Or for a woman to be a man? On reflection, it is evident that even nature has not given them similar personalities. If they are able to take on each other's identity, then this world would turn into another Ramlila. Law is there to take care of all other conflicts, but in this case even law is blind.] (38, translation mine)

The story travels into the past as Kripanarayan's voice takes over, or when Kutumb contemplates a sexual relationship with the priest who promises to find a remedy for her husband's infidelity. Amidst fear and nightmares she seeks validation for her conduct in her husband's infidelity. There is almost a surrealistic possession of her own inner being as she struggles with choices

Another narrative voice is that of his sister Chhuno. And the imagery is beautiful, born out of the domestic environs.

> एक बार कलेजे वाला चूल्हा भख गया तो जो भी पका लो। मीठा चावल, भुनी खिचड़ी, पुलाव, कोरमा, पसंदे
> "उनकी कलफ़ लगी सरसराती साड़ी तक बौखलाई रहती है" (53).

> ['Once the heart's fire is aroused, you can cook anything on it – sweet rice, khichdi, pulaf, pasande,' and then follows a phrase such as, 'Her starched rustling sari is also always bewildered'.] (53, translation mine)

*Dil-o-Danish* is firmly located in a torn domestic environment and professional interests are referred to only marginally, signified merely as the 'room'. Kripanarayan's two families are placed almost side by side but the space earmarked for each is ironically reversed. Kutumb who occupies the haveli lives on the margins of his heart, while Mehak who lives in the cramped space in a poor neighbourhood constantly pulls at his heartstrings. But his inner debate is always centred on the 'legality' of Kutumb's claims, an issue closely interwoven with the notion of respect, and reputation in the community and the rights of his wife.

Kripanarayan's mother had given her own 'kangans' to Mehak, which Kutumb insists on claiming as her own while Mehak's box of jewellery is firmly under the lawyer's control. Later when he parts with it, he hands it over to Khan Sahib not to Mehak, demonstrating the injustice incorporated in the whole relationship. The two women are both treated as property, only the care lavished on each differs in direct proportion to the legality. Mehak has no right to go into tantrums, not even when her children are taken away from her. But it is by finally breaking these taboos that she rises above her fate: first by participating in Masooma, her daughter's wedding, when she had been strictly forbidden to do so (184–185), and later by visiting the Vakil Sahib on his death bed, when Kutumb has succeeded in winning him back – a victory which has killed much in him. Mehak wins both admiration and sympathy – for her grace, her courage and her defiance of the norms. She refuses to stay confined to the space earmarked for her. At her first stepping out when she closes the door of her house and goes to meet Khan Sahib, she wonders why she had taken so long to move out of that room? (174).This spatial shift is also the moment of transformation. In fact there are four scenes with a strong visual and dramatic presence: the birthday party which is like a carnival; the retrieval of the kangans a closed-space entangled domesticity; then the wedding reception, a public event in the open and finally the dying man's bedroom.

These explore the possibility of reversal lurking in the representation of physical space, the ugliness of victory, the significance of both enclosed and open spaces and the encroachment into the anguish of being itself.[4]

Lying on his sickbed, Kripanarayan relives his moment of defeat. He asks his sister to act as commentator-narrator on the events that took place on the evening of Masooma's wedding. Mehak's visit, he feels was directed more at his public humiliation than at asserting her maternal right; her defiance was the final blow to his masculine pride. Kutumb's gnawing at him was like the action of termites, while Mehak's was a beautiful audacity that said volumes without using any words. The action defied the regime of tradition, redefined individual right in feminist terms, moved beyond legality and respectability and symbolised a break with whatever inheritance, circumstances and space had marked for her.

There is a brief debate between Kripanarayan and his wife on the forces of '*taqdeer*' – destiny and of '*tadbeer*' – the forces of human will. Destiny, he feels represents all that is derogatory and backward, while a personal act of courage (*tadbeer*) defies it. Mehak tramples on his public face by making an appearance at her daughter's wedding, while he is left helpless locked in his own sense of destiny (180–181). It is thus that modernity knocks at the door, shattering existing frameworks through the remaking of values.

Urban spaces are beset by many challenges and several of them combine to shrink both personal space and time, some of them attack concepts of tradition such as the electric crematorium. Khushwant Singh comments on the huge use of wood, the Delhi dead make – 'they consume a sizeable forest of timber every day .... The only takers for the electric crematorium which costs less than a quarter of the expense of disposal by wood are the dead of the anglicized rich or the unclaimed bodies of beggars' (378). Right from the bank of Jamuna, through Majnoon ka Tilla to Rajghat memorials of the famous leaders line the land, consuming precious space. He goes on to comment on pollution, the smoking chimneys of the filtration plant, the spread of diseases and now AIDS, with more than 70,000 new immigrants every year, Delhi is 'the nation's orphanage'.

Modernity also underlies the whole text through the narrative of the sexual in-between, the hermaphrodite (*'hijda'*). Not only is Bhagmati one, but royal kings have had their own pleasures. The hermaphrodite springs up from nature, makes its way all through history now to take its place amidst modern sexual norms. Else, one may ask why does the writer pursue it all through his narrative? It also demonstrates the gradual shift of the peripheries towards greater centrality, disrupting the very idea of any fixities where definitions of the masculine and the feminine are concerned.

The positive values of modernity have laced all ideas of tradition right from Massudi Lal, the first narrator, who also has a Muslim name Abdullah, whose Hindu wife gradually consents to a relationship with him under the Auliya's influence and the verses of Khusro which bridge separate identities. Then the untouchable who stands converted to Sikhism, another bridging device between castes and religions, which the people created for themselves. These men comfortably move in and out of their two identities. The strongholds of power represented by palaces are shattered both for Bahadur Shah Zafar and the British in 1857. The walls of forts no longer protect. And the Civil Lines located outside Chandni Chowk in Daryaganj, yields to newer construction, driving out the British administrators to a new location and later giving birth to Lutyen's New Delhi.

No space is free from encroachments. Revolutions take place, just as wars had been fought in the lanes of Delhi, two assassinations in less than fifty years – one of Gandhi, the other of Indira Gandhi – mark the turmoil of the violence that besets a crowded space when victims are locked in houses and streets and in blind alleys. Riots in urban spaces take advantage of combustible material and the density of population. It works better if more people die. Trains, petroleum, bombs – who ever invented them so that men could be killed and burnt?

Finally, I draw your attention to the covers of the two novels I have discussed. The covers represent Delhi foregrounding monuments with settlements in the background the sloping roofs, hutments, open spaces of times gone by and the more symmetrical Red Fort and – comparatively newer – Old Delhi (as compared to Mehrauli and Purana Quila, Indraprastha and Tughlakabad).

Though both the writers work with urban spaces, 'presence' is produced in different ways. Singh works through history and the making of Delhi through shifts, mergers, replacements, rebellions, refugees and constructions as it presents a seductiveness hidden behind the ugly clutter moving through its various births, while Sobti locates it in the heart of Old Delhi, in Chandni Chowk, in the 1920s and from that limited space makes forays into various directions in time, in memory and the life span of Kripanarayan who is shaken by the challenge to the received notion of masculinity, the fading romance and Mehak's assertion of her right and Chhuno's defiance of the taboos on widowhood. Each negotiates the claims modernity makes on them in different ways – succeeding or failing no one knows. Modernity knows no successes or failures– it simply doesn't stand still to take stock, it is not a rupture but an evolving continuity.

## Notes

1. Bhisham Sahni's *Basanti* (1987) is a fine example of the Rajasthani immigrant population bringing in its own community culture, caste patterns and gender roles. What Basanti gains in the city is a certain degree of freedom though she still remains trapped in gender roles.
2. In the 'Foreword' to the Paperback Edition of *Delhi*, Singh writes: 'It took me twenty-five years to piece together this story spanning several centuries of history. I put in it all I had in me as a writer: love, lust, sex, hate, vendetta and violence – and above all, tears. I did not write this novel with any audience in mind. All I wanted to do was tell my readers what I learnt about the city roaming among its ancient ruins, its congested bazaars, its diplomatic corps and cocktail parties' (Singh 1990).
3. Aesthetic pleasure immediately establishes a contact with a presence outside. One is reminded of Antonin Artaud's theatrical experiments when he sought to reach the passive viewer through violence. It is this 'presence' within art which produces meaning over and above its philological and semiotic base.
4. In an essay 'Force of Flight', written in 1973 to accompany a series of paintings by Paul Rebeyrolle (1926–2005), Foucault, when describing prisons, wrote of the desperation which

haunts a captive and the final resort to hanging which remains the only way of 'dying upright' (quoted by Elden and Crampton, 8). Spaces of captivity, he felt, could be reversed and the inside-outside syndrome reworked.

## References

Elden, Stuart and Jeremy W. Crampton., eds. 'Introduction' *Space, Knowledge and Power: Foucault and Geography*. internet checked on 28 August 2009. 1–16.

Foucault, Michel. 'Of Other Spaces'. *Diacritics*, Spring, 1986, 22–27.

Gordon, Colin., ed. *Michel Foucault: Power/Knowledge: Selected Interviews & Other Writings 1972–1977*. New York: Pantheon Books. 1980.

Gumbrecht, Hans Ulrich, 'Will My Present Have a Future?' *Producing Presences: Branching Out From Gumbrecht's Work*. Dartmouth, Massachusetts: University of Massachusetts, 2007. 339–351.

Hosagrahar, Jyoti. *Indigenous Modernities: Negotiating Architecture and Urbanism*. London: Routledge (Indian Reprint), 2005.

Mendes, Victor K. and Joâo Cezar de Castro Rocha., eds. *Producing Presences: Branching Out From Gumbrecht's Work*. Dartmouth, Massachusetts: University of Massachusetts, 2007.

Singh, Khushwant. *Delhi*. New Delhi: Penguin, 1990.

Sobti, Krishna. *Dil-o-Danish* (Hindi). Delhi: Raj Kamal Prakashan, 1993, 1999.

*Note:* My grateful thanks to both the writers: Khushwant Singh and Krishna Sobti, for granting me permission to use these covers as illustration.

दिलो-दानिश
कृष्णा सोबती

# The 'lonely crowd': Perspectives on *Life in a Metro*

*Shaila Mahan*

An acute awareness of the pressures of life in the contemporary urban situation is a keynote of modern artistic creations. Hence, the city has become an integral part of such creative expressions. The rapid expansion of Indian cities and the artistic representations of the urban lifestyle are closely linked phenomena. With globalisation, city life, specifically metropolitan Indian life, has undergone a sea change. Alienation is a direct offshoot of the intense pressures of globalisation and market economy and obviously Indian urban life is no exception to this sense of separation and alienation. Loneliness and restlessness are in evidence everywhere and fractured human relationships are now an increasingly common experience. In fact, loneliness is no longer just a problem of the individual but is endemic to urban, more specifically, to metropolitan existence. Dr Roberta Hestenes at Eastern College refers to this phenomenon as 'crowded loneliness.'[1] Various artistic expressions have grappled with this sad yet rapidly rampant reality of life in metros.

The relationship between cinema and modernity in the Indian context is both complex and multifaceted. Despite its usual escapist fare, Bollywood cinema has now begun to depict this new age reality by investigating the fluid and fragmentary character of life in contemporary Indian metros. Anurag Basu's *Life in a Metro* is one such representative film which deftly explores the complexities of cosmopolitan human relationships as reflected in their struggle for existence. The film deals with the contemporary conflicts of a globalised Indian city life. This well crafted, multi-narrative film showcases the aspirations, goals and 'emptiness' of its major characters as they go about their daily routine in the metropolitan setting of Mumbai.

The present paper attempts to deconstruct the film's narrative in order to highlight the desensitisation of human beings by market forces interacting in metro spaces, causing havoc to their emotional fabric. The film depicts how most characters suffer an emotional void and vacuum as they strive to acquire materialistic comforts and the inevitable cracks that their marital/romantic relationships develop from a ruthless pursuit of 'success', defined primarily in terms of money, sex and power. My aim is to give a flavour of the film and reflect its multiple layers through the eye of its major female protagonist, Shikha played by Shilpa Shetty. I also plan to explore the variety of cinematic tools that have been used to depict the trials and tribulations of individuals who seem 'lonely in a crowd.' Saleem Peeradina's remark about the source of vitality of a literature: 'A literature that is just beginning cannot be vital unless it stems out of, and is involved in the life around it' can be aptly applied to the seemingly post-modern films like the present one under study (Peeradina, x–xi).

*Life in a Metro* (hereafter referred to as *Metro*) describes the contemporary Indian urban experience. Made in Mumbai itself, the film has used the Mumbai metropolis as its backdrop and it tells the stories of characters one comes across in our everyday lives. It showcases dilemmas which are similar to the ones frequently faced in a city like Mumbai and in doing so it mirrors the overpowering loneliness of life in a Metro. The song 'Rishtey' that appears just as the credits are rolling virtually sets the tone of the film. This gripping song with its English version is given below to reflect the urban loneliness that runs as an undercurrent all through the film:

*Rishtey to nahin, rishton ki parchayian milen*
*Yeh kaisi bheed hai bas yahan tanhayian milen*
*Ek chat ke tale ajnabi ho jaate hain rishtey*
*Bistar par chhadaron se chup so jaate hain rishtey*
*Dhundae se bhi inn main nahin garmayian mile*
*Yeh kaisi bheed hai bas yahan tanhayian*

*Not relationships but their shadows are what we get*
*What a strange crowd, where all we get is loneliness*
*Even under one roof, we turn into strangers*
*Shrouded under the sheets, our bond turns cold and silent*
*Even a desperate search yields no warmth*
*This horde has has nothing but loneliness*

This song quintessentially reflects the film's fundamental theme of a 'lonely crowd' – it highlights how leading a life in a metro virtually dehumanises and desensitises relationships so much that instead of love and warmth it is only loneliness and shadows that appear to dominate life in the urban jungle. This song is particularly applicable to the loveless existence of Ranjeet and Shikha, whose eight-year old marriage has turned meaningless and bitter. Shikha is well educated and a trained dancer who could have earned well had she pursued a professional career. But soon after their marriage, they decide that she would stay at home and take care of the house and their daughter. As she remains in the confines of her home, gets neglected by an indifferent husband and is bogged down by family chores, Shikha is a typically 'desperate housewife' who seems terribly lonely. She sacrifices all her talents and ploughs all her energies into an unhappy marriage that appears doomed to failure. With even physical contact, leave alone emotional intimacy, deserting the couple, Shikha gets attracted to Akash, himself a struggling theatre artist separated from his wife: it is clearly an attempt to fill up the emotional void that Shikha feels as her husband's indifference leaves her terribly isolated and desperate for companionship.

If Shikha is unhappy and lonely, her straying, errant husband seems hardly better off. Ranjeet is involved in a steamy affair with his office junior Neha. Their clandestine coupling provides physical pleasure but leaves neither of them any closer to forging an emotional bond. During one of their escapades, Neha asks

Ranjeet about their future, which leads to an argument. He insults her and leaves. This ugly scene, where both Ranjeet and Neha accuse each other of exploitation in the name of love, brings out the essential hollowness of their affair and depicts how both remain utterly lonely even as they carry on with a relationship that has the potential to bring them a sense of calm and companionship. Instead, as they lead a fast-paced, metropolitan life overcrowded with action, they are unable to overcome the desolation of their inner, emotional selves that drives them to seek solace through their affair.

Through this triangular tangle the film reflects powerfully the false image that people, trapped in loveless marriages, often have to live up to in front of the world. This dilemma is particularly echoed through Shikha's trauma. Outwardly, she has to pretend that her marriage with Ranjeet is a happy union, full of love and companionship; and yet, deep within, Shikha is desperately unhappy and lonely. This external–internal contradiction, is a reflection of the façade that's entrenched in many an unhappy marriage in middle class India, is portrayed with great irony in the scene of their marriage anniversary party. This well-shot sequence succeeds in bringing out the fissures and the hypocrisy of their marriage. Ranjit deliberately stays away from the anniversary party given by Shikha who hopelessly calls him up and pleads with him to come soon to pose as a happy couple in front of the friends. But as he fails to show up she makes excuses on his behalf and lies to her friends that Ranjit is unable to come because he's stuck in the traffic and hopefully he'll be there by the time dessert will be served.

Clearly there's no affection or respect left in the Shikha-Ranjeet marriage, as it has grown utterly dysfunctional. Similarly, the Ranjeet-Neha liaison is an association of convenience and compromise which leads to no emotional rapport and can in no way fill up the void in Ranjeet's life. Indeed, even Shikha's attraction towards a much younger Akash seems mainly a physical pull. She herself vents out her deep sense of guilt and dismay by saying that she feels like a slut, after their brief and guilt-ridden encounter at the house of Akash's friend turns semi-physical. Moreover, their relationship does not blossom, it comes to a sudden standstill as Shikha is bogged down by moral pressures that rule out the possibility of true romance.

Another interesting but unfulfilled character is that of Rahul who from the very start is projected as a small town person with great aspirations. He has come to metropolitan Mumbai to fulfill his father's dream of constructing a hotel. So, quite unscrupulously, he too becomes part of the urban rat race. He lends his apartment to his office superiors to conveniently sleep around with their girlfriends and mistresses in a bid to improve his own career prospects. Ironically, his boss Ranjeet also borrows his key to meet Neha, an office colleague who Rahul loves secretly. Little does Rahul suspect that it is Neha who is sleeping with his boss. When this truth gets revealed, Rahul is quite shattered. In a separate development Neha accuses Ranjeet of 'using her' when he turns down her request for marriage. In a fit of anger he blurts out the real basis of their relationship: its no emotional bond that they share, instead its an economic 'give and take' transaction. He blatantly states that she gets all kinds of 'perks' like 'out of turn promotions', 'business class travel' and other such privileges for the sexual favours she confers.

This refusal pushes Neha to attempt suicide. This tragic twist is a callous yet realistic manifestation of modern urban fragmented existence. But this turn of events makes Rahul voice his discontent with the metropolitan reality – *'Bambai shahar mujhe raas nahi aaya'* ('Mumbai hasn't suited me at all) ... and he finally decides to leave the Metro to return to a small town and lead a simpler life. In a separate incident with Shruti, Monty philosophically states the harsh reality *'yeh shahar hamey jitna deta hai badle mai usse kahin zyaada le leta hai'*. (This city takes away a lot more from us than what it gives.)

As a matter of fact, none of these associations give any kind of emotional gratification to the characters involved in this topsy-turvy urban milieu. On the contrary, this tangled web of relationships leaves all the characters depressed and disconsolate in one way or the other. None of them derives any lasting sense of satisfaction or emotional fulfillment. From this complex mess of rotting relationships, one may get an impression as though *Life in a Metro* is an unmitigated saga of miserable, mis-matched human beings; that urban life is totally hopeless. However, the director also sets up an absorbing contrast in the Shruti-Monty relationship that's simple but heart-warming. Searching for a perfect match for herself, Shruti meets Monty through Shadi.com but is unimpressed by his naïve and unsophisticated behaviour. In her quest for the right guy, she is attracted towards Rishi K, a colleague who is an RJ; her boss also encourages her to have an affair with Rishi. She feels cheated and is heartbroken when she discovers that Rishi K is actually gay and has used her to pretend to his parents that he is a heterosexual. As fate would have it, the dejected Shruti accidentally meets Monty once again. This time she is drawn to him and after a lot of fun and melodrama the relationship between the two reaches a happy climax. The end of the film depicts Shruti and Monty with a kid moving on a scooter on the crowded streets of Mumbai.

In cinematic terms, this positive couple may seem just a device to provide the viewer with some comic respite from the brooding saga of fractured relationships. But through their humorous and witty interactions, the Shruti-Monty sub-plot actually serves a deeper purpose: it conveys a subtle yet powerful message that even in the middle of Mumbai's maddening crowds and heartless pursuits, the possibility *does* exist of leading a happy and contented life

Although *Metro* suggests that living and loving in a big city is a chaotic and confusing experience, the director Anurag Basu manages to present city life in a tidy and rather well-contained package that features some great cinematography. He has attempted a difficult genre of episodic film. The plot comprises of a number of different stories that run parallel to each other and merge into a common climax. But through some deft cinematography all these stories are cleverly interwoven. It's a web of people whose lives are closely knit and something in someone's life affects the others. This is why we don't get stranded into multiple storylines without a clue.

Besides this, the director makes use of various cinematic tools and devices like music, light and shade, colours, use of space, body language, facial expressions, dialogues and silences to enhance the urban angst and loneliness that most of his characters feel. By a clever handling of the camera, he is also able to reflect powerfully the pervasive sense of isolation that most people experience even though they are perpetually surrounded by a crowd in Mumbai. There is a fine fusion of background score, sound mixing and cinematography that develops the desired feel in most of the crucial sequences of the film.

Basu specially exploits the efficacy of music as a means of communication in his film. In *Metro*, music is used as a crucial tool to stress the vital relationship between sound and image in the cinematic context. It is done with such finesse that the music goes a long way to supplement, enhance and expand upon the film's narrative. A number of songs like *'In dino'*, *'Alvida'*, *'Baatein kuch ankahee'* and *'Kar saalam'* are well placed in the film and emote their otherwise unexpressed feelings. They not only bring out the conflicting emotions of the characters but also push the story forward and highlight the subtext of the scene. In fact, the sound-track against the visual montage serves as an objective voice of a documentary maker.

*'Inn dino'* especially focuses on the dilemma of Shikha who is torn between her husband and child on the one hand and the simultaneous attraction towards Akash, on the other. Some of the most evocative lines of this song capture not just Shikha's dilemma but also her essential loneliness:

*In dinno*
*Dil mera mujhse yeh keh raha*
*tu khawab saja*
*tu jee le jara*
*hai tujhe bhi ijazat karr le tu bhi muhabat*
*berang se hai bhari zindagi, kuch rang to bharoon,*
*Main apni tanhayi ke vaaste ab kuch to karoon*
*Jab mile thodi fursat, khud se karr le muhabbat*

*These days,*
*My heart tells me to learn dream and live life for a moment,*
*You too have the freedom to fall in love*
*Empty of all colour, life needs to be filled with colours,*
*I need to fill the void in my life*
*And when there is a moment to spare,, Fall in love with myself.*

In fact, Anurag Basu uses an innovative device throughout the movie: that's 'the metro band' which appears in many scenes of the film. This rock band plays at important junctures in the film and acts as a sort of a *Sutradhar* for the film. It not only furthers the film's storyline but also makes it a bit easier for the viewer to appreciate the subtle nuances that the director wishes to convey.

Another effective cinematic tool employed by the tech savvy director is the use of interior monologues at many engrossing moments of the film. One such extended monologue by Shikha brings out the essential hollowness of her marriage with Ranjeet. Their broken relationship is established at the start of the movie by using snippets and extracts of Shikha's memories. This powerful and evocative monologue highlights their past interactions, the rifts and cracks that are tearing them apart. In an interesting and innovative fashion the monologue followed by the dialogues highlights the deep fissures between them. Shikha comments on their relationship: *Ranjit aur mere dost kehte hain hum ek ideal couple hai … shaadi kuch aur sikhae ya na sikhae acting karna sikha deti hai* … culminating in *ab to hamari khamoshi bhi aapas mai jhagde karti hai.* This powerful voiceover is followed by a volatile scene that shows their growing tension and distance. When Ranjit tells her … 'Go to hell' …. Shikha retorts: 'I'm living in hell'.

The director also makes use of open and closed spaces very effectively. When he wants to show the claustrophobic, loveless relationship of Ranjeet and Shikha or an illicit affair between Ranjeet and Neha or even the sensuous scene between Akash and Shikha he uses dark, closed spaces. In the end, the closed space of a taxi indicates the constricting confines of marriage that Shikha is unable to break through. In contrast, the happy-go-lucky pair of Monty and Shruti are shot in lighted open spaces. Similarly, the crucial scene between Rahul and Neha when the former describes his dream to the latter is shot in the open.

The film's cinematography not only gives us great pictures but also successfully conveys a sense of the city that's racing fast, well ahead of human bonding. There is juxtaposition of urban crowded landscapes and skyscrapers on the one hand and of the isolation resulting from the wounds inflicted by the harshness and insensitivity of life in a metro on the other. To escape this deep sense of loneliness, people in urban India now depend on a variety of methods; one of the more popular among them is listening to FM radio stations as they move about in metros. In fact FM has now become almost an integral part of modern urban life. And Basu cleverly uses FM broadcasts by the RJ Rishi K as a further reminder of how people living in big towns now look for such extraneous entertainment to combat their loneliness.

The shots of the Bombay skyline, skyscrapers, fast paced and incessant movement of traffic and RJ dialogue are used by the director to capture the nonstop nature of life in Mumbai which is forever crowded yet its residents remain utterly lonely. The radio talk of RJ in this regard strikingly highlights the ironical existence of the people of Bombay: '*faasle kam ho rahe hain parr dilo ke faasle bad rahe hain sensex se bhi tej*'. Bombay becomes the metaphor of the modern city existence. Kerby Anderson succinctly points out towards a similar trend in United States. In his perceptive article 'Loneliness' he argues: '... in rural communities, although the farm houses are far apart, community is usually very strong. Yet in our urban and suburban communities today, people are physically very close to each other but emotionally very distant from each other. Close proximity does not translate into close community.'

Before concluding, it needs to be emphasised that *Metro* reflects that the city and the urbanscapes of life and its tribulations have now entered the mainstream of Hindi cinema. The city figured earlier too, but it was a sort of minimal presence, a space one took refuge in, but where one was never really 'at home'. Its values were projected in sharp contrast to rural centres in the narratives of Hindi cinema; as, for instance, in many films of Raj Kapoor like *Awara, Boot Polish*, and others. In these movies, the village symbolised innocence and purity while the city signified cleverness and manipulative behaviour.[2]

This bi-polarity has certainly changed and in films like *Metro* the city is no longer a 'place of arrival' but where one simply is. The feeling of awe and wonder at the sight and pace of the city, its anonymity, are now passé. There is no longer the feeling of shock; instead the city is a place that totally engrosses its inhabitants and inexorably draws them into its vortex. Unlike the earlier films, these films don't place the rural at a moral pinnacle as a counterpoint to urban values and lifestyles. City life is now something that seeks its own redemption and draws from its own resources and conflicts. Deconstructing the narrative of the film leads us to some broad conclusions. Since it is unfashionable to give neat solutions, Basu like a typical postmodern creator offers no moral judgements or prescriptive solutions to the complex dilemmas that confront his characters. His theme and filming techniques focus mainly on the anxiety within modern urban living. His film does not provide an answer to the anxiety, nor does it tell the audience how to deal with that anxiety.

In brief, this film is about our postmodern human condition. The characters are very much alone in the large city environment. They are alienated from one another even though they are involved in each other's lives. There is an underlying sense of dystopia and confusion. The city is too huge and life moves too rapidly to give each individual character adequate space. Each character cries out to be heard. The characters want to love and be loved, and yet are so dysfunctional that they cannot do so. Each character has to play by the city's rules, in order to survive from day to day. The meaning of love hence becomes distorted and lost.

It seems that Basu the filmmaker wants to create realistic cinema by offering a 'slice of life art' so to say. His film merely tells the stories of characters we meet in our daily lives, deals with love, affection, ambition, sex, desire, passion, stress, infidelity, romance – all the everyday emotions that erupt from fast paced city life, the urban metaphor shows its edge in every frame of the film. *Metro* deals with serious problems and issues. The Shikha-Ranjeet-Neha triangle, the ups and downs in the relationships of Rahul, Neha and Ranjeet are all serious matters. In contrast to this gloomy saga of broken relationships, is the humorous love chemistry that erupts between straight-forward Shruti and the happy-go-lucky Monty. This subplot is not just an attempt to provide a relief for viewers; instead its also a ray of hope that lights up this dark, almost depressing tale of human relationships fractured in the quest for money and power. The fact that its two relatively simple characters who eventually find happiness indicates that even in the otherwise ruthless 'life in a Metro' (where most people are driven by ambition and a relentless pursuit of worldly success), it *is* possible to live with utter simplicity and yet achieve a degree of success and happiness, *without compromising one's dignity and fundamental values.*

As a sensitive, postmodern filmmaker, Basu passes no moral judgment, takes no clear cut ethical stand. Instead, he leaves it for viewers to introspect, reflect and arrive at their own individual solutions. If refined art need not be didactic and a good film, like a good piece of literature or poetry, does not make any overt statement, *Life in a Metro* eminently deserves to be called refined cinema. Its an entertaining yet meaningful film for it only suggests rather than prescribing solutions. Like a real metropolis, *Life in a Metro* has good parts, a few less than enticing parts, and some parts that make the film a really thought-provoking experience. After watching *Metro*, one realises that living in a metro is really what you make of it.

## Notes

1. This term was coined by Dr Roberta Hestenes and first used it in her lecture 'Building Clwktian Community'
2. For a historical and analytical perspective on Bombay in Bollywood cinema, refer to an incisive study by Ranjani Mazumdar, *Bombay Cinema: An Archive of the City* (University of Minnesota Press, 2007)

## References

Anderson, Kerby 'Loneliness,' http://www.leaderu.com/orgs/probe/docs/lonely.html.site visited May 18, 2010

Gokulsing, M Dissanyake, W. *Indian Popular Cinema: a Narrative of Cultural Change*, Trentham Books, 1998.

Jungen Christian. 'Urban Movies: The Diversity of Indian Cinema,'. http://www.fipresci.org/festivals/archive/2009/fribourg/indian_cinema_chjungen.htm site visited May18,2010

Mazumdar Ranjani, *Bombay Cinema: An Archive of the City*: University of Minnesota Press, 2007.

Peeradina, S., ed. *Contemporary Indian Poetry in English*: An Assessment and Selection. Bombay: Macmillan Co. India Ltd., 1972.

Rajadhyaksha, A and Willemen, P. *Encyclopaedia of Indian Cinema*. New Delhi: Oxford University Press, 1995.

# Power and Resistance in Azar Nafisi's *Reading Lolita in Tehran*

*Maheeka Nanda*

*Reading Lolita in Tehran* is a memoir by Azar Nafisi. Her narrative is based on the memory of eighteen years in Tehran, from 1979 to 1997 as she reminisces from her office in Washington DC. In her poignant declaration she urges the reader to imagine herself and her companions 'against the tyranny of time and politics' in a manner in which they 'didn't dare to imagine' themselves (6).

Nafisi returned to her homeland from the United States of America at a time when political unrest was at its peak. She could ominously sense the anxiety and the morbidity in the atmosphere at the airport. The realisation that her country had changed so drastically from what she remembered from her childhood brought in both disappointment and guilt. Nafisi felt complicit in the unfolding of the present political drama. The memoir unfolds the Iranian Revolution of 1979 that overthrew the authoritarian and repressive regime of the Shah of the Pahlavi dynasty and brought to power the Islamic Republic Party (111–113). This political group imposed an authoritarian regime under the aegis of the exiled religious leader Ayatollah Khomeini. As Nafisi describes, the establishment was completely averse to individual, political and religious freedom. Brutal violations of human rights soon followed, as people were executed without being given a fair trial (96–97). The control of the Islamic Government was organised through constant surveillance by the patrol cars of the Revolutionary Guards (26–27). They ensured that the citizens follow the dictates of the supreme command. Revolutionary courts carried out prompt mass murders in the name of God, law and morality (96–97). Through the subsequent consolidation of its rule, the regime imposed certain laws that were inimical to women and children. Literature and art were condemned to 'blind' censorship (24), while the education system was overhauled to meet the cultural requirements set by the regime (147).

As a teacher Azar Nafisi would warn her students never to 'belittle a work of fiction by trying to turn it into a carbon copy of real life; what we search for in fiction is not so much reality but the epiphany of truth' (3). However she goes paradoxically against her own pronunciation and compares life in the Islamic Republic of Iran to Nabokov's 'Invitation to a Beheading' and 'Lolita' (3). She reminds us of the dance in the 'Invitation to a Beheading' where the jailer invites the prisoner – Cincinnatus for a dance. Cincinnatus whose main crime is his uniqueness is subjected to the cruelty of a rule that imposes homogenisation. This dance then becomes 'the main movement of the novel' for Nafisi (76). She says that 'as long as he accepts the sham world the jailers imposed on him, Cincinnatus will remain the prisoner and will move within the circles of creation. The worst crime committed by totalitarian mind-sets is that they force their citizens, including their victims, to become complicit in their crimes. Dancing with your jailer, participating in your own execution, that is an act of utmost brutality' (76–77). The Iranian citizens had to comply to the dictates of the regime in order to survive, as voices of dissent were promptly silenced.

The memoir takes one to the tumultuous space of Tehran, where the both the personal and the public are meticulously surveyed and controlled. As a consequence individual is expected to be unconditionally subservient to the authority of the regime.

This reminds one of Foucault's explanations of power in *Power/Knowledge* (1980) where his concerns are focused on the 'how of power' (92). He describes that in 'any society there are manifold relations of power which permeate, characterise and constitute the social body, and these relations of power cannot themselves be established, consolidated nor implemented without the production, accumulation, circulation and functioning of a discourse' (93). In Iran's case power was exercised by a discourse that hijacked and politicised a religion that laid out the field for subjugation and repression of the Iranian citizens. The interpretation of the regime was considered supreme. It could not be altered or be made accommodative to the very least. Michel Foucault's exposition becomes relevant to the case of Tehran when he suggests '...we are forced to produce the truth of power that our society demands... we are also subjected to truth in the sense in which it is truth that makes laws ...In the end we are judged, condemned, classified, determined in our undertakings, destined to a certain mode of living or dying, as a function of true discourses which are bearers of the specific effects of power (93–94). This I believe describes the creation of the modest Islamic woman in the Republic. Nafisi mentions her grandmother's refusal to go out of the house when Reza Shah made the unveiling of women compulsory. It reminds her of her own denial when the act of veiling was enforced. She says '...it was not the piece of cloth that I had rejected, it was the transformation being imposed on me that made me look in the mirror and hate the stranger I had become' (165). In both the cases the women had no control over their public appearance, a fact that displays the enormity of political power. This finds resonance in Foucault's critique of power in manner of its 'on-going subjugation, at the level of those continuous and uninterrupted processes which subject our bodies and govern our gestures, dictate our behaviors etc' (97).

During the period of internal oppression, the people of Iran were also challenged by external aggression from Iraq (Nafisi 157–160; 205–207) Eight years of war, further deepened the roots of the regime, while little was done to protect the citizens from the Iraqi air attacks (160). To make things worse a group of government emissaries would circle the site of bombing. They would prevent the people from mourning and blaming the government, and would chant in the name of the spiritual leader (211). The position of the Iranian citizen is close to what Agamben (1998) describes as the 'homo sacer (sacred man), who may be killed and yet not sacrificed' in the book *Homo Sacer* (8). The 'homo sacer' is one who is created by law and yet not protected by it. The 'homo sacer' is a 'state of exception' or 'exclusion' (15–18), which has become the norm today. This in turn forms 'an inner solidarity between democracy and totalitarianism' (10).

Resistance forms a crucial aspect of negotiation with such circumstances. As Foucault avers, resistance lies at the heart of power (92–108). Resistance then can either be overt or covert, is exercised by the people of Iran who negotiate on a daily basis with the humiliation and dread imposed by the regime. Bottles of bootlegged vodka, smuggled satellite dishes and movies become means of resistance. As Nafisi describes people would rush to watch movies in an alien language, edited to non-recognition by the censor and would attend music concerts where dancing or moving in any form was strictly prohibited (206, 299).

People became defiant by celebrating the state's misgivings. The writer's dear friend Laleh, celebrated her expulsion from the University of Tehran through a sumptuous lunch where she called herself a 'free woman' (162–164). Laleh who refused to teach with the veil (before it became mandatory), sowed and baked to make a living as she had been denied the license to practice child psychology. Nafisi's enigmatic mentor Mr R., a legendary figure since he taught the nuances of cinema at the University of Tehran, withdrew completely from public life. He found comfort in his invisibility, his erasure and escape from the gaze of the state.

As is evident in Azar Nafisi's account, literature became a means of escape from the morbidity of their lived reality for many. It became an essential aspect of people's lives, 'a necessity' (72). She joined a Persian literary group where people from diverse political and cultural orientations would read Rumi, Sa'adi, Khayyam, Hafez, and the likes through the dark nights of the bombing. Classes were organised at her home, where some of her brightest female students would get together to discuss works of literature (10–11). They would ponder over the link between 'fiction and reality'. The discussions gave the women a sense of relief from the homogenising outside, a reality that had made the individual 'irrelevant' (169). Her home became an oasis of warmth and sharing through the personal accounts most of romance, hardship, hope and anxiety. The space of her living room came alive with a view of the Elbruz Mountains, as they discussed *A Thousand and One Nights*, *Pride and Prejudice*, *Daisy Miller* and others over hot cups of tea, and pastries (6–11).

The conversations about writers brought to Nafisi memories of events and people many of whom were lost to the tyranny of time. Their dialogue about Fitzgerald took her to the classes at the University of Tehran, during the early days of the revolution. Some her students questioned the relevance of *The Great Gatsby* in the Islamic Republic of Iran. The novel according to the regime loyalists glorified greed and adultery. Nafisi promptly proposed a trial of the book in her classroom. The prosecutor Mr Nyazi asserted that the book was unacceptable to the 'Islamic culture', as Gatsby was a synonym for lies, cheating and the immoral American culture. The defendant Zarrin called for a distinction between 'fiction' and 'reality'. Literature for her could not be branded as immoral on the basis of the values of its characters. The very aim of a novel was to unsettle one from a secure comfort zone. It made us question or rather reframe the values that we take for granted. Nafisi stated that the story was primarily about the 'loss of dreams'. It had to be accepted on 'its own terms', to 'celebrate and love it because of its amazing and anguished beauty'. She iterates that 'a great novel heightens your senses and sensitivity to the complexities of life and individuals and prevents you from self-righteousness that sees morality in fixed formulas about good and evil' (133). Gatsby epitomised the complexities that linked love, dreams, money and betrayal. The entire act of the trial lent a voice to the sensitivity regarding human sentiment, a sensitivity that was steadily being smothered.

As a teacher Nafisi had encountered students from different cultural and financial backgrounds; their interactions were invariably shaped by literature. At Alzahrah University she was disappointed by the lack of originality in the answer scripts as students had mostly repeated her lectures verbatim. Her angry address to the class was later countered by a tiny yet firm student Razieh, 'but you must think about where we are coming from. Most of these girls have never had anyone praise them for anything. They have never been told that they are any good or they should think independently. Now you come in and confront them accusing them of betraying principles they have never been taught to value. You should have known better' (221). Razieh narrates to Nafisi that her students valued her classes a lot and had looked up to the unconventional protagonist – Catherine Sloper of *Washington Square*. The 'plain rich American girl' had belonged to a different era and social background yet gave a refreshing view of an alternate life (221), a life, which most of her students could have accessed only through their imagination.

The author discovered later that Razieh had been executed because of her political views. Mahtab – Nafisi's student, who had been Razieh's companion in jail, fondly remembered their conversations and laughter over the trial of *The Great Gatsby* (218). The magnificence of Razieh's courage to laugh in the face of death is a testimony to the redeeming powers of literary dialogue. How it brings about camaraderie and joy and makes one transcend the horror of violent spaces.

The writer's proximity with her students, friends and family strengthened her will to bear with the monstrosity of both the war and the regime. Nafisi met her mentor at the risk of been arrested for meeting an unrelated man, read forbidden works of literature and hoarded obituaries of those who had been victimised. However the fact that her students and her children had no respite from the cruelty of the regime pained Nafisi the most. Unlike herself and her mother they had no fond memories of their country. The yearning for fearless memories forced many to flee the country. The memoir ends with the writer's imminent return to the US.

Azar Nafisi chronicles struggles, memories and spaces. Through this act she resists the lies perpetuated by the state. Literature and language assume the form of an instant refuge when there is no other escape. They make one fight against the overpowering control of fear. Nafisi would encourage her students to play with words. One of their favourites' had been Nabokov's creation 'Upsilamba'. The word which has no formal meaning is described by the author as 'the impossible joy of a suspended leap' (21). To Manna, 'the poet' the word brought 'the image of a small silver fish leaping in and out of a moonlit lake', while Mitra described it as a 'blissful sigh' (21). For me the word describes a blissful zone where the individual is not bound by a body, she can exist as a thought or anything she wishes to be. 'Upsilamba' then would be accessed through one's courage irrespective of space and time.

## References

Agamben, Giorgio. *Homo Sacer: Sovereign Power and Bare Life*. Trans. Daniel Heller-Roazen. Stanford: Stanford University Press, 1998.

Foucault, Michel. 'Two Lectures'. Trans. Alessandro Fontana and Pasquale Pasquino in *Power/Knowledge: Selected Interviews and Other Writings 1972–1977* Ed. Colin Gordon. New York: Pantheon Books, 1980. 78–108.

Nafisi, Azar. *Reading Lolita in Tehran*. London: Fourth Estate, 2003.

# Contributors

**Madhuri Chatterjee** teaches English and is in Rajasthan Education Service. She worked on the theme of homecoming in John Updike for her doctoral thesis and has later moved on to exploring Bengali women's autobiographies and the contemporary travelogues. Her areas of interest include Latin American writers.

**Santosh Gupta**, former Professor and Chairperson of the Department of English at the University of Rajasthan, has recently completed a project on Modern Prison Narratives. Her other areas of interest are Modern Fiction and Critical Theory. Dr Gupta has worked extensively on psycho-analytical approaches and has participated in conferences both at home and abroad. She has co-edited *Contemporary British Writing* and *Literary Constructs of the Self.*

**Jasbir Jain**, formerly of the University of Rajasthan, Jaipur is an independent intellectual. A Fulbright Senior Fellow and life member of Clare Hall, Cambridge (England), she has worked extensively on drama, fiction, critical theory and feminism. Currently she is engaged in research on the problems of periodisation in Indian literature and diaspora studies.

**Vijay Lakshmi** is a well-known creative writer. Her stories have been anthologised in several collections and her own collection *Pomegranate Dreams and Other Stories* has won great critical applause. Lakshmi lives in the United States and teaches English at the Community College, Philadelphia. Her doctoral work was on Virginia Woolf as a Literary Critic. Currently she is working on a novel.

**Rama Rani Lall,** formerly of the University of Rajasthan, has worked in a wide range of areas. While her doctoral work was on the Satiric Fable in English, later her interest in American drama took her to the States for an interface with American theatre and writers. Lall has published work on both western and postcolonial writers.

**Shaila Mahan** is currently an Assistant Professor in English at the Directorate of College Education in Rajasthan. Besides presenting papers and participating in numerous national and international seminars, Dr Mahan has published several research articles in journals and edited volumes. Her major areas of interest include ELT and Indian Writing in English.

**Charu Mathur** teaches English at the University of Rajasthan, Jaipur. Dr Mathur worked for her doctoral degree on *Perspectives on Women in the Selected Plays of Eugene O'Neill and Tennessee Williams.* Besides American drama, her other areas of interest are Indian drama, postcolonial literature and women's writing.

**Joya Mitra** is a creative writer and an activist. She has travelled widely in India, especially the Himalayan foothills. Mitra, an active member of the CPIML since the 70s, has also served a four-year prison sentence, an experience recorded in her *Killing Days.* Initially a poet, her work is concerned with environment and culture and is located in the feminist perspective. She has published several novels, collections of short stories and of poetry. Mitra is also a translator and has translated Amrita Pritam, Bhisham Sahni and Mamta among others.

**Bharat Bhusan Mohanty** is currently an Associate Professor in English in Chilarai College, Golakganj, Assam. He has authored the book *Edward W. Said's Orientalism: A Critique* and has translated Assamese Sheelabhadra's collection of stories titled *Madupur Bahudur* and the novel titled *Godhuli* into Odiya, which have been published by Sahitya Akademi and National Book Trust of India respectively. His recent research project entitled "Folk Theatre Beyond Boundaries" is in press.

**Nishevita Murthy** is a research scholar in English at the Indian Institute of Technology (IIT), Mumbai. Her doctoral dissertation on historical novels derives from her interest in critical theory and postmodern fiction. Her other areas of research interest include fantasy writing, studies in Tolkien and medievalism in contemporary literature.

**Maheeka Nanda** is pursuing her M.Phil in International Relationships at the Jawaharlal Nehru University in New Delhi. She is interested in cinema and literature and has travelled to Canada to present a paper on partition narratives.

**Raji Narasimhan** is a well-known writer, literary critic and translator from Tamil and Hindi into English. She has published five novels of which *Forever Free* was shortlisted for the Sahitya Akademi Award, as was her critical work on Indian English Writing, *Sensibility Under Stress*. Amongst her well-known translations are Rajee Seth's *Niskavach* and Pushpa Maitreyi's *Alma Kabutri*. Her own work has been translated into German and Gujarati.

**Rajee Seth** is a creative writer in Hindi and writes fiction and poetry. She is the recipient of several literary awards for her contribution to Hindi including Vagmani, Bhartiya Bhasha, Hindi Akademi and Katha Sahitya. Seth's work has been translated into several languages and she herself has translated Rilke's letters into Hindi during her fellowship in the Indian Institute of Advance Study at Shimla.

**Sudha Shastri** is an Associate Professor at the School of Humanities and Social Sciences, IIT, Mumbai. Her doctoral work was on intertextuality, and she has published extensively in this area. Shastri, besides being an accomplished dancer, is also an innovative teacher. The courses designed by her have won her recognition. Amongst her areas of interest are narratological studies and Shakespearian drama.

**Geetanjali Shree** is a fiction writer. She has four short-story collections and several novels to her name. While she writes her fiction in Hindi, her discursive works are both in Hindi and English. Her works have been translated into English, French, German, Serbian, and several Indian languages. She also works with theatre groups in Delhi, where she lives, when she is not travelling all over the world.

**Nidhi Singh** teaches English at the University of Rajasthan. Her doctoral work was on Randolph Stow and in 2010–11 she was an Indian Council Senior Fellow in Australia firming her interest in Australian Studies and engaged in exploring diasporic experience. Her interests include postcolonial studies and currently she is working on First Nation communities in Canada.

**Sarbani Sinha** is an activist journalist working for the *Hindu* and based in Chennai. Her articles take up issues of social concern and her work on Sundarbans and critiquing of anti-people action has been widely appreciated. Sarbani is also a translator and has translated Joya Mitra's story for the present volume.

**Gerda J. Unnithan-Kauffman**, born and brought up in The Netherlands, married in Kerala (1957) to Dr T.K.N. Unnithan. Background in history, literature and later in counselling, she was Director, Students Advisory Bureau, University of Rajasthan from 1962 to 1996. Her major interests are in voluntary services in early childhood education, gender issues, human ecology and rural health. She is the recipient of the Knighthood in the Order of Orange Nassau for distinguished services.

# Index